Carolyn,

Healing thyself
creates a better
world for all.

Dedicated to you.

Love & Light,

Mary

Healing Point of View

MARY BURKHART REED

authorHOUSE®

AuthorHouse™
1663 Liberty Drive
Bloomington, IN 47403
www.authorhouse.com
Phone: 1-800-839-8640

First published by AuthorHouse 4/30/2010

ISBN: 978-1-4490-2215-0 (e)
ISBN: 978-1-4490-2213-6 (sc)
ISBN: 978-1-4490-2214-3 (hc)

Library of Congress Control Number: 2009909437

Printed in the United States of America
Bloomington, Indiana

This book is printed on acid-free paper.

The awesome front and back cover was created and designed by Robert Kane Chan of Kearneysville, West Virginia. The swan-lake background was photographed by Mike Wade from the United Kingdom. Front cover photo of the author's eyes was taken by Mary Jo Bennett of Hedgesville, West Virginia. The back cover photo of Mary Burkhart Reed was taken by Julie Strong from Martinsburg, West Virginia.

Acknowledgments

I thank my Aunt Alvernon for arranging the meeting with my Dad's living siblings over ten years ago. Much thanks to Uncle Buck, Aunt Margaret, Aunt Daisy and Aunt Carrie for the information about their parents, their family life as they were growing up and for the photos of the Burkhart family.

Many thanks to my Aunt Ruth, Aunt Esther, and Uncle David for the information they shared about their parents, their family life and for the photos of their family. I appreciate my mom for sharing her childhood and information about my dad. I also thank all my family who have passed over and contributed in guiding me to write this book.

Thanks to Beatrice for sharing her broad knowledge in marketing and giving alternatives for producing the summaries for the book. It was very refreshing and helpful to have my sisters, Marie, Virginia, Betty, and Ruth give me input.

I am grateful to my daughter April for her help in getting the photos ready for this book. It was very satisfying having my daughters Loretta and Jeanelle share and support me in finishing my creation. I am indebted to many friends who encouraged me and gave suggestions especially Jessica, Renie, Robby, Dan, Joyce, Betty, Dale, Kimberly, Lynne, Brenda, Toni, Patsy, Pat, Julie, Linda, Silvia, and David.

It was wonderful having Lisa Madden as my main editor. Also thank you Dave for the final edit of the last chapter of the book. Last but not least, thank you to the Nile Design Team of Jessie Klingler and Anne Marie Pruett of AuthorHouse for their support and excellent job done.

Table of Contents

Intentions of Book

The intention of the *Healing Point of View* is to give the reader techniques and healing modalities that I have used to successfully heal myself. These I make known by giving the reader an overview of my family heritage and of my life. The book begins at a very high-stress point in my life when I began to question my circumstances and how I unconsciously created them. History repeats itself and I share how lightning struck approximately nine years before that. What was my past? What did I create?

The past is explored through my point of view of both sets of grandparents, my parents, my family and my life. There is also a chapter on Jesse, a Vietnam combat soldier, whom I was in a close relationship with for nine months. He had a great impact on my life with many life-changing lessons. He, unlike most veterans, revealed his war experiences and I share those to impart an understanding of what war was like for him and other veterans.

There is a smorgasbord of my points of view, which may help to open the reader's eyes to a different perspective to aid in self-healing.

I hand you my life; pick and choose what may help. If even one point of view helps, then writing this book will have been worthwhile. It certainly did open my eyes.

My hope is that this book will provide a variety of techniques and readings that will help you to become more self-empowered, happy, grateful, and aware. Peace to you.

Love and Light,

Mary

Prologue

Back on Saturday, May 23, 1999, I was crying to my soul. It was a horrible, loud, and anguishing cry, "What had I done to deserve the events that had taken place?" The only thing I could think was that I needed God to help me.

My boyfriend, whom I had just broken up with after a nine-year relationship, asked me what was wrong, but I kept wailing and crying, so he left the house. Whatever the reason for his departure, whether it was guilt, fear or helplessness, I didn't care. I began to repeat over and over Psalm 23:

"The Lord is my shepherd; I shall not want.

He maketh me to lie down in green pastures: he leadeth me beside the still waters.

He restoreth my soul: he leadeth me in the paths of righteousness for his name's sake.

Yea, though I walk through the valley of the shadow of death, I will fear no evil: for thou art with me; thy rod and thy staff they comfort me.

Thou preparest a table before me in the presence of mine enemies: thou anointest my head with oil; my cup runneth over.

Surely goodness and mercy shall follow me all the days of my life: and I will dwell in the house of the Lord for ever."

How did I get into this situation?

I had just met with the president of the company where I had worked as a controller for over six years.

He said to me, "First, I want to apologize for doing this right now. I know you just broke up with your boyfriend, but I put this off too long. What are your intentions? You are not focused. You talk too much. You are very knowledgeable and I wish I had two of you. You influence others around you."

He wanted me to talk less and be an example to the rest of the staff and he was also willing to pay me more if I would work more hours.

But I didn't want to do that because I had seen one of the supervisors do this, and even with more money along with extra hours, it did not make him happy. In fact, he was always complaining he didn't have enough time to do everything he had to do. His marriage had broken up and he was miserable.

I felt overwhelmed and frustrated by my job because the president was in the process of buying three new companies and it was difficult trying to reconcile the books for so many. I had asked him if he would allow me to hire another accountant to handle the new companies, but he had refused.

What had just taken place was that the president of the company had been mirroring my relationship with my boyfriend. There was no support. That meeting was very humbling to me.

After I told the secretary about certain parts of this meeting, she asked me, "What are your intentions?"

When I called my daughter, Jeanelle, she too asked me, "What are your intentions, Mom?" (She had just heard about Gary Zukav's *The Seat of the Soul,* and she sent me the book, which I would highly recommend.)

I then asked myself, why is everyone asking me what are my intentions?

And now, I like to take time to ask myself before speaking or doing something, "What is my intention?"

At this time I was also attending the Virginia School of Massage in Winchester, Virginia to become a massage therapist. I was taking the deep tissue massage course in the evenings and weekends. Deep tissue massage brings up deep issues stored within the body and on April 29, 1999, when my partner was doing deep tissue massage on my back, I could feel my heart beating strongly. But I didn't say anything. I sensed the deep work would get to the heart of the matter.

The next morning I had a profound dream and knew for sure that my relationship with my boyfriend was over. I didn't tell him this until May 17, a little less than a week before my company's president asked to have the meeting with me.

Was it karma? Did I create this?

I certainly did. So I began a search back through my past for the answers to my questions as to exactly how I had arrived at this crossroad in my life. Because in addition to that fateful meeting and the breakup of my long-term relationship, my boyfriend's father found out he had cancer on June 29, died on August 3, and on September 11 my mother had a stroke at my house.

But I'm not finished. One of my friends confessed all her sins to me and then on November 30th one of my best friends, Cheryl, died of cancer.

Let me start with Cheryl. I had arrived home from Texas late the night before the 30th of November and I was going to call her the following evening after work. But at work I received a call from a fellow worker and friend of Cheryl's who told me that she had died the day before. I was in shock because she had told me about the cancer less than two months earlier.

She had told me that she was angry about doing the job of two people and not getting paid for it. She also had requested to her boss that she be given some help, but they didn't hire anyone. We were going through the same thing, mirroring each other. Yet she was such a responsible person that she worked extra long hours to get the work done whereas I had refused to. I had done this because I know that you set your own boundaries. *You can't blame someone else if they use you. It is your choice.*

I thought about how when I called her at her office she would answer the phone in a sharp and angry tone, only relaxing when she discovered it was me on the other end. I was very concerned about her anger. After she told me her story, Cheryl wondered if she could release the anger and cure her cancer. I told her that Louise Hay had written in her book, *You Can Heal Your life*, that anger does indeed cause cancer, it eats away at you. Hay had cured herself from cancer; it certainly wouldn't hurt for Cheryl to release her anger.

Cheryl told me that if she did die from cancer, she felt as though she had done everything in her life that she had wanted to. She had lived life to the fullest.

The day I heard about her death I pulled an animal card to get the message that I needed at that time and then read from the *Medicine Cards*, book by Sams and Carson. When I pull an animal card from the deck, I go to the book to read the lesson or medicine that this particular animal represents in the Native American tradition. If I draw the card upside down, I read the contrary lesson.

The card provided me with much relief and I composed the following poem for Cheryl that was read at her funeral service by her boss.

To Those Who Are Left Behind
Shock and grief took over me when I first heard
That Cheryl Johnson was deceased.
I cried and cried but still no cease.

Cheryl was so loving, so thoughtful, so generous and so giving.
Why had she stopped living?

God what message is there for me?
I drew from the deck of animal cards in search for peace.

Why had my friend died?
The hummingbird card did not lie.

It said:
Hummingbird …
Joyful little sister
Nectar you crave!

All the sweetness
Of the flowers
Is the love you gave.

The hummingbird stands for JOY.
When Cheryl Johnson passed away,
There was much JOY in heaven that day.

For those of us who are left behind,
We too can shine as Cheryl Johnson had done.

She accepted death because it is only a transformation.
God is always there for your information.
So as we grieve, sob and cry,

Know that God is always on the job
With Cheryl Johnson by His side.

A friend always,
Mary B. Reed.

Her boss said that there was not a dry eye in the house. I was so thankful that he read the poem since I did not attend. They told me that people had to stand in the church because so many people had attended the service. She had given so much to others and to her community.

So, during this period of breaking up with my boyfriend, meeting with the president of SES, my boyfriend's father dying, attending massage classes during nights and weekends, the stroke of my mother, and the death of my friend, my other friends were calling me. I would answer the phone, but for me it was a time of deep depression and I really didn't want to talk. While I was questioning life, God was sending angels to help me.

This was not the first time in my life where lightning had struck in rapid succession. Nine years earlier during a three-week period, my boyfriend broke off our relationship, my ex-father-in-law died, I lost my job, and someone confessed all their sins to me. I had just moved and taken out a loan to buy furniture. A lot of growth took place back then, so it looked like it was a situation of here we go again!

I wanted to heal. When history repeats itself you can make a choice to learn from it so you won't repeat it. I had reviewed my childhood many times, but now I wanted to know more about my grandparents and my parent's childhood so I could have a broader point of view.

Wedding of Eugene & Ida Burkhart
Photo by The Gerbrick Studio, Martinsburg, West Virginia

My Paternal Grandparents – Eugene and Ida Stuckey Burkhart

Granddaddy's baby picture

Granddaddy Eugene Burkhart

Since my father died in 1987, I interviewed his siblings to find out about his parents and childhood. My Aunt Alvernon arranged for me to speak to my Aunt Margaret, Aunt Carrie, Aunt Daisy, and Uncle Buck, my father's only living sisters and brother. Aunt Margaret told me that she had wished that she had asked her parents about their childhood, especially since she had a stroke and has lost parts of her memory.

I only saw my dad's parents once a year during the summer when we were not in school. Once in awhile they might come to see us. Granddaddy Burkhart reminded me of John Wayne. He was a tall and handsome man who was always kind and friendly to me and would try to get me to talk with him.

My aunts and uncle told me that he was a very humble man who owned two sawmills where all the children worked at as soon as they could shovel sawdust. One sawmill burned to the ground in 1936, and Aunt Daisy and Grandma poured water on the house so it wouldn't burn down, while the younger children were escorted to the middle of a big field.

Uncle Buck was the youngest and he said, "He always seemed to get along pretty good with most everybody, but of course when you worked with him that was different. I didn't work much with him other than on the farm."

He continued, "He was somebody that would instruct you what to do and he wanted you to do it. Like pitching hay on a wagon. If you didn't pitch it up that way, he would throw it back at you. I saw him do it many times. Make hay then pile it. Then you pick it up and set it on the wagon. You don't throw it up on the wagon. You set it up on the wagon."

Aunt Carrie remembered that, "He was mean to the boys."

Uncle Buck said, "If Dad had something in his hand when you disobeyed him, then he would use it on you."

As Uncle Buck recalled a time when his older brother did not listen to their dad, who happened to have a crowbar in his hand and used it against his brother's back, you could see the pain on his face and the grimaces and shame on the bent heads of my aunts, who were all shaking their heads in agreement.

I am sure there was an expression of pain on my own face when I heard this story, and I felt the energy of the meeting shift way down. I wanted to bring the energy back up, but I didn't know what to say.

What is your own, personal reaction to this story? When one person suffers, we all suffer because we are all connected.

This story reminded me of the time my son and I went fishing. We were poling the boat back to the dock at my dad's river lots on the Potomac River. We weren't able to get back to the dock because my son and I were not working together. He was about seven or eight years old and was in great fear, and expressing it, which made me very nervous. I told him to shut up and stop poling, but he continued to do both, and finally out of frustration, anxiety and the fact that he hadn't listened to my pleas to stop, I hit him on the head with my pole. He then sat down and stopped poling and I was able to get the boat back to the dock within a very short time.

Back at the dock I immediately asked Dad for a plastic bag with some ice in it to put on my son's head; and he just laughed at me. I felt horrible that I had hit my son on the head, I didn't want to hurt him and it probably hurt me more than it did him. I wished that I had dropped the anchor, sat down, and taken some deep breaths until both of us had calmed down.

Hindsight is always better, but it is too late. The past is over, so what is important is to go forth with new insight, understanding, and a different response from the lessons that are learned.

My Aunt Margaret, the second born and oldest living child at age 90, had positive memories. "I thought he was a great dad, because I worked with him ever since I was big enough to shovel sawdust. I loved my dad very much and I worked with Dad all the time. I wasn't with my mom very much. One thing that I thought was very unusual was when he saw this pretty yellow dress in town in the store. He said, 'Margaret, I think that dress would look pretty on you.' So we went down and parked the truck a couple of blocks away, and went up and he said, 'Go on in and try it on. I think it will look pretty on you.'"

Granddaddy also helped Aunt Margaret pick out her light pink wedding dress and a gray and pink suit since he thought she might be cold in the dress. "I thought he was a special Daddy," Aunt Margaret said.

This story made me feel so good about my granddaddy. How does it make you feel? Remember, we are one.

Uncle Buck said when his father went to deliver the products from his sawmill, he always went with him because his father always had a bag of candy in his truck. "That is where my teeth went," Uncle Buck confessed.

My dad always had candy around too. My older sister and I had false teeth when we were in our twenties. It must run in the family, although my other sisters still have their teeth. Granddaddy would tease us by taking his false teeth out and showing them to us.

Aunt Carrie said that when Granddad would get mad at Grandma, he would not speak to her for weeks. Even so, they celebrated more than 50 years together. They bought a new car every other year and a new truck when they didn't buy a car, according to my mom.

Granddaddy closed the mill down in 1942 due to government regulations and paper work. He went to work for Fairchild Hiller Corp. for several years, but the paint fumes got to him, he quit, and went to work for the B & O Railroad Shops in Martinsburg. During this time he had two heart attacks, and Aunt Margaret recalled that the doctor told him that since he had survived two heart attacks he might as well eat what he wanted to. My granddad lived to be 81 years old.

Granddaddy had asked me to come and live with him after Grandma died in July of 1974, but I said no. So my sister Marie and her four children moved in with him. Marie said that Granddaddy worked hard and expected everyone to work together until the job was done before you could go to school or play. Breakfast dishes had to be done before the children went to school. Marie agreed that he was a wonderful man, but one day one her of sons spoke back to her, and Granddaddy went after him. Marie jumped on Granddaddy's back to stop him and told him that he could not beat her son. Granddad expected children to show respect for their mother.

When Granddaddy Burkhart passed away on July 23, 1976, my granddaddy, Reverend Frazier, gave an eloquent and touching eulogy. He had tears in his eyes and broke up as he spoke of the love, kindness, and generosity of Granddaddy Burkhart, who had started to go to church when he was 42 and became the superintendent of the Sunday School and a trustee where Granddaddy Frazier preached.

Granddaddy Frazier said that if you asked Granddaddy Burkhart for an apple, he would have given you a bushel of apples. We were all in tears, especially my younger sister who had thought she wouldn't be affected by the funeral since she really hadn't known him all that well.

Granddaddy is tall man with hat.
Photo by The Gerbrick Studio, Martinsburg, West Virginia

Picture of Ida and Eugene's 50th anniversary
Photo by The Gerbrick Studio, Martinsburg, West Virginia

Grandma Ida Stuckey Burkhart

Grandma Burkhart's mother died during an influenza epidemic in December of 1898 when she was eight months old, so she was raised by Lexie Kesecker. Grandma was an amazing woman and a wonderful cook who prepared meals and did laundry for the seven to eight men that worked at the sawmill. Since we did not have a phone she never had advance notice that we were coming. There were six or seven of us, and another sibling or two might come with their children, but Grandma always had something to cook. She had a building built to hold her large, double refrigerator/freezer.

She always had a smile and cheering words to greet you, and she tried to make all fifty of her grandchildren a quilt. Every time we would visit, Grandma would take us into the parlor room where she made the quilts. She had made more than thirty-five quilts the last time I can recall being in the parlor. My sisters and I never saw a quilt after Grandma died, but the love and desire to make us one was all that I needed.

My mom told me that Grandma had designed and made a concrete slaughter containment space for when they slaughtered the pigs and cows. She also helped the men put a new roof on their house. Mom said she worked like a man. She raised chickens and cows; she sold eggs, and took in laundry to make money. She also made money by selling gas to local residents at the sawmill. Back then Grandma had to pump the gas by hand. She played the organ by ear at church and taught Sunday school at the Jones Spring Calvary Church. My mother's sister had her for Sunday school when she was ten years old and liked her very much.

Aunt Daisy loved her mom and told about the dresses that she had made her from feed sacks. Grandma would also buy them a store-bought dress each year. Aunt Carrie said she remembers her mom killing two rattlesnakes when they moved into the home place. She also said that the place was haunted and you could hear chains upstairs, but Grandma nicely told the spirits to get out, that they were going to live there now, and so they left.

When Grandma bought their house and approximately five acres, Granddaddy got mad. The outside of the house was not painted and they had to put new siding on it, later adding a new kitchen and turning the old kitchen into a dining room and bathroom. A lawyer friend told Grandma that her best investment would be land. So Grandma and Granddaddy invested in land with their excess money, and later sold part of it back to their children.

"Well, I think she was a wonderful lady and she had a job trying to raise us kids," Aunt Margaret said.

Uncle Buck was the last of nine children and when Grandma was pregnant with him the doctor wanted to take him because he was concerned that Grandma would die. Uncle Buck thinks it was some kind of blood disease, but Grandma wouldn't let the doctor take him. Instead she stayed in bed for months so that she could give birth to Uncle Buck.

Grandma also loved her flower garden and had a gazing globe in the front yard that we would all look into to view the world and ourselves in distortion. She also had this small, white rocking chair that my sisters would run and compete for when we arrived at her house.

An interesting thing to note is that when my father died, my cousin, who did the eulogy, didn't have much to say about Dad since he felt he was of low character. Instead he praised Grandma.

Burkhart Family
Back row Louise, Raymond, Daisy, Mary, Eugene Jr. (Buck)
Front row Dad (Newt), Margaret, George, Eugene (Granddad), Ida (Grandma), and Carrie Burkhart. Photo by Gerbrick Studios Martinsburg, West Virginia in early 1950's.

Daniel, Rachel, Venusta (mom at 4yrs old)

My Maternal Grandparents – Daniel Abraham and Rachel Rinaca Frazier

To help me with the history of my maternal grandparents, I talked to my mother and also had a friend interview her later. I received information on my mother's father, Reverend Daniel Frazier, from a paper my Uncle David and Aunt Esther had written for Shenandoah University, which his sisters also contributed to. I also interviewed my mother's sisters, Aunt Ruth and Aunt Esther.

Daniel Frazier
He is 16-18 years old.

Granddaddy Daniel Abraham Frazier

I especially loved Granddaddy Frazier, with his wooden leg, because he was the only one that I felt who loved me uncon-ditionally. He had asked my grandma if he could take me to the store to get some candy, but Grandma said that I needed to be cleaned up. Granddaddy took me to the store anyway, introduced me to the owner, and let me pick out any candy I wanted. My sister Marie was sick from eating too much applesauce, so I chose the pink Canada mints that Granddaddy said would help her stomach.

My mom said that honesty was the most important thing to her dad. This might have something to do with the fact that when Granddaddy went to work for the railroad in July of 1918, he lied about his age. Within a few weeks his leg was cut off below the knee when it slipped under a train wheel. He felt he lost his leg because he had lied about his age. From my point of view, this was a defining event in Granddaddy's life, which caused him to stress honesty to my mom and I suspect to all of his children as well.

Education was important to Granddaddy. Mom said that he made her change schools when he did not think she was learning from the teacher she had. Granddaddy knew because he was certified in the Commonwealth of Virginia to teach all elementary subjects plus Biology, English, Greek, History, Latin, and Mathematics in the high schools. He was also a substitute teacher in the state of West Virginia. He worked as both a substitute teacher and a preacher when he was younger.

Granddaddy's father, John Mordichai Frazier, was also very well educated. John's mother died when he was 11 and it is believed that he went to live with a family by the name of Lincoln, and they educated him or saw to it that he was educated. He taught at a school and was a rural mail carrier around 1897 because he scored the highest on the test. The job required not only mail delivery, but to read letters to people that could not read them. Great Granddaddy was not to let anyone know the contents of the letters he read, but it was suspected that after reading a very confidential letter to someone, that person may have poisoned Great Granddaddy with some crackers, because after eating them, he became paralyzed and died.

My Granddaddy Frazier was a United Brethren minister. He was called to the ministry in 1918, but did not obey until August 7, 1920. He wrote, "The second call to the Ministry was in July 1920 while praying and asking God to make me a good Sunday school superintendent. God spoke and said 'How can I make you a good superintendent, when you will not do what I want you to do?' That was plain enough. That changed me completely."

Granddaddy preached in Virginia and West Virginia. On February 19, 1973, the Central Church in Jones Springs, West Virginia presented a version of "This is Your Life." Elwood S. Frye served as master of ceremonies and he wrote the following:

This is your Life
Daniel A. Frazier, affectionately Dan
A friend of sinners, and a prince of a man
Clergyman, minister and servant of God
Walking each day where the Master trod.

One who serves with pure delight
Whose home is open both day and night
Always abounding in faith and love
Down to earth, with affections above.

God gives us men like Brother Dan
Men who are willing, and men who can
This is your life, one without end
Daniel A. Frazier, dearest friend.

I heard Granddaddy preach at least once, but I don't remember the sermons. He was concerned that the bibles would all be burned, so he memorized the book of Revelation, but after an operation, he could no longer quote it, so he recorded it on a cassette tape. My aunt gave me a copy of the recording so I can hear my granddaddy's voice anytime I want to.

Can you listen to a deceased relative's voice anytime that you want to?

During the Maysville flood in June 17, 1949, the church was swept away, with the bell a ringing. The church busted up by a swinging bridge, then hit some trees downstream, and broke into pieces. My aunt said that Granddaddy thought someone had gone into the church and was ringing the bell for help. The two-room schoolhouse up on the hill by the parsonage was converted to the church and named Fout Memorial Church, although the townspeople called it Maysville Church.

Granddaddy then built a stonewall facing downtown Maysville that had the letters E.U.B. in scarlet, red and white marble colors relating to Isaiah 1:18 (King James Version)

"Though your sins be as scarlet, they shall be white as snow; though they be red like crimson, they shall be as wool."

Even though Granddaddy was supposed to be paid $1,130 a year when he had the Hardy Charge which consisted of six churches in West Virginia from September 1927–1930, he was only paid $640–$800 a year. In spite of these conditions, my mom said that her dad would spend money to get boxes of candy and oranges for poor children in the community. Granddaddy had a heart full of love and gave in the ways that he could.

Since the income from preaching was small, Granddaddy tilled a garden, hunted, and fished so that he could put food on the table. He also raised chickens because he wanted brown eggs and he wanted to know what the chickens were being fed. When he lived in Maysville he also raised pigs.

When I went into the fenced-in area where the pigs were, he told me not to touch the electric fence. But I did anyway because I wasn't used to avoiding a fence, and I received a bolt of electricity that ran through my body. No wonder the pigs stayed in the fenced-in area! It was in this same place that a bumblebee landed on my outreached palm and stung me.

Granddaddy was very sensitive and would collect stones that felt right and he would keep them in his pocket and on his fireplace mantle. Coins were another thing that he collected, and he gave each of my children a silver dollar for the year that they were born.

The car accident, which my grandmother died from, left Granddaddy with a ruptured spleen and kidney, a punctured lung, and broken bones. After he recovered from the accident he ordered blue pencils that had the inscription:

JESUS and HIS CHURCH, first
OTHERS, second
D.A. Frazier, last.

He also served as a treasurer for the Conference Christian Endeavor Unions from 1925 until it merged with the Conference Board of

Christian Education and became its treasurer from 1931 to 1962. Also he was the treasurer for Conference of Youth Camps. With this duty, he attended the Youth Camps and was a great friend and leader to the youth.

He also made gravy for every meal. It wasn't a meal unless he had gravy. And even though that isn't considered to be a healthy food, he lived to be 82 years old.

How important is your outlook on life?

At his funeral, the minister said that Daniel was known for his meekness, sincerity, and humility.

Rachel, Venusta, Daniel

Grandma Rachel Rinaca Frazier

Grandma Rachel & Mom

Grandma Rachel married Granddaddy on May 30, 1924, while she was working for or staying at the Will Shifflet farm, which was near where Granddaddy grew up. They both attended East Point Church and East Point School near Elkton, Virginia. She always had her hair up in a bun and I was astonished one morning when I saw her hair before she put it up – it hung down below her waist. My mom said that her mother had never had her hair cut. This may be because back then women of the church didn't cut their hair for religious reasons.

When she came to our house one time, she rolled my hair up using strips of cloth to curl my hair. I was thrilled to have this done by Grandma, and then she asked my sister Marie and I to come spend the week with her before the rest of the family came up. I was delighted to go, as I had never been away to spend the night somewhere else.

Well, being with Grandma Rachel was almost like being at home. I had to dust the woodwork and scrub the bathroom floor on Saturday. My aunts had to do chores too. My grandma sounded just like my mom except she didn't put me down and there were no fights between Granddaddy and her. It was great to be away from the fighting and complaining, though my grandma did fuss and boss just like my mom did!

Grandma was the best baker alive. My Aunt Ruth said that when Grandma's cakes were auctioned off they would bring up to $200. She always had baked goods in the pantry and the smell in there was delicious, especially when there was banana cake. Mom said she baked bread a couple of times a week because there were always people stopping in to visit so Grandma kept the pantry full.

My mom and my Aunt Esther said that Grandma was a workaholic. She was also very close-mouthed about what went on in the family home, just like my mom was. They both were also tight with money, even more so since they had lived during the Great Depression. Grandma canned a lot from the garden they planted every year and she was famous for the plate-sized dahlias that bordered the garden that people could see from the road, and would often stop to look and marvel at. She also made quilts from leftover scraps of material.

Aunt Esther said that her mom had very high morals and a strong belief in God. Even though Grandma had only gone to school up until the eighth grade (which was as far as the schools went back then), she taught the adult Sunday school class that she spent Saturdays preparing for. She also read bible stories to her children while they kneeled at her feet and said their prayers.

I remember that Grandma sent us a pop-up Christmas story and the first page had a stable. The next page had farm animals and Mary and Joseph were on the third page. The fourth page had Baby Jesus, the fifth was the angels and shepherds, the sixth page had the three wise men and a camel. The last page had the words to "Silent Night" on it. We read this book every Christmas Eve and ended it by singing "Silent Night."

Grandma was very kind and giving. She took people in and fed them when Maysville flooded, she helped in preparations for the festivals and suppers that were held to raise money to pay Granddaddy's salary, as the community was so poor. She would often be called on to stay overnight at someone's house when someone was dying or sick.

When I took an energy medicine class in September 2007, the teacher asked me my name and then told me that my Grandma Rachel was standing behind me. He said she had always been with me, but at this time she was around a lot. The teacher also said that my gift to facilitate people's healing came through my Grandma Rachel's bloodline. During this time, ironically, I had been looking to buy a house and land in the area that she lived and died.

Grandma Rachel died when she was 42 years old in an automobile accident between Petersburg and Moorefield, West Virginia. Another woman also died in the crash and my grandfather was in critical condition staying in the hospital for over a month. He was unable to attend the funeral of his wife, which was one of the biggest funerals ever held in Elkton, Virginia.

My mom and I could not sleep the night of the accident, so we were awake when the police came to the door. The police told my mom that her mother had died and that her father was in critical condition.

Was the connection between Grandma Rachel and me so strong that I could not sleep that night? My three sisters and Dad were fast asleep.

In summary, the Burkhart's had money and discipline and work came first. When I asked my Aunt Carrie what she received from her parents, her first response was hard work. When I asked her if Granddaddy had ever hit Grandma, she said she never saw him hit her, but that he was mean to the boys. They both worked hard and together to earn money and invested it wisely in property. They also raised milking cows for meat and milk. They were entrepreneurs and experience smart. They were both of German descent.

The Frazier's were highly educated but did not have much money. In fact, they were very poor, but they were healers and community was very important to them. They worked together to survive and to raise their children, and they were penny pinchers and frugal with their possessions because they had to be. They were from German, Irish and Scottish descent as well as from French-Huguenots that had moved to England.

There were indoor bathrooms at both homes, but I was always told to use the outhouses. Both sets of my grandparents were workaholics, lived off the land, raised chickens, and pigs, God had a place in their lives and they were all intelligent and generous with what they had. Both granddaddies liked to tease. Every time Granddaddy Frazier saw Aunt Carrie, he would sing to her, "Carrie me back to ole Virginia." Both of my grandmas made quilts.

I learned some interesting things in my search to discover what my grandparent's were like and how they led their lives. One was that both Grandma Frazier and Granddaddy Burkhart were both perfectionist which I have been accused of being. Another was that my Granddaddy Frazier heard God's voice. I have heard (and believe) that we do choose our parents. Why did I choose mine? What was I to learn from them?

My Parents – Newton and Venusta Burkhart

Dad as a baby on his Mother's lap with family
Back row Margaret, George Next row Daisy, Ida (Dad on her lap), Mary, Eugene
(Louise and Raymond in front of Granddad Burkhart) Photo taken in 1925
Photo by The Gerbrick Studio, Martinsburg, West Virginia

Daddy

Dad was a tall, handsome rebel, and a fisherman who worked for the B & O Railroad as a yardman. He was the seventh child out of nine and he was born on a mountain in Berkeley County in an unpainted house. My mom said he was lost for two days when he was a baby. He was found behind a stove.

Dad was out shoveling sawdust in his father's sawmill when he was six or seven, just like his brothers and sisters. Aunt Margaret said they started at 7:00 in the morning and quit exactly at noon for lunch, then back to work until 6:00 p.m. Dad also had to pick up rocks in the field after his parents bought their house in Jones Spring, so they could have a garden. Mom said that Dad didn't mind, but it was rough on his sisters.

During school time Dad and his siblings stayed with their Grandma Maggie Burkhart, who lived to be 93 years old. Every Friday after school all the children would walk up to the Mountain Lake Lodge where their parents were staying. Aunt Daisy said that her grandma would give them some bread to eat on the way. It took them over two hours to walk in the woods and go across fields to get there.

Aunt Carrie said that her Grandma Maggie was mean, but she also said that if she had had to take care of nine children who didn't listen, she would probably be mean too! Aunt Margaret said that her grandmother was precious. I think that their positions in the family affected their perspective of Great Grandma. Aunt Margaret said that being the first girl and only the second child gave her grandmother more time to bond with her, whereas Aunt Carrie was the fifth girl and the eighth child that Great Grandma was watching, which didn't provide much time for bonding.

It just goes to show that it is all about your point of view (though position in the family does make a difference in how you are treated.)

Dad had meningitis when he was in the seventh grade and Mom said that she didn't see him in the one-room school for a year. Dad had to go back to the first grade to learn to read and write all over again. Mom said he looked funny sitting in the front row because the seats in the front were smaller for younger children. He quit school when he was in the sixth grade at the age of 16 or 17 years old.

"I can remember your dad crawling up the stairs at the house and at the store," Aunt Carrie recalled. "He had to learn to walk all over again. And Daddy said, 'Newt was lazy.'"

My father's parents got him a bike to help him build up his legs, and even though Dad had a limp, it was not real noticeable later in his life, though it did keep him out of World War II. He tried to get into the services but was turned down with a rating of 4F.

Even though Dad quit school in the sixth grade, my daughter said that he had a photographic memory. When she went for a ride in an engine one day along with her aunt and cousin, the engineer said that my dad would look at a paper with a list of 30 – 40 freight cars that had to be hooked to the engine in a specific order and then throw it away. His supervisor would get mad and would later check to see if Dad had the right number of cars in the order they were supposed to be – Dad always had the cars exactly right!

Dad was also the black sheep of the family. In the book, (which I will refer to as *Destiny* hereafter) *The Secret Language of Destiny: A Personology Guide to Finding Your Life Purpose*, by Gary Goldschneider and Joost Elffers, it says for the year and date of my father's birth that the pitfalls for him could be "morally weak, self-absorbed and immature." I would agree that Dad had all of those traits. He was very sexually active; he gambled, drank excessively, and was very seldom at home.

His grandson asked him one day, "Why did Grandma have to drink salt water so my mom and her sisters would have food to eat?"

My dad wasn't aware that this had taken place and was so embarrassed that he did not show up at our Christmas dinner that year.

Destiny also stated that Dad's gifts could be "tough, action-oriented, accomplished." I would also agree with his gifts. He was only working at the railroad for six weeks when he was promoted to foreman. When he purchased four river lots along the Potomac River in Brunswick, Maryland, he kept the place neat and trimmed. He built a flat bottom boat in our basement with no plans. He also, when in an argument with my mother over money, beat her which left bruises the size of softballs the next day.

According to the book, Dad's karmic path was "The Way of Resolve," and his core lesson was "standing up for what they believe in or for those they love." His goal was "to take up any challenge and not back down." Both of these things he did since he fought the National Park Service for 17 years to keep his land along the Potomac River. His parents also offered to sell him a house, but he turned it down. I don't know why, but I feel it must have been because he didn't want to answer to his parents.

There were stories and pictures in *The Brunswick Citizen* and *The Frederick Post* about Dad's fishing accomplishments and his fight with the National Park Service to keep his land. *The Washington Post* also carried a story about Dad on January 16, 1986 entitled, "To Catfish Burkhart, Life's a Holiday Along Potomac," by Eugene L. Meyer.

Five months after the newspaper story, on May 21, 1986, a man who was the boyfriend of one of his renters, I will refer to him as Dun, beat my dad up. A witness told my mother that she saw a National Park Service man give Dun money along with a bottle of booze. Dun had also bragged around town that the Park Service was going to let him live on my father's land for the rest of his life.

A friend of Dad's called me about the beating and to let me know that my father was in Frederick Memorial Hospital. God had already prepared me for the sight I was about to see when a college classmate of mine had fallen asleep at the wheel and gone over an embankment and through the windshield of her car. When I went to see her, her face was twice as big and she was unrecognizable. So at the hospital I was looking for a man the size of my dad but with a head twice the size it should be.

My father asked me, "How did you know it was me?" I told him the story of my friend going through the windshield.

Dad said that he had come home, was getting out of his Cadillac when he reached back in to get the newspaper, when he felt a two-by-four hit him in the back of his head. When he came to, Dun was kicking Dad's ribs and face with his cowboy boots. Dad said he managed to roll away from Dun, stand up, and was headed towards his trailer when Dun took off running because he thought that Dad was going to get one of his shotguns and shoot him. But Dad called an ambulance because he thought he was going to die.

Mom said that Dad's shirt was soaked with blood and so was the carpet in the trailer. Outside on the ground there was a two-foot by three-foot area that was solid blood. The surgeon wanted Dad to stay in the hospital a week before doing the required surgery, but Dad refused and left after two days. He returned a week later for the surgery. Dad's entire face needed reconstructive surgery. It took six hours to complete. Two hours longer than the surgeon had expected. Every bone in my father's face was broken and the surgeon had to take Dad's false teeth and wire them together so he could reconstruct his jaw. Dad also had a couple of broken ribs, but after a day in intensive care and two days in a regular room, my father left the hospital to recuperate at home rather than staying at the hospital for a week as the surgeon suggested.

When my children saw him five days after the beating, they said he looked like a monster and they wished they hadn't seen him like that.

My mom said when she went to the hospital, the only way she could be sure that it was Dad was to look at his left hand where it had been burned when he was young. It was smooth and a different color from the right hand.

While Dad was in intensive care, I went to see him and could see the fear on his face because he could not talk with his mouth wired shut. He was trying to communicate with my mother that he wanted water, but my mother didn't understand. I gave him water and then he wanted paper to write on, but again my mother didn't understand. She told me to help him since I seemed to know what he wanted. I asked him if he wanted a pen and a pad of paper. He nodded that that was what he wanted, and he was more secure knowing he could at least communicate through writing. I knew that because I would have felt the same way.

The doctor wanted Dad's false teeth to be wired shut for a month, but Dad only allowed his jaw to be wired for two weeks. He made his own decisions, as he always had throughout his life, and not what someone else thought he should do. Right or wrong, my father did it his way so when he was in the hospital I gave him a musical statue of a duck with its wings up and ready to take off which played the song, "My Way." I have it now, and from time to time I wind it up and think of Dad.

When the trial came, Dun had three top lawyers. Dad's friends wondered how a man who had been accused of murder in Virginia and served 15 years in prison could afford three top lawyers. The witness who had seen Dun get money along with a bottle of booze from the National Park Service man refused to come forward because she was scared for her life. Dun got off scot free. All of Dad's friends were in shock that he had gotten off, not to mention how did he afford all those lawyers?

Did the Universe return to Dad in one fell swoop what he had given my mom all those years? Was his karma paid up?

The National Park Service had a man working for them who thought he was above the law – *may all men and women in government live within the law, uphold the Constitution of the United States, and respect its citizens.*

Dad discovered that he had lymphatic cancer during an X-ray for the reconstructive surgery. He died of cancer on September 16, 1987, while his three sisters where there to see him. *The Brunswick Citizens* newspaper ran an article on Sept. 24, 1987, "Catfish Burkhart: 'a rugged individual' is Dead," by Pete Maynard. The article contained a picture taken in 1978 of Dad with a string of bass and read:

Picture of Dad with string of Bass.
Photo by Pete Maynard

"The writer makes no claim to have known Newton "Catfish" Burkhart very well. No claim, even, to have liked him or not liked him, personally. But by most accounts he was, in his way, an admirable person – an individual who stood up for his rights (and his wrongs) in an admirable way. He was an "individual" in the best American tradition.

Newton Burkhart, who died last week at the relatively young age of 62 – perhaps in part because of injuries suffered in a tremendous fight some time ago – came into the news when he battled the National Park Service to a standstill a few years ago.

Burkhart in 1959 or thereabouts, had bought a piece of property along the Potomac River, about a mile down river of the present Brunswick campground. There were other houses along the river in that area then, it was an established campground with both shanties and more or less standard houses, owned mostly by people who enjoyed fishing on the river.

Then came the Park Service, with a new policy of turning the canal area into a "natural" area, with no houses on it.

Newton Burkhart objected. Others sold out to the Park Service, faced with threats of legal action. Burkhart refused to sell. And continued to refuse to sell. He wanted to keep his home on the river. It was his, despite what some government people wanted!

By the time the fight became a legal one, Burkhart had some powerful friends – people who enjoyed his company, people who shared his love of the outdoors and the river.

Former Congressman Goodloe Byron regularly came to see "Catfish" Burkhart and go fishing with him – and to give him advice on how to hold off the Park Service lawyers.

Even Supreme Court Justice Douglas, the great proponent of the park along the C & O Canal, was sympathetic to his cause, and on his bikes along the towpath always stopped to get refreshments at Burkhart's riverside home, and talk with him.

There were others too, in high places.

Counting on the support of his friends, Burkhart went public with his refusal to knuckle under the Park Service. There were articles in newspapers and interviews on TV. Reporters enjoyed the drama of the "little man" against the forces of the big government.

When the Park Service finally brought to court its case for condemning Burkhart's land, "Catfish" Burkhart refused to attend to defend himself. They had their minds made up, he said. When a check for the appraised value of his land was sent to him, he refused to accept it.

And he won! Despite Park Service protestations that Burkhart was no longer the owner of the land, the government never did evict him. Maybe it couldn't. Maybe it didn't dare …

What kind of man was this "rugged individual?" The writer talked to retired railroader, John Sell, who for many years knew him as a fellow employee and friend.

"He was no angel," Sell said. "But the people who worked with him on the railroad thought an awful lot of him. He had a lot of very good friends.

"He was a generous man. If he liked you, there is no limit what he would do for you.

"He loved that river, and enjoyed taking people out in a boat. He was one of the best fishermen around, and he knew that river of his, he knew where the fish were.

"When he caught more fish than he needed, he never wasted a one. He'd give fish to needy people, every time. There are a lot of people who have had food on their table because of Catfish Burkhart! And, he had cleaned them himself! In summer he'd take live fish up to put in the Rod and Gun Club pond near Petersville, so the kids could catch them again.

"He never wasted a fish, and he never wasted a boat. When there was a flood, and boats would come loose and drift down river, he'd be along the bank with binoculars watching, and when he saw one he'd go 'capture it, fix it up, and rent it.'

"Burkhart had a remarkable memory, like many a man who didn't have a lot of schooling. He was a good 'yard foreman' (the proper name for freight train conductor) and when he got a list of cars to be made into a train, he'd take one look at that list, and then without looking again – and without a mistake – switch that whole train right, car by car. He was one of the best switchmen I ever worked with."

Why did they call him "Catfish?" Because, John Sell said, "he caught so many."

A personal reminiscence. One cold winter day probably eight years ago, Burkhart called me at the newspaper office. "Pete," he said. "I got something I want to show you. An iceberg on the river."

I expressed my doubts.

"Come on down to my place, we'll take a boat up the river and I'll show you!" he said.

Was it ever cold! And the river was full of ice floes, which he dodged with skill. The current was pretty strong.

But upriver we went, the outboard roaring, and near Weverton there was indeed quite a sight. Ice piled up on an island – in layers a foot or so thick – until it towered 15 or 20 feet in the air. An iceberg!

"I wanted you to see that," Catfish Burkhart said."

Not only was Dad known as Catfish Burkhart, he also called everybody, including us girls, and his grandchildren, "catfish." On Jan. 11, 2001, 14 years after Dad died, a lady sent me an article from *The Brunswick Citizen* that showed a picture of my dad with a string of fish that he had caught, along with the story "Proof," under the title, "What You Did 25 Years Ago!"

What are my feelings about my dad? I felt sad for him when he came to family gatherings. He was always hiding behind a pair of dark glasses and arriving late. I could see that he felt he didn't fit in, but that he wanted to be there. He wanted to be part of the family that he had created, but he was ashamed of the beatings he had given my mother and the life he was living. Weeks before Dad died he said to me, "I never told you girls that I love you, but I loved you all very much."

Dad didn't have to say that to me, but I am glad that he did. There was a wall of non-acceptance, and not being what others expected him to be.

This wall was apparent even when we went to visit Dad and Mom at the river. Usually Mom was visiting Dad at the time, even though they had been divorced in 1969. Dad always offered to take us on boat rides, especially when we brought friends with us. He would also fix something to eat or buy us food. Uncle Buck said he made the best fried catfish he had ever eaten.

At these times, I would observe the interaction between my sisters and my dad. I could see the wall of non-approval, just being there in body only. I had this wall also, even though I loved Dad.

This wall has shown up for me in other relationships. Do you have a wall in any of your relationships?

I loved Dad when he would get down on his knees when I was little, let me climb on his back, and take me for a ride. I liked it when he would put me up on his shoulder for a ride, but I was afraid of falling. It was fun when he raked leaves and tossed me in them and when he helped me to build a snowman. The few times I went along with Dad somewhere, he always bought me the candy of my choice.

I enjoyed being with Dad when he would gut the fish and I would clean them, since he would also pay me a nickel or a dime depending on how many fish I cleaned. It was alone time for Dad and me. He taught me how to fish with a stick, string, and hook. Yes, I caught fish with just those three things! Then Dad taught me how to cast with a rod and reel. The boat rides were fun and it was an adventure standing in the Potomac River and in the dam at Harper's Ferry (when it was drained) catching hellgrammites for bait. I was Dad's "go for it." Any time he wanted something and Mom wasn't around, he would tell me to get his shoes, newspaper, drink, etc. There was a bond there because

Dad knew I loved him, even though I hated what he was doing when he would hit my mom. Because of the fights I really didn't want my dad around. I wanted peace.

I feel very proud that Dad did not let the government, society, his parents, or Mom tell him how to live his life. He did it his way. But the price he ended up paying was the wall of disapproval (his and ours).

We are taught not to judge, but we do it anyway. Open your heart and melt the wall away. Just ask God to help you.

Senior Picture of Mom

Mommy

My mom is also a rebel, unique, feisty, determined, loner, victim, controlling, sacrificing, generous, penny pincher, broad world perspective of events, herbalist, and smart. Mom was three years old when the Great Depression began, and 18 years old when it ended. The Depression had a great influence on my mother because her father was a minister who was located in a very depressed area of West Virginia, and therefore they were very poor.

When they had guests for dinner, Mom was told not to eat very much in case there was not enough food. Because of this she felt like she never got enough – she was always hungry. My Aunt Carrie said that a friend of hers only had applesauce and something else to eat, whereas her mom always had the table full. Even now my mom has a fear of not having enough food, so she has lots of canned goods and boxes of food sitting everywhere.

Her mom made all her clothes from feed sacks. She said her mom skimped on the cloth so they never fit right and were always too tight somewhere. Her underwear was made of broadcloth and was also too tight. Back then, underwear and sheets were ironed because the material was so rough. To this day, my mom would prefer going nude, but wears loose-fitting clothes.

Mom was born during the era where children were to be seen and not heard. She said her mom had a switch that was long enough to reach across the kitchen table. If she started to say something, her mom would respond that she didn't want to hear any sassing then the switch would come across the table at her.

Her parents had all these rules, laws and controls:

1. No lying – if you did, you received two beatings.
2. Cannot accept money from anyone (a pride thing). She couldn't even accept money from her grandfather.
3. You make your bed, you lie in it.
4. Don't tell anyone about what is said in this house. (Since her dad was a preacher, it was private and nothing was to be said to anyone outside of the house.) Mom will sometimes go to tell me a secret and then not tell me. She has done this so many times, that when she says she is going to tell me a secret, I know she will not.
5. You had to act better than others and put on a front.
6. You were to practice self-control.
7. Go to school everyday. If you can't go, then you get a dose of castor oil. First you took a bite of pickle then the castor oil followed with another bite of pickle.
8. Curfew: You had to be in bed by 10:00 p.m. When Mom didn't get home in time, which according to my Aunt Ruth was quite often, both parents were waiting to talk to her. Aunt Ruth would go hide in another room so the screaming and hollering of her parents would not be so loud.
9. Children were to be seen and not heard.
10. In church you sit still.

11. Tuck five dollars away for an emergency.
12. Shouldn't tell kids so they don't get upset.
13. No matter what. You stay with your husband.
14. Keep mouth shut. No complaints.

Oddly enough, even though Mom did not like these rules, she passed most of them on to us. But with the castor oil we got orange juice! Some rules, laws, and control don't need to be passed on. They stop as soon as we decide they are not necessary or do not enhance our relationships with our children. One rule Mom didn't pass on was about having to stay with your husband–no matter what.

Mom is obsessive about cleaning. One time she spent an hour vacuuming one square foot of carpet in my dad's trailer. When Mom was young, nothing was wasted or thrown away; therefore, she has a hard time throwing anything away, whether it's a plastic bag or a take-out container from a restaurant.

In the third grade, her father was brushing her hair and asked her why her head was red. She told him that boys were pulling her hair. Her father then asked her to say her multiplication tables, which she had learned even before first grade. When she couldn't repeat them correctly, her dad put her in another one-room school where Frank Newbraugh taught. My daddy also went to the new school.

One Room School

Her mother packed her lunches at Jones Spring, but Mom complained that the pie was always squashed and the fatback sandwich she hated. She would throw the fatback away and only eat the bread. Her grandmother would buy peanut butter and crackers, but her mom never would. In the fifth grade Mom knocked herself out when she slipped on ice at the flagpole, where ice formed below where the schoolhouse roof sloped.

In the eighth grade Mom weighed 105 pounds and mowed the lawn for a lady who paid her 50 cents. Her mother would not let the lady pay my mother more than that, despite the fact the mowing took half a day with a push mower with no motor. The lady gave Mom her first slip that was salmon-colored and satin. She also gave her a hound's tooth black and white skirt, a red vest, and panties. The lady gave things to my mother that my grandmother could not buy for her.

My mother was an only child for 10 years before her sister Ruth was born. Two years later Esther was born, then three years later her brother, David. My mom said she wished that her mom had stopped having babies that she had to take care of, because that just meant more work to do. Despite my mother's feelings about this, she had her first baby when she was 18 years old.

Mom's first job while she was still going to school was at an apple plant in Jones Spring as an apple trimmer. There was a truck that would come by the store and pick up anyone that wanted to work that day. Her job was to peel off any skin that the machine missed. She also worked at Musselman as a peach facer, where she picked the best looking peaches to put on top of the bushels of peaches.

When she was 17, she worked at Perfection Garments. She put socks on a machine that would put toe and heel parts on the socks. In her senior year, Mom quit school in April because her pregnancy was starting to show. She lived in an apartment in Martinsburg, West Virginia, and with Aunt Annabel and Uncle George in Brunswick, Maryland.

During the war, women, old men and children did all the work. There was no sugar and people had to use honey, which was two to three times more expensive. You couldn't get merchandise and you had to use coupons. Fuel and shoes were also scarce during the war. A friend told me about how when her family had holes in the soles of their shoes, they used cut-out cardboard inside the shoes to avoid getting their feet wet.

Mom had my oldest sister Virginia, during World War II in August, 1944. She was given ether during the birth and she ran a high fever. Something went wrong every time that Mom had a baby. She was in the hospital for eight days after having Virginia because the doctor didn't know what to do. The doctors told her to get the situation solved now, but she didn't stay. (Years later my mother had her eyes read and was told that she had a hole in her stomach.)

In July 1945, a few weeks before the end of the war, my mom had Marie. She again returned home before the doctor wanted her to. Her sister Ruth was helping her. Mom was hanging up clothes she had washed by hand when the news came over the radio that the war was over.

Mom's shortest stay in the hospital was a little over a year later in 1946 when I was born. And then a year later in October 1947, my sister Betty was born. Mom said that they stayed in the hospital longer than they should have.

Virginia, Betty, Great Granddaddy Rinaca, Marie, Mary

In September of 1954, my mother's mother died in a car crash. Her father remarried the following year to a woman named Hazel. My youngest sister Ruth was born in July 1956.

Ruth had a twin sister that was stillborn; her name was Jane Marie. My mother said that she was sick within an hour of getting pregnant. She believed that Jane Marie was born dead because she slipped on the stairs and fell down three or four steps when she was eight months pregnant. Her abdomen began to swell and after a month she went to the doctor who gave her medicine to force labor. The labor was 12 hours long and Mom was numb for years after that.

Mom's blood was so poor that they gave her a transfusion of two pints, but they did it too fast and she went into shock. She did not stay in the hospital very long, she signed herself out because she didn't have the money, but she said that the blood did give her more strength.

During this time her sister Esther took care of the four of us. A day after the birth, Jane Marie was buried in one of the four burial plots Dad had bought. Mom was not present since she was still in the hospital.

While I was writing this book, my Aunt Carrie took me to see my father's gravesite in August, 2008. There was only a four-by-five-inch metal marker on my dad's grave, and none for Jane Marie.

I felt an emptiness and sadness for Jane Marie. It was as if she didn't exist, but her death did have a profound effect on my dad. Because of her death, Dad was more of a father to Ruth than he was to the rest of my sisters and me. In fact, Ruth lived with Dad until she graduated from high school. When I asked about Jane Marie's marker, the gravesite keeper didn't even know that there was a baby buried there. Since then, a three-by-two-foot memorial gravestone has been erected for Dad, Mom, and Jane Marie.

When Ruth was six, Mom started working as a nurse's aide at the Vindoona Nursing Home. I wasn't living at home since I was already married, but my three sisters still were. Two years later Mom left Dad when she came to the conclusion one night that he was going to kill her. Dad went down into the basement to get a piece of wood to hit Mom with, and she went over to a neighbor's for help. This was only the second time that she had sought outside assistance.

The first time was before Ruth was born, Mom and the four of us went down to the courthouse to file charges of abuse against my father because he hit my sisters when they interfered in Mom and Dad's fight. But when it came time to sign the papers, Mom refused, and when we got home, Dad beat Mom severely.

After the board incident, Mom moved to Baltimore and filed for divorce. She found a job at a nursing home, then she had a job at London Fog, and after that she worked at Gilbert's Optical. Even after the divorce Mom would spend time with Dad at the river. He would also go to Baltimore to spend time with her. When Dad was dying, Mom took early retirement so that she could take care of him.

Mom also had a boyfriend named Edwin at the time that Daddy was dying. Edwin took care of her when she was sick and had a hysterectomy. She also took care of Edwin who died ten years after Dad.

My sister Betty had Dad sign a will leaving everything to Mom. We had all agreed that Mom deserved to have whatever he owned. Shortly after his death, on the day of his viewing, the National Park Service showed up with several men with guns telling Mom to get off the property. My sister Marie told them she was getting a camera to take pictures to give to the newspaper, and so they all left. Mom did not attend the viewing because she was too upset over the incident.

After Dad died in 1987, Mom stayed at the river except during the winter, which she would spend in Baltimore. But in 1996, after a January snowstorm, the snow melted too fast and caused a flood. The federal government put a gate across the towpath and would not let the town of Brunswick plow the snow so that Mom could get her things. So at the age of 70 my mother lost all of her possessions in the flood. She stayed at a local motel for a year as she attempted to settle things with the National Park Service.

A reporter saw my mother at the post office and asked her if she could do a story on her. On April 11, 1996, the following article ran on the front page of the *Brunswick Citizen, Vol. 23, No. 15:* "Brunswick's last river resident gone – Flood gets done what Park Service couldn't do," By Caroline O'Connell.

Mom said in the article that since Dad had died, the Park Service had harassed her every couple of days for two years, then they quit in 1989 and never bothered her again.

FEMA searched with Mom for a new place to live, and she moved into a trailer along the Potomac River in West Virginia in 1997. She has lived there for more than 10 years.

What are my feelings regarding my mom? I love her very much. She always had a nutritious meal ready for us when we came home from school. When I was sick she went out of her way to do whatever she could to make me better. She praised me on my artwork and on my school grades. Mom also had hot chocolate to warm us up when we came in from sled riding.

She also made snow ice cream after the first snowstorm and on Christmas Eve she always read us the "Story of Christmas," book that her mother had given to us which we ended by singing "Silent Night." On Easter Mom always made golden rod eggs for breakfast, pickled eggs, and colored eggs. I was always proud of the clothes that Mom made for me and other students always told me how pretty they were. I loved it when Mom and I would walk downtown and she would always stop on the way back and get us both a small scoop of ice cream.

I did not like it when my mother would compare me to my sisters, who studied while I did not. I felt we had different abilities and I was always proud of all my sisters.

Why do we compare ourselves with others? Why do parents compare one child with another, and according to what standard? We are perfect the way we are. We are all a work in progress.

I was also frustrated with Mom because I could never do anything right except the time I spent four hours cleaning the spice section of the cupboard. I would say the word "angry" best describes how I felt when Mom called us brats and told us that we were the reason that she was not happy. And if it were not for us, she would be happy.

I also hated it when my mom would tell Dad to get out when he was drunk. Then when he tried to leave, she would stand in front of the door and shove him away. A fight always followed. Sometimes my two older sisters would join in. It never made any sense to me. Three to four people getting hurt and nothing being solved. If Mom didn't approve of Dad, she had two choices as far as I was concerned. Accept him as he was, or leave. She did leave once, but came back and never accepted him for who he was – and so the battles continued.

I am very proud of my mom because now she is noticing when she is negative and trying to change it when I am around. She has also sought natural ways to heal herself, since she has bad reactions to pharmaceutical drugs. She is a survivor. She is also much more loving now, ever since I told her that when I was a child she never hugged me. (A psychic told me that my mom had trouble showing affection since she had been a General in many lifetimes and could not show emotion.)

I am so grateful that I chose my mom to be my mother. There are many lessons I have learned which I will expand upon as I continue to tell you my life story.

Newton Veneta Burkhart

Photo by Margaret Burkhart Malatt

Mom and Dad's Relationship

My parent's relationship started when Mom was eight and Dad was 10. The first time that they met was when Mom went with her father to visit the Burkhart's. Mom loved going there because she had so much fun with all the Burkhart children. She said that she thought that Dad was cute the very first time she saw him. He shared his chewing gum with her every week which Mom enjoyed because her own parents would not buy gum. She said he rationed it out to her.

She said that she followed Dad around like a little puppy dog. He would take her for bike rides on the back of his bike. Unfortunately one time her foot got caught in the spokes and she still has trouble with her feet from time to time.

Mom hunted Dad down to get married when she was seven months pregnant. Dad did not want to get married.

Mom's karmic path, according to the book *Destiny*, was "The Way of Originality," quoted from page 652:

"Those on the Way of Originality are here to delve into and assimilate the content that lies in the realms of their unconscious.

"...those on this karmic path must overcome their fear of being different from others in order to pursue their individuality.

"Thus they become quite adept at hiding their more unique personality traits and conforming to what's expected of them. These souls often use their tremendous determination to keep themselves squeezed into the little boxes in which they believe they must live.

"These men and women often live out their own more peculiar sides by surrounding themselves with eccentric or even unstable individuals."

The *Destiny* book hit Mom right on the nail in regards to these quotes. Mom, the rebel, did conform to what society thought she should be, but she was a rebel; therefore, I am sure she pushed her mother's buttons.

When Mom was pregnant her mother told her, "You made your bed. Now lie in it." Mom's father was a preacher so she didn't want to make it hard on him. What would people think if she got a divorce? So she stayed in her marriage for 30 years.

Dad also contributed to the little box that Mom believed she had to live in by telling her not to leave the apartment or to invite anybody in. *Did Mom choose Dad because he was unstable?* Mom said that Dad was mean, but she also said that he was exciting. Dad would gamble then he would come home and ask her for more money. He knew she had some, and he would look for it, even tearing up the linoleum in his search. If he didn't find any, then he would beat Mom up. She would eventually give him some money, so the pattern continued.

I've already talked about how my mother would shove my drunken father away from the front door, and then a fight would ensue. This happened several times a month. After reading one of Dr. Phil's books, I kept wondering what Mom's rewards were. One was that Dad would take Mom places with him, whereas she usually stayed at home. And another was that Mom felt some control because Dad had to ask her for money.

The day that Dad received his divorce papers I saw him in a restaurant, crying. He said to me, "If I ever get married again, I will marry your mother."

As I said before, Mom and Dad still got together after their divorce, but Mom said she quit worrying about him, and life went better for her.

But it still bugged her. In September of 2008, I asked her what it was that still bugged her and she said, "What is God going to say when he raises the dead? Maybe I should ask Aunt Carrie to pray for him."

So 24 years after my father's death, my mom is still worrying about his soul.

From my point of view, Mom and Dad were two rebels who both wanted to be in control. Both had low self-esteem, and Mom wanted to conform and Dad did not. Mom tried to change Dad, but he did not change.

What is love? Perhaps it has to do with accepting people unconditionally and appreciating their good qualities. You cannot change someone else. The only one you can change is yourself.

Picture of me in 1ˢᵗ grade

My Life: Birth through Sixth Grade

You can imagine how excited my mother must have been to have a third baby in three years with a husband who beat her, who didn't want her to let anyone into the house and who was never at home. But she gave me life, took care of me, and I am so grateful to her and Dad for the opportunity to create in this lifetime.

My mom told me that when I was born her father said to her, "She looks like the Virgin Mary." So they named me Mary Lee Burkhart. Mom also said I was the first to talk in complete sentences. But the earliest memory I have is being whipped by my mom when I was three or four. I must have had an out of body experience, because I remember seeing myself crying and holding my teddy bear as I stood next to the kitchen sink. I felt like nobody cared. I was alone.

Another experience I remember was when I was five years old and my two older sisters were about to leave for school. I had been at the kitchen table and I was headed towards the living room when I tripped and fell backwards into a rinse tub that Mom had just poured boiling water into.

It was on a Monday (wash day) and Mom had no clean sheets, so she sent my older sister over to the neighbor's across the street to borrow a clean sheet. I was more embarrassed because my mother made me take off all of my clothes. Mom also asked the neighbor to call a taxi since we didn't have a car and we never had a phone.

I was angry at Dad because when the taxi came, instead of going straight to the hospital in Frederick, Maryland, Dad had the taxi take us to where his oldest brother, George, lived. He wanted George to know that he had to take me to the hospital. Uncle George peeked into the window while I held the sheet close to me.

When we arrived at the hospital, I must have had another out of body experience because I could see my dad carrying me and walking up the steps into the hospital. They put a salve on the burn, bandaged me up, gave me some orange juice, and asked me if I wanted to stay in the hospital for the night and keep the other girl company so they could observe me.

I said no, but they kept trying to convince me to stay. I kept repeating no, and I did so because I didn't think that my parents would come back and get me. After all, I was a brat and I was the reason that Mom was so miserable. So why would they come back and get me?

My mom ended up getting a taxi for several days and taking me to the doctor to have the bandages changed. The burn did not leave a scar, even though I would scratch it when no one was looking. On our hikes at the river, I always tried to be at the end of the line so I could scratch.

Since my mom was so negative and always complaining, I stayed as far away from her as I could. In the summer I would climb trees and go into the woods near our house to get away and have peace and quiet. I knew all the paths, so if I heard or saw someone else in the woods, I would take another path. This was because my mom had said to stay away from strangers.

I was a loner. My sisters would argue or fight and I tried to avoid that as much as I could. Mom often said, "You have selective hearing, you never come when I call." I honestly never heard her. Then one day when Mom and I were alone in the house and I was playing on my bed, I heard this voice say "Mary." It did not sound like my mother's voice, but no one else was in the house, so I went downstairs and asked my mother what she wanted. She replied, "Nothing."

So I returned upstairs and continued to play, and again I heard this voice say "Mary." So I went back downstairs and asked my mom, "What do you want?" She again said that she hadn't called me. I went back upstairs to the bedroom again, and heard the voice call my name again. So I asked my mother once again, "What do you want?" She again said that she did not call me, but she said, "Maybe God is calling you." So I went back upstairs petrified that God might call me again and what would I say? What did He want? What would I do? But I didn't hear the voice again.

Was God trying to get my attention? I don't know. I didn't go to church. Mom didn't go because her church mailed her a notice that she was no longer a member because she had not tithed to the church.

She was mad and still is. "That is not what churches are for. That's just not right."

The only thing we had on any wall was a plaque with a picture of Jesus that said, "I Am The Way, the Truth, and the Life." Her father gave it to her, and when I was married he gave me one also.

Vaccination time had come and the doctor gave me the smallpox shot four or five times, however it never took. The last time we went the doctor said, "If it doesn't take this time, don't bring her back."

On the first day of school my sister took me to the church stop to catch the school bus. We were going to the new Brunswick Elementary School on the other end of town. When the bus monitor asked me my name, I didn't have a clue what she meant. My older sister, Virginia, told her that my name was Mary. *I still remember my name is Mary!* I was clueless in school as well.

I was assigned to this wonderful teacher who asked, "My class is too full, would anyone please volunteer to go to the other class?"

Well, she was so nice that I volunteered. My sisters told me that I shouldn't have moved because that teacher was mean. And they were absolutely right, but I was lost in school. I remember learning the alphabet and how to write in cursive rather than print. My teacher called my sister Marie into the room and in front of me, told her to ask my mother to help me with my homework.

When I got home, my mom asked, "What homework do you have to do?"

I honestly answered that I didn't know.

I would get in trouble in class so that I could go to the coatroom that was in the back of the classroom. It was more fun in there than sitting still at a desk.

Besides being a loner I was very bashful. I was too afraid to raise my hand to go to the bathroom. One day in second grade I had to go so bad, but I was afraid to ask. I kept hoping that the teacher would stop and give us time to go, however that didn't happen. I sat at my desk in agony. What was I going to do? I decided I could pee in my little plastic zip purse. I was actually caving in on myself mentally, hoping that no one would see me do it. I don't know how long I agonized over it, but it seemed like an eternity. Finally, I peed in my purse at my desk.

I put myself through a lot of pain, agony, and torture all because I was too bashful to raise my hand. I then decided I would never do that to myself again and the next time I had to go to the bathroom, I raised my hand and asked permission. That was so much easier and was the first step of getting out of my shell.

Since we only saw our grandparents once a year and no one came to the house, I didn't develop social skills. I was in fear most of the time in view of the fact that my mom overdid the fear thing because she was paranoid.

It was also in the second grade that my mom attended the only school functions with me. I was in the Christmas play and my mom had to buy me pajamas, which she complained about since we slept in our underwear. The play was at night so Mom got a taxi to take us there. I don't know if she used the neighbor's phone or if we walked down the hollow to the Brunswick City Park to get to a pay phone.

The play was "'Twas the Night Before Christmas." My lines were, "My Ma in her kerchief and I in my cap had just settled down for a long winter's nap. When out on the lawn there arose such a clatter, that I sprang from my bed to see what was the matter." I was so excited to have my mom in the audience.

One morning that year my mother said, "You don't look too good. Do you feel all right? Do you want to stay home today?"

Well, I certainly did want to stay home. But I regretted that decision. Dad came home and they argued and pushed each other near the basement door. Dad hit Mom and she fell to the floor. Then Dad sat on Mom and pinned her thighs on the floor and started slugging away at her with his fists.

I can still see this sight. I was terrified. This picture has haunted me because Mom was not pushing against Dad so he wouldn't leave the house. He was brutally beating her so she would give him money. I didn't want to stay home any more from school unless I was sick, and even then I usually went to school. Being there was better on my psyche than being at home.

Bedwetting was a problem for me once in awhile until the second grade. Since I slept with two of my sisters, I would say that I hadn't done it. But one night I knew I had wet the bed, I realized I was having a dream about having to go to the bathroom. So after that, anytime I dreamed I had to go, I would just get up and go. I never wet the bed after that, and I bet my sisters were glad!

That summer I received one of my greatest lessons. Several of the neighbors were over playing at our apartment house with my sisters and me. Someone found a turtle and we all stood around. Then someone said that someone should kill the turtle, so I did it. And my mother whipped my ass. I felt so bad about killing the turtle afterwards, and I told my mom that they had told me to do it.

She said, "If someone told you to jump off a bridge, would you do it?"

I of course said, "No." But I knew I had done it, because I wanted attention. No one ever paid any attention to me because I was the third child. My older sisters always got all the attention. So it was then that I decided that I would never do anything other people said to do, just to get attention.

If it doesn't feel right, don't do it.

I think it was this same summer that I learned the power of prayer. One day the same neighbors started chasing my sisters and I. They all ran into the second cellar door and locked me out. You could not lock the first cellar door, so I banged on the second one but my sisters would not let me in. Without knowing, I stood directly under the window where the coal was poured into the outer basement room. I prayed to God and asked if he would protect me and not let anyone hurt me. I heard giggling and looked up and two of the older kids let go of a rock that was almost three times the size of my head. I didn't have time to move and the rock hit me on top of the head and fell to the floor. I did not feel a thing.

When my mother saw the rock she got madder than hell. I told her that my sisters had locked me out. She made both of them carry the rock to the neighbor's house and the two of them could barely lift it. They could only raise the rock up about six to eight-inches off the ground and had to stop several times to rest because it was so heavy.

My mother said, "They could have killed her. Look at the size of that rock."

At the time I personally didn't know why she was so upset. I didn't have any pain, so why was Mom hollering? When I think about the size of that rock today, I know that if that had been one of my children, I would have been hollering too. I know God sent Angels to protect me that day, because I felt no pain.

The following winter the older boy who helped drop the rock was picking on me while Marie and I was sled riding. Marie beat up the boy and told him that if he ever picked on me again, she would beat the shit out of him. That boy never bothered me again. Was she trying to make up for locking me out during the summer, or was she just taking up for me … or both?

It was in the third grade that I no longer felt lost in school. We were put in groups, with Group I being the above average students, Group II, the average and Group III the slower students. I was in Group II and was able to answer questions the teacher would ask me. I was having fun, until the teacher put me into Group I. What a bummer. I rebelled and didn't study, but to no avail. The teacher kept me in the first group.

Also in the third grade my bus stop was changed from the church to the store. I think it was because my sister, Virginia, had a friend on the store stop. It was five more blocks to walk, but in spite of this I could get candy at the store if I had money before going to school. One day the owner asked me if I wanted to come back behind the candy counter and pick out any candy I wanted. My sixth sense told me not to, but he was so nice and his wife was there, and he was going to let me choose any piece of candy I wanted.

So I went behind the candy counter and the owner started feeling my breast, and I got out of there fast. His wife just sat there and laughed. I never went into the store after that unless someone else went with me.

I have never told anyone this story until now. Years later a neighbor of the store owner's told me that the wife never wore underwear and would raise her skirt and flash the neighbor's boyfriend when he would come see her.

Before this happened, I thought that the owners were the nicest people I had ever met. I was too embarrassed and ashamed to tell my mom.

There have been other times I did not listen to my sixth sense, but now I put forth the effort to do so – especially since it has always been right.

In the sixth grade my whole class went to Camp Greentop for the week. Everybody went except for me. My mother said she did not have the money to buy clothes and supplies for me to go. I only had two dresses that had been handed down from my two older sisters to wear to school and since she was always saying that she didn't have any money, I did not insist. The following year my younger sister insisted and Mom sent her.

That always bothered me, until I read the book, *Ask and It is Given*, by Esther and Jerry Hicks. It was then that I realized that my vibration was not high enough for me to receive. Also, the Universe gave me what my thought was, "Mom can't afford it." And the Universe also gave my sister what her thought was, "Mom can afford it and I am going."

Missing Camp Greentop was a blessing because I was treated very special by Mrs. Carter. The joke at the school about her students was that they were Carter's Little Liver Pills. I loved her and could tell that most of the students loved having her as a teacher. Wow! School could be fun. When teachers enjoy what they are doing and love their students, what a difference it is to be in their class.

The first six years of school I hated because I could not see the chalkboards, so I was always looking at the papers of the people on my right or left. I didn't do it to copy their answers, but to get the questions that the teacher had written on the board. When I took a spelling test, at best maybe I would get six out of 20 words, mainly because I did not study. So for the most part, school was a struggle.

During this time I also hated being at home. I wanted peace so I tried to do everything right so as not to rock the boat, and then maybe Mom wouldn't bitch. I tried to be perfect (ha, ha) but it didn't do any good. When Mom and Dad would fight, I would run upstairs and hide in the back room where Mom stored things. If I could not get upstairs, I would hide behind the chair in the living room and put my hands over my ears. I didn't want to see Mom or my sisters being beaten or hear their screams. I would also pray and ask God to please let my mom live.

Even though I would hide most of the time, there were many times I could not avoid seeing the fights. One of those times I saw my dad choking my mom against the wall until she passed out. He waited until she came to, and then left.

A couple of times when we were younger Virginia told all of us to get out on the roof above the porch during a fight. It scared me and I wondered why we were out there since the roof slanted down. Dad wouldn't hurt us unless we interfered with the fight, which I never did. I just stayed out of sight and didn't say anything. Mom was horrified when she discovered that Virginia was taking us out of their bedroom window and putting us on a slanted roof.

One day Marie put pots and lids all over the steps and dared Dad to come up after her. She was hoping he would come up, fall, and break his neck. At nighttime, Marie would roll her head back and forth until she fell asleep. She told me that once in awhile she still rolls her head. Needless to say, Marie had her own fold-up bed that she slept in alone.

When Mom thought we were old enough, she would leave us at home when she went out to get groceries. Virginia was in control then, but the rest of us didn't like that. We were playing and I went to go in the front door, but Virginia locked me out. I was determined that no one was locking me out so I just busted the front door open. I knocked Virginia on the floor and was going to hit her, but I realized that I didn't want to hurt her. So I just got up off of her. I wanted peace.

The front door was easy to burst open and we all knew that anybody who wanted to could come in. So at nighttime, Betty or Marie would go around and make sure that all the doors were locked. They would put pan lids propped up against the doors to warn us if anybody came in. I remember going around with Betty every evening to check all the doors. The back door to the basement was a sliding door that anyone could have come in. I still have dreams once in awhile about securing that door. Is it about protection of my backside?

I think it was when I was in fifth or sixth grade that my father got his first car – an old Studebaker that my two older sisters were embarrassed to be in. So when Dad drove through town, my sisters would duck down so that no one could see them.

It was around this time that we also got a television. Mom would let us watch the Musketeers and American Bandstand – we all learned how to dance watching American Bandstand.

Senior Picture of Mary
Photo by Charles F. Magee

Seventh through Twelfth Grade

It was in the seventh grade where I was finally with a different group of students. Throughout grade school I had been with the same group of approximately 30 students, but in seventh grade I thought to myself that these new students didn't know that I was stupid. This gave me a whole new lease on life. It was also the first time I had more than one teacher, and I loved moving to other rooms with different teachers. The only bad part was that I still couldn't see the blackboard.

I expanded a lot during this year because of a wonderful teacher named Miss Lloyd, who was an old maid. My friend thought she was nosey because she would ask personal questions, but I loved her. To me it made me feel as though someone cared. Miss Lloyd taught the Core Class which included history, English, and other. She had the class write their autobiography, which forced me to look at my life at that point in time. I didn't want to tell her what my family life was like! She also had us read and discuss a poem about being able to look at yourself in the mirror and liking yourself so you wouldn't have to hide on a closet shelf.

I was fortunate when we had to prepare reports on a country in South America. Miss Lloyd did not require you to hand it in until you gave your oral report. My report was not done, but after hearing some students give their oral reports and hearing the questions that Miss Lloyd asked, I then knew how to do mine. I worked on my report every evening, hoping that Miss Lloyd would not call on me yet because I was so excited and wanted to add more. So of course, when I gave my report on Peru it was great!

Miss Lloyd was one smart cookie. She knew that students would learn from other students and she probably had great intuition and knew on whom to call on to give a report on each day. It was in her class that I realized that I was not stupid. My mom was always saying, "You can't do anything right. You are stupid; can't you get anything through your head?"

Mom's programming had a tremendous effect on me and to this day I am trying to overcome that and create my own life and program. I can do it.

In Miss Lloyd's class, I began to notice that I almost always knew the answers to her questions and I also noticed that the other students didn't laugh when a wrong answer was given. Therefore I began to raise my hand when I knew the answer and Miss Lloyd put a comment on my third report card saying that she was glad that I was participating in class more. I also decided to study my spelling words. I very seldom missed more than one or two, usually getting 100 percent on the spelling tests. It was amazing what studying could do!

It was also in the seventh grade that I began to have monthly periods. I used rolled-up toilet paper because I didn't want what happened to one of my classmate's to happen to me (a large blood spot on her white skirt.) A month later I overheard my mom explaining to my older sister what to do, so I told her that I was having periods also. Oh wonderful! Coming into womanhood is so great. (Just kidding about that part!) However, it did give me the ability to have my wonderful children later.

One of my closest friends moved up on New York Hill in Brunswick, Maryland, and we would walk to school together. After she moved up on the Hill, she would come over to my house and beg my mom to let me go over to her house to spend the night. She would not take a no answer from my mom, she would just beg her until my mom gave in.

I thought that this was strange. I would go over to her house and her mother would threaten her verbally the entire time I was there.

"Just because Mary is here, don't think that I won't remember."

I went over there often, and one time my friend came to school when we were in the twelfth grade with a scarf around her neck. She was hiding a six-to-seven-inch long knife slit that her mother had made with a butcher knife in her neck. When she climbed out on the porch roof to get away from her mother, her older brothers took the knife away.

It was 20 years before my friend told me that her mother was on drugs and when she would ask me to stay; it was because she thought that her mother was going to kill her that night. She would take turns asking different friends to stay.

After report cards came out, I would go with her to see our teachers and she would beg them to change her grade to an "A." I always wondered why, but she told me 20 years later that if she didn't get straight "A's" her mother would make her take off all her clothes in front of her older brothers and then she would whip her with an ironing board cord. My friend would then have to wipe up her own blood off the floor. Sometimes her mother would whip her for something she had done weeks before and she would get mad if my friend couldn't remember what it was that she had done wrong.

I often wondered what was worse, being beaten or watching someone else being beaten. Either one I didn't want to experience. My friend told me later that she only wanted her mother to apologize to her, but her mother said that she didn't have anything to apologize for. My friend's desire for her mother to apologize to her so that she could feel better was giving her power to her mother.

It is more empowering to forgive, feel better and then go forth and create what you want, instead of dwelling in the past. You become self-empowered.

My friend and I ran around together, we went bowling at a duckpin bowling alley where you had to wait for the pin boy to reset the pins and clear away the downed ones. Not long after, a new bowling alley was built with automatic pin setters. We went by the Brunswick City Park one time where a group of men were playing ball, and it was there that I met my husband in the summer of 1961 when I was 15 years old and he was 24. He and several other guys who were playing ball asked us if we would go to the store and get them some chips and drinks.

My friend started talking to my future husband and he offered to drive us home. We began dating after that, with some reservations from my mom, since he was nine years older than me. Every time we went out on a date, we took at least two of my sisters with us. We went roller skating, dancing and swimming at the Braddock Heights amusement center. We also went to the Fort Drive-In movies in Harpers Ferry, West Virginia.

I became very ill in March of 1962. I had taken the NEDT test (which showed whether you were college material) on a Saturday and was running such a high fever I could barely take the test. The next day I got severe cramps and started vomiting. That is when Mom asked me if I had had sex with my boyfriend. I said yes, and she assumed that I was pregnant. (I was not.)

Old Dr. Carpenter came to the house and gave my mom some pills to give me. I was taking pills every hour and throwing them up. He said that if I didn't get better he would put me in the hospital. The cramps lessened a day later and then for the next three days I threw up.After that I went downstairs and sat in a chair. When I looked at my hands, they looked green. I would learn a few years later that I had had an appendix attack (and lived!) It was during that time that my mom told me that her dad thought I looked like the Virgin Mary so they named me Mary. *Wasn't that a lovely time to find that out?*

Mom also revealed to me that she had been pregnant with my oldest sister and had to hunt Dad down to get married. She also told me that she wanted to get married when she was 16, but her mother said no. She always wondered if she would have been happy if her mom had said yes. That is the reason why my mom said that my boyfriend and I could get married.

We had obtained the marriage license and planned to get married on a Saturday, except that my monthly period came around and I told my boyfriend that I was not pregnant on a Monday. That evening he showed up and asked me to go with him. His friend Peachy and her boyfriend were in the car. I think that Peachy convinced my boyfriend to go ahead and get married before my mother found out that I was not pregnant, so that she wouldn't charge my boyfriend with the rape of a minor.

So that night, on a rainy April 9, 1962, I got married. I knew after the minister pronounced us man and wife that I had made a mistake. My husband did not bend down and kiss me, after what seemed like an eternity, I stood up on my tiptoes and kissed him. To add more insult to the marriage, when we stopped to get something to eat, I left my pocketbook in the car and it was stolen. My pocketbook had all the money my mom had given me that I had saved from the past four Christmas's. Every year she gave me five dollars as well as a stocking full of candy, nuts and an orange.

I wanted to cry, and I did, for almost every day of my marriage for the first four years. I felt violated every night. My husband's idea of foreplay was to give me a kiss and start having sex. When I suggested foreplay and what I would like, he called me a slut and a whore. There had been foreplay before the marriage, so where was it now? I had made a commitment before God, and I was keeping it.

Mom wanted me to finish school since I was in the tenth grade when I got married, and she had never finished school. When my husband picked me up on Saturday, we pretended we were getting married that day, though I did tell Mom later that we had actually gotten married on Monday. I took my possessions, which consisted of a handful of hangers with clothes on them and one box of things. My new husband's mouth fell open and he said, "Is this all you have?"

He said that he would fix that and with his next paycheck he bought me some clothes. That was very sweet of him.

There was one box of my personal possessions that had been missing a couple of years before I was married. It was my paper doll box, and I had loved playing with them, some of which had been my Aunt Esther's. At the beginning, I would always choose which beautiful doll was the prettiest, which one was the smartest, and after awhile I decided that they were both beautiful and smart. The dolls were equal. I would rush home to design and make clothes for my paper dolls. I loved them and when I played with them I could have peace and quiet.

One evening my mother said to me, "Mary, sometimes a person gets so wrapped up in something that they lose touch with reality. People need to live in the real world."

The next day when I came home, the box was missing. I ran downstairs to Mom and asked her, "Do you know what happened to my paper doll box?"

She said that maybe it got mixed up in the trash box and got burned, so I went down to the basement and searched through the barrel that held paper to start the coal furnace, but it was not there. I cried. I knew my mom had warned me the night before and then the very next day she burned my paper dolls. I didn't need them anymore because I had learned the lesson that we are all equal – even the paper dolls. One doesn't have to be prettier, richer or anything else. These are judgments, which in the Bible in Matthew 7:1 says, "Judge not, that ye not be judged."

I am still working on that. We are all equal.

While writing this book I had lunch with my mom and when she saw someone wearing bleached out jeans from below the buttocks, she said that they shouldn't sell jeans like that and no one should buy them. I thought for a minute about what I should say. Normally I would have said something like they have a right to choose what they want to sell and the buyer has a right to buy what they want. But instead I told her, "You have a right to your opinion." This felt wonderful and I was not making a judgment on my mom, which would have been a double judgment.

After I was married I saw a television special on how a family of monkeys that had been kept isolated would react when they were introduced to other monkeys. The family of monkeys would run to a corner in the cage and huddle close together.

I was stunned because that is exactly what my sisters and I would do when someone came to our apartment. We would all run upstairs, huddle together, and lean over the banister to see who was there. After Mom would encourage us to come down, we would come down one by one. When I was in the eighth grade, I stopped doing that because I was more interested in seeing who was there.

It was in the eleventh grade that I finally got a pair of glasses. My husband bought them for me. When I came out of the eye doctor's office, I was so excited to see I kept pointing at things that I could never see before. My sister had gone with us and asked me to stop pointing because it was drawing attention to us, but I didn't care. I could see!

In the eleventh grade whenever I was sick and didn't go to school, I knew that my friend and maybe a couple of other girls would show up at my apartment, which was in the old Brunswick Elementary School where my two older sisters had gone. My friend would also stop by some mornings and we would walk to school together.

One morning we were walking to school when my friend convinced me to skip school that day. So we turned around and went back to my apartment. She wanted to go to Lovettsville, Virginia, but on the way there she stopped by a house where her aunts lived. Even though no one had actually told me, I knew it was a whorehouse. I hoped that Dad wasn't there. My friend's mother was a whore; it was how she supported her family after her husband left her, and even maybe before that. People used to say that there was a church on every corner, a beer joint and a whorehouse to match in Brunswick, because it was a layover town for men who worked on the railroad.

So when my dad found out that I had been in the whorehouse, he blew a gasket. He told me that if my husband couldn't keep me straight, then I would have to come back home and he would.

I didn't say anything, but it was all I could do not to burst out laughing. Here was an example of do as I say, not as I do. Dad was one to talk about keeping me straight since he was very seldom home, but he was mad because he was very proud of all of us girls and he would brag about how smart and good we were. We were a part of him, so therefore there was something good about him. We were something to be proud of.

There is no right or wrong; we are all equal.

I felt this when I was in the whorehouse listening to my friend's relatives. This Daily Buddhist Wisdom email I received expresses it beautifully:

"I come from the East, most of you (here) are Westerners. If I look at you superficially we are different, and if I put my emphasis on that level, we grow more distant. If I look on you as my own kind, as human beings like myself, with one nose, two eyes, and so forth, then automatically that distance is gone. We are the same human flesh. I want happiness: you also want happiness. From that mutual recognition, we can built respect and real trust of each other. From that can come cooperation and harmony." – *His Holiness, the Dalai Lama*

My husband and I moved to Lovettsville, Virginia. This move gave me a deep appreciation of school and I never played hooky again. Since we didn't have any money and I wanted to graduate from Brunswick High, I wrote a letter to the Board of Education asking if I could still attend Brunswick High without paying an out-of-state tuition. They granted it, and my typing teacher picked me up each day at the end of the road where I lived. Yahoo!

In the twelfth grade, I had my third episode with severe cramps that doubled me over accompanied with vomiting. My husband left for work and told me he would be back to take me to the doctor's again. (Approximately a year earlier I had the same symptoms and when we went to the doctor in Brunswick, he couldn't find the source of the pain, even after giving me a shot. My husband then had to carry me out to the car because the shot knocked me out.)

This time he took me to Leesburg, Virginia, to his doctor, who pinpointed the pain immediately and told me that I needed to have an appendix operation right away. The surgeon met me at the hospital and I was operated on so fast that I didn't have time to worry about it. *Thank you, God.*

My husband's aunt was a nurse and she examined the appendix after the surgery. She told me that I was fortunate, because there had been no surgeons at the hospital and that they had just caught the one who operated on me before he was supposed to leave town. *Thank you, God.* She said that my appendix looked like link sausage, which meant that I had had several attacks.

President John F. Kennedy was assassinated when I was in the twelfth grade. I had just had a couple of teeth pulled and one of them had abscessed. I was spending the day with another of my husband's aunts who had taken me to the dentist, and we were eating lunch when the news came over the television. I was in shock, as were most Americans. I used to rush home to see his news conferences on TV.

Our senior class trip was to New York City to see the World's Fair, but I did not go since I thought I didn't have the money. But winning the design for the front of the 1964 Senior Class book made up for it. I put the world in the circle of the six with the energy looping around it. Even though after I got married I changed my course to commercial, because I had two years of French and two years of Algebra, I was presented The Academic Course diploma. At the time of my graduation, an academic diploma was required to go to college.

No one in my immediate family attended the ceremony on June 10th, except for my in-laws and my husband. His mother, grandmother, stepmother, father, sister, and stepsister also attended. Since I knew that no one would attend my sisters' graduations, I attended all of them to show family support and honor them. At my two older sisters' graduations I sang in the glee club.

Births of My Children

The most wonderful results of my marriage are my four children. Even though I was not happy in my marriage, I didn't want to put that unhappiness on my children the way that my mom had done to my sisters and me. I have no regrets that I stayed with my husband and kept my family together.

In numerology, my life path number is a six, which is Love and Responsibility. The Life Path is the major lesson to be learned in this life – the defined path which will provide the maximum in growth and development according to the *Numerology, The Complete Guide, Vol. 1,* by Matthew Goodwin. This validates why I chose to stay and raise my children with their dad. I had always wanted four children. When I had my first psychic reading, my guide said that my children, my husband, and I were friends in a past life in Canada. It was then that our souls had agreed to come back as a family in this lifetime.

When I graduated from high school, I was two months pregnant with Loretta. I dreamed while I was carrying her that she was born with a newspaper rolled up in her hand. She is an avid reader, has a selective photographic memory, is intuitive, and is also a rebel. While writing this book she told me that she was spoiled. Maybe so, for her dad bought her something every week when she was young.

On the day Loretta was born, my husband left me off at the hospital on his way to work. When visiting hours came, he stood outside the nursery window, which wasn't opened for 20 minutes. I was hurt that he did not sit with me until it was time for the curtain to be opened.

For the first three months, Loretta would get colic every evening so we walked the floor with her and tried many remedies. Fortunately she started sleeping through the night within a few days after bringing her home.

A year later, on Valentine's Day, my husband brought Loretta and me a small box of candy. I was hurt that he didn't get me a larger box of candy – especially since I was carrying our second child. I was also jealous of the attention that he was giving Loretta. She had his love, not me. I didn't like how I was thinking, or the jealousy. Even though money and things don't give you love, I was expecting it from my husband since he didn't show any affection.

I began to hate myself for the way I was thinking. During this time I had a profound and disturbing dream where thousands or more people had died. There were so many dead people that their heads were cut off and put in toilets for viewing. As people passed by the head in the toilets that were in a long outhouse, the heads were flushed away. I was quite shaken up by the dream and I started singing in my mind, "Yes, Jesus loves me. The Bible tells me so." It was the only thing that would calm me down. Even though I did not love myself, I knew God did. After that dream, I started reading the Bible from front to back and I started to go to church.

Was the dream telling me that the body and mind were not important? One of my classmates was in the dream following me in the outhouse. She was the one who had stood up in class one day in the seventh grade and her white skirt had a six-inch bloodstained circle in the back of it. I had felt such compassion and embarrassment for her womanhood to be exposed. In a dream class I took I was told that every person in the dream represents you. Was she in the dream to express compassion for myself? Was she in the dream expressing the exposure of my dark side? Or was it exposing my human side? Was she there to expose the vulnerable feminine side of me? To be able to look myself in the mirror and love myself is so important to my soul.

A few months after the dream, Loretta became very sick. The first day she had vomited 12 times and she had 12 bowel movements that went straight through her diaper and rubber pants onto the floor. The second day the same thing happened and when I gave her a bath she licked the water off her arms. This terrified me. Even though it was a Saturday night, my doctor made a house call and gave me suppositories to help, but it didn't seem to matter.

The next day she was still doing the same thing. I was exhausted from cleaning the floor and changing diapers on top of being four months pregnant. I put her in the crib in our room on Sunday night and I could hear the bowel movement dripping down onto the floor. I cried and asked God to please help Loretta. He answered my prayers because Loretta did not have another bowel movement that evening. The next day my husband's stepmother was driving us to the doctor, when she saw Loretta she gasped. She was just skin and bones. But she made it.

As the doctor said, "I believe we have a winner."

Thank you, God.

My son Larry was born in August of 1966. His birth was my hardest labor. The doctor was going out of town so he induced me on Tuesday night. When the doctor came in to see me, he said that I was having labor contractions. That was at 9:00 p.m. and Larry wasn't born until approximately 3:30 p.m. on Wednesday afternoon. Since my doctor had his meeting, he gave me a shot to relax me, but it had the opposite effect and another doctor delivered my baby. I would not recommend that any pregnant woman have induced labor unless she or the baby is in danger.

Larry, like all of my babies, was jaundiced after birth. I found out several years ago that I have O+ blood type and all my children have A+ blood type. Larry's jaundice was so bad that they said if the count went up any further they would have to do a blood transfusion. The hospital did not have the capacity to do this, so I went with Larry to Sibley Hospital in Washington, D.C. in an ambulance.

I did not stay at either hospital since we didn't have insurance at the time. But this was probably the one time I should have stayed. I was in great pain. I would put on a girdle because my behind felt like it was going to fall off. Two hours later I would have to take it off because of the pain. I did this routine every two hours for several days. The first day I went down to see Larry at Sibley, but the day he came home I could not go because of the pain. My husband fed Larry that night because I was still in so much pain and I was crying. That was the only time my husband got up to feed a baby during the night.

Larry was a good baby. He was competitive and full of energy like Loretta.

She would pick up two of Larry's toys and say, "Which one do you want to play with? I will play with the other one."

Larry would sit there and try to decide. This was pretty smart on Loretta's part, but I told Larry that both of the toys were his and that Loretta should ask him if she might play with one of them. The two of them were active all day, mostly playing on toys that they could ride.

Potty training was very easy for Larry. I asked my husband to take him to the bathroom with him and show him how to go, because he was ready. When my husband did this, Larry was trained on the spot. He was just a little over a year old. He also started walking at ten months.

When Loretta was four and Larry was two and a half, two older boys (one was a little older than Loretta and much bigger) started throwing rocks at them. I would tell the boys to stop, tell my own children not to throw rocks, and smack my children's butts. These boys continued to do it until one day when I heard a knock at the door.

It was the boy that was close to Loretta's age. He said, "Mrs. Reed, Larry hit me with a rock."

I know that he expected me to whip Larry, but I just said to him, "He did? You taught him well."

"But Larry hit me with a rock," the boy said again. "Aren't you going to whip him?"

I said, "No, you were a good teacher," and I shut the door.

The boys never threw rocks at my children again. Larry became a baseball pitcher and he pitched in many playoff games from Little League on up. He pitched for Jefferson High School at the West Virginia

State tournament. He could thank those two boys for helping him to develop his accuracy in pitching at a very young age!

I decided to take birth control pills after Larry was born. I tried to play softball but I wasn't very good, but it gave me enough knowledge and skill to teach Loretta and Larry how to play ball. During this time, May, 1968, I was baptized, along with Loretta and Larry at the Zion Lutheran Church in Lovettsville. Even though Loretta was only three and a half, she remembers them putting water on her head and wiping it with the cloth.

All my teeth were pulled after I had Larry. I had both upper and lower false teeth put in, just like my Granddaddy Burkhart. *Hurray!*

When Virginia saw me with my teeth she said, "Mary, you have a beautiful smile. I never saw you smile before."

That was because one of my front teeth had been crooked and eventually broke off while I was in the ninth grade. I would hold my hand in front of my face when I smiled or talked. The guidance counselor at school had asked me about my teeth. She suggested that they could get some help, but my mom said absolutely not. She was not accepting charity.

My husband joined the Lovettsville Volunteer Fire Company and I joined the auxiliary. This was a very political organization. Some of the members only wanted women who had husbands that were volunteer firemen to have the right to vote and be a full member. Of course there were two sides. One side was for open membership with full privilege and one side was for restricted membership with limited privilege.

This was the first time that I spoke up at a large meeting and stated my reasons for letting anyone who wanted to be an auxiliary member to be able to become a full member with full privileges. I was grateful that after my speech more than half were in agreement, but the rule was that you needed a bigger percentage to change the rule. I think we missed it by two votes. It was a great challenge for me to stand up and state what I believed in, just as my dad had done, even if it was on a much smaller scale. *Yea! I did it.*

In July, 1968 I got the nerve, with the help of Celie (my husband's oldest sister) to take a helicopter ride over the Gettysburg battlefields. It was exhilarating and awesome. *Thank you, Celie.*

In September, 1969, my third child Jeanelle was born three weeks past her due date. She looked like my husband's brother. She was the easiest labor of all the children. After the doctor had finished examining me, I had my first labor contraction while his hand was still on my abdomen.

He said, "You are having a labor contraction. That was pretty long and hard. Let's time the next one." He checked the next contraction and said I could go home and get my things then go to the hospital. I had her four hours later.

All my labor pains that were hard were in my back, with all of my children. I was hollering when the nurse came in and checked me. She said, "You are not doing anything. Shut up and be quiet," and she left the room. Within a few minutes, an explosion of water came from me and I called for the nurse.

The nurse said in a nasty tone, "What do you want?"

I told her that my water had broken. She examined me and told me not to bear down, that the baby's head was about to come out. As she was running to wake up the doctor, she said to the other nurse, "She wasn't doing anything a minute ago and now the baby's head is there."

Both times that Jeanelle gave birth, they were easy ones because she said, "I am going to give easy births." *Now I know the secret.*

I wish I had known that before, because I would have said that for all of my deliveries. *Because I did not feel loved by my husband, was that why my first two were so long and hard?* It is about my feelings and thoughts, not my husband's. My husband was not responsible. I was responsible. I must love myself first, before I can feel love from someone else.

Jeanelle is Miss Clean. When she was able to walk, if she spilled water on her dress she would get another dress to put on. Jeanelle would also keep the house clean. She actually did more work around the house than the others. She was very perceptive. She would tell me at a very young age that I was using psychology on her to get her to do something, but that she would do it anyway. *Thank you, Jeanelle.*

She must have a small bladder like me because we competed for who would get to use the bathroom last before going somewhere. Donna Sims, a psychic, told me that she is more like me than I know. She is now going to massage school in Colorado to become a massage therapist like me. She is also very intuitive, just like Loretta.

Since Celie was living with us at the time Jeanelle was born, she felt like she had two mommies, and this overwhelmed her. Celie was very caring and loving, but also domineering. I had to ask her not to be Jeanelle's boss. One mommy was all that Jeanelle needed.

When Jeanelle was tired she would get very cranky and cry. Loretta would try to console her. But I just let her cry because I knew that she was just tired and she would eventually stop. When she got mad at me, she would tell me that she hated me. I would just let her alone and told her it was okay how she felt. Later she would tell me that she really loved me. I of course, knew that.

I came into a lot of independence when Jeanelle was around nine months old. I had taken the written exam for my driver's license four times but I never took the driving part because I didn't have someone to practice driving with, even though we had both a car and a truck. My dear friend Nell took me out one day. She got down on her knees, prayed, and thanked God that she was still alive when she got home. When I finally did get my driver's license, thanks to Celie, I commented that this was the first time I was not pregnant when trying to get my license. But I was wrong. I was pregnant with my daughter April.

It was during this last pregnancy that the relationship ended between my husband and me, even though my plans were to make the most of it until the children were grown. Our landlord told us that we had to move since our family had outgrown the two-bedroom house.

We had been looking with no success for a new home. I never said no to any of the houses we looked at because I could always see potential in all of them, even though I didn't like any of them. When we went to see Betty at her apartment, when I was seven months pregnant, my husband said to my sister, "If I find a house I like, I don't give a damn if Mary likes it or not. I am buying it."

It was that statement that did it for me. I was so humiliated and any love that I had had for him died on that day.

In February of 1971, I delivered April. My husband came to see her, but spent most of the time with me. I wanted to say, "Get the hell out of here." But I didn't.

April is generous, loving, smart, has a photographic memory just like my dad, and is intuitive too. When I was in labor, my doctor ended up delivering another baby before my baby. He gave me a shot to relax me that almost put me out. Or should I say, did, since I could not open my eyes or say anything, although I could hear him.

April was two weeks late and the day before she was born my doctor said, "This baby is ready to come. Choose a day and I will deliver the baby. You cannot carry this baby any longer because of your varicose veins, which are popping out." I was happy when I started labor that night and gave birth to her the next day before noon.

I had my tubes tied two days later. My husband told me he would not have signed the papers for the operation except that the doctor told him that I shouldn't have anymore babies because of my varicose veins. I did not tell him that if he hadn't signed the papers, our sexual relationship would have been over and possibly we would be divorced (way before it actually happened).

Clown (Mary) at Pack 83 meeting

Bolivar, West Virginia – the First Ten Years

My husband was very excited about finding a house. He drove by it to show it to me, but I did not look at it. My eyes were directed straight ahead at the road. I did not look at the house located in Bolivar, West Virginia until we moved our things into it on Memorial Day of 1971 when April was three months old.

Because I had had a miserable childhood, I didn't want to inflict that upon my own children. So my decision was to make the best of it, since I wanted my children to be happy and have both of their parent's together. In view of the fact that I considered my love for my husband to be dead, I concentrated on my children's happiness. I was both living through and growing up, with my children.

In the fall of 1971, Loretta started the first grade and Larry started kindergarten. There was no pressure to get A's, but I did expect them to do as well as they could. One of Loretta's teachers in high school told me that she would come to his class and read a book while he was teaching.

He asked her a question and to his surprise she answered it absolutely correct. He said after that he never said anything about her reading in class. Like my mom, Loretta was bored in school too.

Loretta read a book a day to me. Larry and Jeanelle were dyslexic and I didn't have the patience to have them read to me, so I hired a tutor twice a week to read with them. When Loretta was ten, I took them all to the library. Loretta came up to me and said, "Mom, look at that book that April picked out. I don't think she knows what she has."

April was four at the time. I saw the book was *How to Make Babies*. I asked April, "What book do you have there?" and she told me the name. When we got home I asked her to explain to the whole family how to make babies. And she explained it to us all, plain and simple.

When Loretta was the same age she asked me how to make babies. We were living in Lovettsville at the time, and as I was explaining it to her, she put her hands over her ears and told me not to tell her anymore. So I didn't. I think the book that April found explained it very beautifully and simply.

After our move to Bolivar, Larry and I were playing ball in the yard. A young girl, that was passing by, suggested I take him over to the field where they were having Little League tryouts that day. We lived behind the Harpers Ferry Junior High School field, so I asked her how old he had to be. She said he had to be eight. I told her that Larry was almost six. She said, "He's better than the ones trying out for the teams."

Loretta and I also played ball, so when she turned eight she went to tryouts in the spring of 1973 and became one of the first girls to play in the Little League. Larry became the batboy for the team and practiced with them until the following year when he became a member himself.

A few years later, after I had started working, I went to one of Larry's games and saw unsportsmanlike conduct by him towards another player. The coach was laughing about it and I felt that the coach was letting go of his frustration of having a mediocre team through my son's actions. I pulled Larry aside and told him if he ever acted like that again, I would not let him play ball. After that, Larry played with good sportsmanship. It is a shame when you have a coach that doesn't teach the players how to play fairly. Larry's first coach stressed good sportsmanship.

Let us hope that our coaches today stress good sportsmanship. The boys and girls are our future. Do we want a world of bullies?

In 1982 he was in the 14 to 15 years-old division at the state playoffs in Weirton, West Virginia. Larry and another boy stayed at someone's home during the playoffs. I asked him to help out the family while he stayed there. He went overboard and was a little tired when the game started. The family sent a newspaper article and a very nice note a year later. They said that their boys still talk about Larry and that they really enjoyed his visit with them. In February of 1984 the father of this family answered questions I had for a college project about the Weirton Steel Corp.

My first vacation (since spending the week at Grandma's) was with Betty and her husband. My husband and I went with them in their camper to Nashville, Tennessee in June of 1972. The Grand Ole Opry show was great. One of the performers was Kenny Rogers. Thanks to Betty we had third row seats. Opryland had just opened, we had fun on the rides, and I thoroughly enjoyed the shows as well.

Picture of Mary at Opryland

In the middle of the night while at the campsite, I dreamt that I was flying. When I woke up I was on the other side of the steps to the camper that had been put in the middle of the camper floor. I was sleeping on the lower bunk on the inside, beside my husband, who weighed at least 220 pounds. The highest part of the steps was facing the bunk bed. How I ended up on the other side of these steps that hardly had any room on either side of them beats me. How I managed to get across my husband also astounds me.

Our trip to Tennessee was cut short because the guys wanted to get back to Harpers Ferry to see the flood that was caused by Hurricane Agnes. Every night we would call home to check on the children. In Tennessee the weather was beautiful and dry. They had been experiencing a drought.

Mom and Dad had come to my house since Dad had been flooded out. The flood was 15 to 20 feet above his trailer. Dad's trailer had two-to-three feet of mud in it and the whole place was a mess.

Wow, the power of water! Our bodies are 75–80 percent water.

After going down to the river and observing the mass destruction from the flood, I became disoriented and ran a red light on the way home. If it hadn't been for the kids I wouldn't have even known I had done so. I just stopped, looked both ways, and proceeded through the red stoplight.

Loretta said that she was around eight or nine when I stopped paddling them. Instead, I chose to tell them why I didn't want them to do what they had just done. Loretta and Larry called them lectures and recalled that they seemed to last forever, whereas a whipping only lasted a few seconds. They would rather have had a whipping! Larry said it didn't hurt that much anyway.

Ignoring the pain, stores it in your body and causes other problems down the road. I should know. I noticed that Marie never cried when she received a whipping from Mom, so I stopped crying too. It would take years of visits to my massage therapist to rid my body of the unexpressed pain that I stored in my body. It would have been much better to cry and let it go. Perhaps that is why Marie rolled her head at night.

It was true for me that the whipping hurt me more than my children. That is why one day I decided that I did not like hurting them. It was not solving the problem. Therefore, the lectures started which worked better than the whippings. It was also a break in the chain from the past.

Jeanelle and April said that they had to be good because Loretta and Larry were so bad. Sounds like what I did in my younger days. It is funny, since I didn't consider them bad, just active, inquisitive, and each with a mind of their own. I considered those good traits. They were always trying to find out how far they could go, just like all children do.

Larry says that I had eyes in the back of my head, because every time he left the yard I would call him. *You can check the back of my head, but I don't have anything unusual there!* If the children were out of sight for too long then I would go looking or call for them. I was very protective of them. I didn't want them to bother the neighbors (just like my mom never wanted us to bother anyone) and I wanted to know that they were safe.

When my children were older and I was taking a nap inside, if I heard someone hollering "mommy," I would be instantly wide-awake and wondering where my children were until I realized that it wasn't them but the children next door. But it would still put me on edge.

My main source of exercise at this time was yoga on TV. But I wanted to get out and meet people, so I joined an exercise class in Harpers Ferry. The teacher invited everyone in the class to come to her husband's karate class where they were going to teach self-defense. I did that and I also took some private lessons.

The self-defense and karate classes were so empowering to me. They gave me confidence and enabled me to let go of a lot of fear my mother had taught me. I only earned two belts because the instructors moved – but what an experience! I highly recommend taking a class to learn how to defend yourself.

I also did duckpin bowling in Brunswick from 1975 –1981. Loretta also bowled and celebrated one of her birthdays there. One time two opposing bowlers humiliated me. On that day I learned that my intuition was right on about this lady whom I had met several years earlier. I had a sinking feeling at the pit of my stomach the moment I met her and I didn't know why. She seemed like a nice lady, but the feeling was right.

She and another woman mocked and laughed at my bowling stance and the way I bowled for three entire games. I did not say a word, nor did any of my teammates. This was another lesson about listening to my gut, because I was so busy with my children that I never expressed any emotion until two weeks later when I just burst out crying. And even though this probably happened during my monthly cycle, since childhood I had been stuffing my feelings.

One of the best things I ever did was to sign up as a Cub Scout den leader when Larry joined in the fall of 1974 when he was eight years old. I only did this because another mother said she would help me, but she quit within a short time because her son developed an eye twitch (that did go away after she quit.) But it was good for me in that it propelled me into the community, tapped my creativity, and helped me to understand leadership.

"Do Your Best," is the Cub Scout motto. I feel that is all we can ask of others or ourselves. During one of the summer activities that involved competition to find out who would represent the pack in what physical event, one of the Scouts laughed at another chubby Scout when he did a board jump. I said, "Cub Scouts do their best. Your best may be five feet and the other boy's may be three feet. If you jump four-feet-six-inches, you did not do your best. If the other boy jumps three feet, he did his best. You would have jumped further than him, but you would not have done your best." I never heard him make fun of the chubby boy again.

Back then the Cub Scout program was excellent, and it appears from looking on the Internet, that it still is. They would give leaders a theme and suggestions. It was up to the leaders to decide what to do for the pack meeting, which was held once a month. At one meeting the theme was farming, so I used one of the suggestions, which was a pig calling contest. I thought it would be hilarious – and it was and more.

The Cub Scout was to call his pig (which was the father, mother, brother or whoever volunteered to be the pig). Then the pig became the caller and the Cub Scout would be the pig. What happened was overwhelming to me. We laughed, yes, but the love and trust that was shown between the caller and the pig when they would hug was awesome and I almost cried (my eyes watered.) There was trust that when the caller would call that the pig would come. This was true for both times it was done. It was a wonderful surprise that I did not expect.

Each time we had sign-ups the new boys would be running around like chickens with their heads cut off. At the last sign-up I did, a mother of an older Scout said to me, "Mary, they always come in like that, but look at the gentlemen they become after being in the program."

She was right and it was very rewarding to see the growth in the Cub Scouts, so I was hesitant about leaving. But she said, "It's time for you to do something else." She was very perceptive.

God sent a domineering leader after my six years as a den leader and assistant Cub master to encourage me to leave. This woman knew everything and the rest of us didn't know what we were doing. I went to the last pack meeting and the Boy Scouts of America presented me with the Statue Award for my work. The representative told me that they knew I would quit after they had met the new den leader. They were right.

Thank you, God. It was time to leave.

In July, 1975 Larry took Red Cross swimming lessons and joined the Jefferson Park Swim Team. He then joined the Hagerstown YMCA swim team in the fall. The whole family became members. Jeanelle and April went in the Polliwog program to learn how to swim. The assistant teacher played with Jeanelle in every class and finally, on the last day she stuck her head in the water.

The following summer Loretta, Jeanelle, and April swam for the Jefferson Park Swim team. Jeanelle and April joined the Hagerstown YMCA in the fall. The swim team helped Jeanelle overcome her shyness. When she went to Kindergarten she would come home and tell me what her teachers said. But when I had a conference with her teachers, they said that they had tried everything to get her to talk, but she just wouldn't do it. She was just like me. We are both the third and middle child.

Jeanelle did not talk until everyone made a fuss about April's talking. April was not shy. She would talk to complete strangers when I would go through the stores with her in the cart. She was always very self-confident, but it surprised me that she won an award when she was in the Miss Harpers Ferry Junior High Pageant. I was surprised because all the winners had competed in many pageants and this was April's first and only pageant. She was awesome and had such poise and grace.

During this time I had an episode with Sears Department Store. I went to Sears to get a catalog and because I didn't have my postcard they would not give me one. After going to my car, I went back in and asked them why they wouldn't give me a catalog even though they knew me, because I ordered from them often. But they still wouldn't give me one. So I wrote to the President of Sears complaining that it wasn't a good business policy. I received a letter back apologizing at least four times and stating that I did not need a postcard to get a catalog.

The next time I went back to Sears, the ladies remembered me. I kept the postcard in my purse and asked for a catalog. The lady told me that she could give me a catalog, but if I had the postcard they would appreciate getting it. So I gave the postcard to them. Sometimes it is best to go to the top of an organization when you know something is not right or when you have a complaint. Consumers have the right to be treated with respect and honor. In this case, it was not a policy of Sears that you had to have a postcard to get a catalog.

Since my mother complained all the time and never did anything about it, I take action. Complaining only makes everyone around you as miserable as you are if you don't communicate to the right person.

On April 24, 1979, I got my first job as a clerk at the Coffee Mill in Harpers Ferry. Most of the clerks were negative and after I was transferred to the candy store I was very happy, because I worked by myself except for weekends. It was great to meet the many visitors to Harpers Ferry.

After a short time, I was then rescheduled to return to the Coffee Mill. I complained and told the lady I would quit, and she said that she would try to put me at the candy store more often. When I got my schedule I was at the Coffee Mill all week, so I asked my neighbor's daughter, who was the manager of the dining room at Cliffside, if she needed anybody in the dining room. She said that she needed a hostess and that I could start right away.

Needless to say, I told the lady who had scheduled me at the Coffee Mill that I quit on August 12, 1979. She told me not to quit, that she would reschedule me, but I told her no thanks. *I guess she didn't think I meant it the first time!* This was so empowering to me, not to be the victim and it was one of the first times that I honored how I felt. My feelings were important enough for me to state what I wanted. This was a big step for me.

A few years earlier I had asked my husband for a $40 allowance to do as I pleased. He gave me just enough money to pay the bills and I wanted some extra. He said that he would have to think about it. That night I found a suitcase and I put it in the closet where I could easily get to it. My husband saw me do it, even though it was dark in the bedroom. He asked me what I was doing. I told him, "Nothing." My sister had left her husband a few months before and that concerned him.

The next morning he said that he would give me an extra $40 a week. The suitcase and the fact my sister had recently left her husband did have an influence on his decision. *Thank you, Sis.* I finally had made a stand for more money to do as I pleased (which basically went for gas and money for the children to buy meals when they went away to swim meets).

In 1979, Loretta performed on the Harpers Ferry Jr. High Track team, played softball for the Shenandoah Valley Girls' Softball league (her team went to the state tournament), and she played basketball. In the fall of 1980, my other children decided to join the Frederick YMCA swim team, which held practices at Walkersville High School in Maryland.

I felt that I was propelled into a new chapter of my life while working as a hostess at Cliffside because at the same time I worked there, I also took an introductory course to accounting at Shepherd College in the fall of 1980. A new manager came to Cliffside for the dining room and the bar. He had been in the service and was used to giving commands.

He would draw up specials for the dining room that were cheaper if the customer ordered them à la carte. The waitresses usually just did that. One day there was a group staying at the hotel as well as crafters' for a craft show. The new manager came up to me, shook his finger at me, and told me not to let anyone have the buffet but the group. I almost laughed at him.One of the customers came up to me and asked, "Why didn't you just bite his finger off?"

The manager also decided one payday that the employees of the dining room and bar should come to him for their checks. I was floored when they told me at the front desk that I would have to find him to get my check. I went to his office, to the kitchen, to the bar and he wasn't there. Then I went downstairs to the lower kitchen and he wasn't there. I screamed at the top of my lungs, and then went back to the dining room. I was told that he was back in his office. I snatched my check from him. The next week the checks were back at the front desk.

I thought to myself that the hassle wasn't worth minimum wage and I certainly had the brains to make more. There was a young college student helping me on weekends who was going to Shepherd College. I asked her how much tuition was for a semester. She told me it was $188, but that did not include books.

When I asked my husband about going to college, he was fearful that if I became educated I might leave. But he also feared I would leave if he said no.

What you fear you do attract to you.

Photo by Beatrice

College 1981 through May 1984

I took a placement test for math and English and started college full-time after my fall class. I almost didn't have to take Algebra, but I missed one too many questions. When I saw the square root sign on the test, it looked familiar, but I couldn't remember it. The next day when I was taking a bath it came to me what it was.

The Algebra professor was from Afghanistan. She skipped the first ten chapters. I couldn't understand what she was saying, but after taking the whole weekend to read the first ten chapters, I then understood her. Going into the final, I had a 100 percent average because she threw out the three lowest quizzes. Also, if you were a senior, she said that you didn't have to take the final. If you had an "A" average and were a senior, some professors would let their students out of their finals. None of my professors did that, although I had a friend who didn't have to take four or five exams.

My most emotional class was "Written English One," that I took the first semester. The professor handed out a test to the class to outline a paragraph, and everyone finished before another young man and me. I was having a terrible time and wondered if I was too stupid to do this. Everybody else was done, why was I having such a hard time? The professor kept asking us if we were done and finally asked us to hand in our papers.

When he went over the paragraphs, the young man's or my paper was on top, and the professor said, "This is the wrong paper." So the two of us were given the wrong test! I was relieved, but I went to my car and burst out crying.

Did I attract this incident because back in the tenth grade my guidance counselor analyzed my results from the NEDT test and told me that I would have a hard time in college? Did I believe her and therefore I had to experience this incident? I feel there are no accidents.

Even though this happened, I learned a lot from his class and the class helped me write other papers and take tests. The first paragraph I wrote which was to show him my writing ability, the professor wrote on the paper, "You will learn how to write." He was right. I wrote this book with the help of my editor, Lisa Madden, and a couple of friends.

During one of my tennis classes, I must have pulled a muscle or somehow my spine came out of alignment because my back felt as though someone had shoved a fist under my left scapular and left it in there. That night I flunked an accounting exam, which happened to be my first and only "F." Since I could not lie flat in bed for three nights, I tried to sleep sitting in a platform rocker.

On the fourth night (Friday) I could lay flat in bed and the next day I went to work at Cliffside, but halfway through my shift I had to come home because I was vomiting. I vomited almost every hour for three days. On Monday at noon I came to the conclusion that if I wasn't going to get better I would rather die. This is the only time I felt prepared to die and it made me understand why some people say they are ready to die. It was a new perspective for me. I wasn't afraid to die under such conditions.

I then ended up getting a sore throat and cold, which ended up being a blessing in disguise. I was supposed to take an exam that day and I found out afterwards from a student that the professor had mistakenly put a problem on the test that was endless and no one could come up with a solution. *Thank you, God.* The following day the professor gave me the test and told me not to do the one question, as there was no solution.

A business statistic professor, who was from Iran, told me I was walking a tightrope and my body was telling me that I needed to rest. He was right. I had never studied in high school except for spelling words, so I was studying now. I was putting too much pressure on myself. It was all self-inflicted to get the grade.

In addition to college I still had a family of four to take care of and bills to pay. My children were awesome helping out wherever they could. Plus, I was taking them twice a week to Walkersville for swim practice and every Saturday I timed at the home meets.

I also spent a lot of time at school because I was taking at least one night course throughout my college career. Furthermore I was trying to attend baseball, softball, and basketball games that my children were in. Additionally I coached the Jefferson Park Swim team for two summers.

When there were college breaks I wanted to do anything that didn't require learning or using my brain. Cleaning the walls and floors was good. When I went to college the first semester, I felt as though I was 18 years old. But when I finished I felt like I was 98.

During my last year Loretta went to college with me. She had the same wonderful history professor that I had, Dr. Frescoln. I took a rose to her one day and told her that my daughter was in her class. She asked me what her name was. When I told her, she said, "I love having her in my class. When she takes a test she gives me her ideas and does not just dish back to me what I gave her."

She was my favorite professor, even though a friend had warned me not to take her class because she was very hard. She had traveled a lot and she gave back so much to the class through her experiences and knowledge about history.

The highlight of my college experience was doing my Business Policy project with Mike and another student. For part of the project, we had to write about the internal and external influences of a company of our choice. Mike suggested that we do it on Weirton Steel, Co. that had just been taken over by approximately 8,000 employees on January,

11, 1984. At the time this was the biggest Employee Stock Option Plan (ESOP), which had been given to the employees with the alternative being that the company was going to be closed down.

Mike had relatives in Steubenville, Ohio that worked for the West Virginia steel company and had access to copies of the McKinsey Report, which provided an analysis of the company.

Mike made an appointment with the director of public relations and was hoping to get to see Robert Loughhead, the CEO of Weirton Steel at the time. Since the company had just been taken over by the employees a few months before, I didn't think we would be able to see Loughhead. I thought the person to see was the president of the steel union; after all it was an employee buyout.

Therefore I made an appointment to see Walter Bish, who at 36 years old was the youngest man ever to hold a presidency of the union. When I met him, I understood why the local newspaper editor described him as extraordinaire.

Walter is a natural people-person with the ability to understand and communicate with people. He talked with Mike, my husband, and I for about four hours in regards to the employee buyout. After we talked with him I suggested to Mike that we call the local newspaper, as our professor had suggested, and speak with the editor.

Glen Zarfos, editor of *The Weirton Daily Times,* was very informative as well as colorful. He also understood the power of a group of people having the same goal. He knew that the company would get energy and support from that togetherness, as well as outside support since they were the underdogs.

Walter Bish went out of his way to be nice to me. He arranged for a tour of the company in May, 1984 to see steel being made. Duke Horstemeyer was my tour guide and Ralph Heise (both in public relations) showed me films on the forming of the ESOP and the first in-plant meeting, and answered my questions. Walter also arranged for me to meet with the union attorney, David L. Robertson, who, according to Walter, had been the catalyst that held the group together. He also had a fantastic memory.

When I met with Carl L. Valdiserri, the company executive vice president, another meeting also arranged by Walter, it was 5:00 p.m. I asked Carl, "Why do some people do more than is required?"

Carl's response was food for thought: "They don't have something else that they would rather be doing."

Carl was also a people-person and one of the things I noticed that I liked very much was that instead of having a chair in front of his desk to sit in, he had a chair beside his desk so that we could talk as equals. *We are all equal.*

After my very full day I called Walter's house to thank him. His wife, Sharon, answered the phone and I told her how grateful I was for everything he had done. I also said that I was having a hard time believing that he had done so much for me. She said that she couldn't believe it either, and she had asked him why. He told her, "She is a nice lady and she will not hurt the company."

Was Walter guided by angels to help me?

Sharon invited me to their house to get an outsider's perception of the employee takeover. She gave me a woman's point of view of Loughhead and what the members of the union were saying and feeling.

Thanks to Walter's help and those that I interviewed, my portion of the report on the internal influences, "Weirton's Weaknesses and Strengths" was well received by our professor and I also had an experience of a lifetime.

Not all experiences were great. There were two really smart professors who were both intimidating, so I quit their classes. One said that most college books were written on an eight grade reading level. When I quit his class I did not feel stupid. I knew I was smart, so during Christmas break I studied the book from cover to cover and the following semester I took the course with another professor who did use a very simple book.

The first professor was up in his head, but I did learn one thing in his class. In a group of 30 people, the statistics are that two people in the group will have the same birthday (both month and day). When I took the same class with the second professor, I didn't have to do anything because I had already learned on my own. But I did learn that it is more important that you know what you are doing and why than the grade level of the book you are reading. And it is very important that a teacher be able to relate the information that you need.

My goal when I started college was to finish in June, 1984, since it would be exactly 20 years from when I graduated from high school.

I made my goal; college took me three-and-a-half semesters and I took Biology I and II during the summer. My high school guidance counselor had told me that I would have trouble going to college. All my teachers stressed how hard college was. What terrible programming; I would have preferred to have encouragement from my counselor and teachers.

I graduated from Shepherd College with high honors. *You can do what you put your mind and effort to.*

Larry graduated from Jefferson High School a month after I graduated from college. He worked for an electrician and a carpenter before he joined the Navy in 1987 and became an air traffic controller. He went to Chicago for training. When he graduated my husband and I went by train to see him. Five of his friends from high school also drove up to see him graduate. The ceremony was very impressive.

We went by train because I had never flown, but we came back by airplane only because I had a bowling tournament the next morning. Now, I prefer flying.

Doing what you fear can sometimes cure the fears; others can be eased or erased by doing EFT (Emotional Freedom Technique) on you. Overcoming fears can serve us well. The less fears we have, the freer we feel.

Photo by Beatrice

June 1984 through August 1989

During this period there were many changes including the first time that lightning struck in rapid succession: The CPA exam; two jobs; bowling tournaments; first visit to psychic; 25th wedding anniversary; first time to a massage therapist; divorce; boyfriend; breakup; two deaths; quitting job; moving twice and losing a job were just a few of the things going on during this period.

After graduation I studied for the Certified Public Accountant Exam and began looking for a job. Two weeks before the exam I was called to jury duty. I did not like the idea of being in the position to judge a person's guilt, but the person did make a decision to choose light or dark, right or wrong. As Grandma and Mom said, the person made their bed, now the person has to lie in it.

My Sociology professor told me that I had been chosen well before the trial because he had done the study of the prospective jurors for the defending attorney. I actually called and told the court that I was going to take the CPA exam in two weeks, and she told me that most cases only last for three or four days. In this case, it lasted the whole two weeks. I actually could have been excused from the jury had I remembered that my dad was fighting the government for his land, but I forgot.

The judge thought that the jury would return a guilty verdict within an hour after the trial ended, but my Sociology professor must have done a good job, because we were in deliberation for two days. At one point I asked the jurors who had already made up their minds, if they would share how they had come to that decision. I was surprised that more than 30 percent said it was because they knew the person did it. That's when I decided that a jury of twelve was a good idea.

One of the jurors asked a question that the defending attorney had posed to the jury, and to my surprise this young, very quiet man spoke up for the first time and answered the question with great detail and precision. I was also impressed with the expert witnesses, but what got to me in the end were the theatrical performances of the lawyers. It seemed as though it was more of a contest as to who could give the best performance, rather than is the person guilty or not.

The next week I was in Charleston, West Virginia taking my exam, which was four days long. Since I was not prepared for taking the Business Law or Auditing exams, I did not pass. However, since I had studied for the Practical Accounting and Theory sections, those were a breeze. I would have to take the Business Law and Auditing exams again before I would pass the CPA exam and become certified.

I couldn't find a job where I lived so I accepted a job in March, 1985 approximately an hour-and-a-half away in Bethesda, Maryland at NonPublic Educational Services, Inc. I worked as an accountant there for a few months and then went to M.A. Bioproducts.

At M.A. Bioproducts, I was hired to replace another accountant. Right after I started, there was a company picnic. The president stood up and gave a speech. I didn't even know who he was. I wrote a letter to the president and suggested that it would be nice if a photo of him had been included in the company packet that was given to me when I started. I also suggested that he could do a film of the production so that the employees could see the broader picture of the operations at the company.

I took the letter to the president's office and his secretary told me to put it in his in-basket. To my surprise he gave me a letter at the end of the day that thanked me for the suggestions and said that he was glad he had hired someone who not only pointed out problems, but gave several solutions as well.

The personnel director called me into her office and told me I should have gone through her rather than directly to the president. Who was she kidding? I was bored, so I decided I would rather drive farther to work than continue to work there. The secretary at NESI had been calling me, trying to convince me to return as an assistant controller, which I did in August of 1985.

I was then offered the controller position, which caused conflict between the secretary and me because I was making more money. But even more than that, she wanted to expand in her position. She then began not to do parts of her job, and while I did do some parts for her, I did end up going to the president to inform him that there were trailers with students in them that were not insured. This broadened the rift between the secretary and me.

Every morning I would surround myself with golden white light to protect myself as the psychic had told me to do. Then I envisioned pink light going to her for love. Before she left for another job, she came into my office, we hugged, she cried, and told me she could not help herself. She knew what she was doing was wrong.

Not too long after, NESI relocated to Woodbridge, Virginia and I resigned in August 1989. Much happened during that period of my life.

Being book smart didn't help me with interpersonal relationships (and I am still learning.) While at NESI I was looking for a job closer to home. My sister, Betty, had gone to see Cindi Wallace, a channeler (psychic) in the Sugar Loaf Mountains in Maryland. Betty had asked Cindi about my job situation and Cindi told her I would not be getting a new job soon.

This upset me, so I went to see Cindi on March 18, 1987. I had her do a past, present and future guide reading. She told me the same thing. She also said that my husband had been my mother in another lifetime in Southern Italy and he/she was very, very domineering. I let her tell me what to do and my wife in that lifetime left me. It was as though I had been castrated in that lifetime. We had come together in this lifetime so that my husband could pay back his misuse of love. Of course Cindi didn't tell me the lesson I was to learn from him or the karma I needed to pay back.

She said I had always honored the mother figure in all of my lifetimes. This was so true for me. I remembered when I was 14 and had talked back to my mom.

Mom said to me, "Mary, I am so hurt. You have never talked back to me before. The rest of the kids have, but you have never talked back to me."

Cindi also told me that the president of NESI knew me when I was an Indian and he was a gun trader. My mother in that lifetime prevented me from shooting him because he was trading guns to the Indians. She said there was something to work out between us. (We always had a good relationship. After I got the job at Keller, Zanger, and Bissell, one of the interviewers, Ed Garrett, told me that it was the president's phone recommendation that had secured the job. "He spoke highly of you.")

Cindi also said my spirit guide said that I needed to let go of control and give it to God. She also suggested that I learn to be calm when I needed to do something and then things would come to me. The next Christmas I practiced this while shopping and stayed calm and kept filling my car with packages the week before Christmas. (I had always tried to do my shopping before Thanksgiving.) It was the first Christmas that my husband's mother liked what I gave her, even though in the past I had given her the size and color she had asked for.

My guide also suggested that I meditate every day. Cindi suggested that I try for five minutes and work up to 15 minutes. The very first time I tried I could not still my mind; it must have been thinking a hundred miles per minute. I just knew 15 minutes had passed, but when I looked at my watch, 15 seconds had passed. I did it again, and again only 15 seconds had passed. Now it is easy to meditate for 15 to 30 minutes.

When I went to Cindi, I started to cry as she started the session because I knew she knew the real me. This experience was very healing to me, to open myself for another person so that they could see the real me. Nevertheless, a reading is what a psychic picks up from you at the moment you are read (except for past life information) and your decisions after the reading determine your life. As the song says, life is a dance that you learn as you go.

On April 9, 1987, my children gave my husband and me a 25th anniversary party. Jeanelle later told me that she knew our marriage was not going to last too much longer, so they planned the party. Just a couple of months prior to the party I had found a cigarette butt with lipstick on it in my husband's new truck. A few weeks after the party, I went with my husband to spend the day with his sister while he worked. On the way home, I found out that he was drinking almost twice the amount of beer than I thought he was drinking which from my point of view was excessive.

When we went to the Moose that day, a very nice brunette woman came in, looked at my husband and began to cry. Another man went over and put his arm around her. It was then that I knew she had had an affair with my husband. I wanted to walk my husband over to her and say, "Take him, I don't want him." but I did not. I didn't want to make a scene and my children were not out of school yet so I was going to stay with him.

In September of 1987, my daughter, April, and I went to see "Cats" at the National Theater in Washington, D.C. I enjoyed the performance so much and it was the first time I had gone to the National Theater. She joined the thespian club and also stage managed after she graduated from school. Ten years later she played a French maid in "Private Lives" and was so funny. Four days later my dad died of cancer in the Frederick Memorial Hospital.

In March, 1988 I returned to Cindi Wallace again. At the first reading she had told me that my spirit guide (angel) said that I should get a weekly massage, but I hadn't done it. I decided to take this advice this time around and I asked where I should go for a massage. She said that there was a holistic center in Frederick. Since I was going to the bowling alley at least three times a week, I asked the clerk which one I should call. She chose one for me, and when I called the center, the gentleman told me that they did not do massages there, but if I waited 15 minutes to call the massage therapist, she should be home.

When I went to see the massage therapist in May of 1988, she told me that she had just met the gentleman at the holistic center and she gave him her phone number. I asked God to give me a massage therapist who was a Sagittarius, Leo or Aries. She was a Sagittarius. *You do get what you ask for.*

She explained that the three layers of muscles in my neck all had knots in them, and that my back was white. After getting weekly massages for several months, she told me my back was finally pink-colored. *Had my back been white from all the cringing I did each time my husband touched my back in bed?*

In August, 1988, my daughter, Jeanelle, and her Army boyfriend from Oklahoma were married. It was a fairy tale wedding, held two months after her high school graduation. She and I had spent months planning it. Her boyfriend had asked my husband if he could marry Jeanelle, and of course he said yes because he was a very confident, friendly, dependable, personable, and caring young man. They now have two wonderful boys and have been married for over 20 years.

My sister, Betty, had taken the LifeSpring course and she encouraged me to take it. So between September and October, 1988 Betty took it again with me. I learned how powerful affirmations that are written, thought, and said out loud are. There were at least 100 people in the class. On the second weekend, before the class that Friday night, I wrote, thought, and said out loud that I was willing to participate.

Well, that evening I barely had my hand up when the instructor asked for a volunteer to come up. While there were lots of people raising their hands high and saying, "pick me," you guessed it. He chose me to come up. I ended up crying when he began talking about being a martyr and he put his hand over my heart. Boy was that right on for me. I had been a martyr my whole life, and most especially with my husband.

In the LifeSpring course each person that volunteers represents an aspect of you. My sister told me after the class that she would never have had the nerve to do what I did. I was surprised, since she is so outgoing and had done many presentations, but this course was not for the weak. It brought up many personal issues you might not want to face especially in front of a large group of people.

My sister told me not to make any rash decisions about my life for at least six months, but I didn't listen. A year prior to LifeSpring, my husband and I had gone to a class in the Baltimore area and one of the instructors had put her hand on my shoulder that had no energy coming from it and said to me, "Love yourself."

For a year I had asked myself, "If you loved yourself, would you be in this relationship?" Each time my response was, "No." But I had not taken any steps to get out. I was making enough money to support myself. April was a senior in high school, and between school and work I really did not see her that much. I asked myself, "Why was I here?" It really wasn't fair to my husband.

I also knew I was using my marriage as a crutch not to get involved with another man. *Have you ever done this?*

So on November 5, 1988, I moved in with my friend in Frederick, the one whose mother had abused her. It was great, and I had a half an hour less to drive to work. *Yea!* We went dancing many nights and bowled a lot. I thoroughly enjoyed myself. After I left my husband, people would hear about the separation and expect to see me depressed. But instead their response was, "You glow. I didn't expect to see that."

In March of 1989, my friend and I went to a Bachelor Auction for the American Cancer Society. It was very interesting and fun. One of the contestants was an Aries who owned his own business, so I initiated a phone call to him. We talked several times, but never got together, still it was another stretch of the boundaries (box) I had built around me.

As a controller at NESI I dealt with a lot of project supervisors around the country and in the office. I had built up a lot of stress. My first massage therapist had quit because she was seven months pregnant, so I was looking for another one. A friend suggested Alice, whom she had never had a massage from, but she said she was very nice.

In April of 1989, I received my first massage from Alice. What an experience! She did a wonderful combination of techniques and I scheduled a two-hour massage every week. During my first massage she asked me if I had ever considered becoming a massage therapist, and I told her no. She asked me the same thing the following week and my reply was again negative.

At the beginning of June after a massage, I bought a white porcelain horse for a male friend of mine whom I would call my White Knight, because I could talk to him about everything. I had been looking for a knight to buy him but couldn't find one. He said one day, "A white knight needs a white horse." While purchasing the white horse, the owner and I were talking and I told him I was looking for a job as an accountant. He asked for my resumé.

I was going to give the Knight the white horse on a Friday night at the bowling alley, but he called and said he wasn't coming because he had left his wife at the beginning of the week. But he did come, and we started a relationship, which only lasted two months.

We met on Friday nights and all day on Saturday. We went on local day trips to parks, Gettysburg, to bowling alleys to bowl in tournaments, and to my Dad's river lot. The relationship was very intense, fun, and passionate.

My friend, I was living with, informed me that she was going to move into a new house and that her boyfriend did not want me to move in with them. The Knight suggested an apartment I could rent in Ranson that a friend of ours had just inherited. I moved some of my things in the middle of July and started cleaning the apartment.

The Knight came over on Sunday, August 6, and told me he was going back to his wife. We made love one more time and I said, "God, I love you."

The Knight said, "You never said that before."

My eyes grew big and I said, "Oh, I thought it many times." He didn't know I felt that strongly and that is why he did not come to see me during the week or on Sundays. He said he would think about our relationship and let me know.

On the following Monday, August 7, the Knight called me at work and hollered and screamed and said, "I don't want a relationship with any woman. We are through. I am not ready for marriage. I only want us to be friends. Don't talk me into changing my mind."

I did not respond and he hung up the phone. The president of NESI came in to talk to me, but I told him I had to go and I left crying.

On the way to the apartment, I stopped by my house for something and to talk to my daughter. April informed me that my husband's father had died and they were burying him on Wednesday. Back at the apartment I sat down and began reading Norman Vincent Peale's, *The Power of Positive Thinking*.

On August 8, Tuesday, Bob Crosby, the president of NESI came in and told me that on September 30 he was closing the Bethesda office. I had already trained the new controller who was in Woodbridge, Virginia since I had decided after going to Woodbridge that I did not want to move or work there.

Tuesday afternoon I stopped by the furniture store and took out a three-year loan at the bank to pay for the furniture I picked out. The owner commented that I really looked good; this was the first time I had seen him since I left my husband. His comment picked up my spirits. I went to the apartment and continued reading *The Power of Positive Thinking.*

On Wednesday, August 9, I was very depressed. After pumping gas, when I went to pay the attendant in the caged window, it was very hard for me and I had to force myself to say, "Thank you. Have a great day."

The attendant told me that only about ten people a day acknowledged him, thanked him, or told him to "Have a nice day."

I know he was an angel and God was speaking through him that day. I cried on the way to work because that gas station is a very busy place and the thought of being treated like a non-human all day made me so sad. Now, no matter what, when I have a transaction with a clerk, I look them in the eye and thank them from my heart and wish them a great day. It is such a small thing, but also a big thing. It only takes a moment.

At my father-in-law's funeral, a nephew and his girlfriend came up to me and told me they were glad that I had come. The girlfriend told me that they had eaten dinner with my husband's father the past week and he had said that he really liked me; he knew I was not going to stay with his son, and was glad I stayed with him until the children were grown. *So am I.*

My father-in-law had served in the Navy and so had my son, Larry. I was so proud and honored to see Larry in his naval uniform and my son-in-law in his Army uniform fold the United States flag and present it to my father-in-law's wife, Ruby. They both looked so handsome.

I went back to the apartment and finished *The Power of Positive Thinking.* God is my source. God is with me. When I saw the Knight on Friday I told him that since he was back with his wife, we could only be friends. He said that he understood. He had been in a car accident on Monday and his nose was damaged. I wondered if he felt like he needed to punish himself and that is why he had the accident.

A week later my sister called and told me that she was worried I was going to have a nervous breakdown, but would I come over. When I did, she confessed what she thought were her sins in order to clear her conscience and the aura field around her.

This was the first time lightning struck more than three times: lost job, end of a relationship, father-in-law's death, furniture loan, and moving.

Losing a job, death, and moving are considered the top reasons for stress. As suggested by the book, *The Power of Positive Thinking,* I made a list of all that I was thankful for. I realized that my positive attitude, massages, friends, family, faith, and the love of God enabled me to get through these events with flying colors.

The Knight stopped by and told me he had gone to a fortune-teller who had told him that he had been John Mosby (a confederate calvary battalion commander in the American Civil War) in one of his previous lifetimes and that I was his wife and we had had a very passionate relationship. I was for the North, and of course John Mosby was for the South. The fortune-teller told him that his white palomino horse had been returned to him and he told her that he didn't have a horse. She said again that his white horse had been returned a few months ago and he remembered the white horse I had given him in June.

The Knight wanted to make love and I gave in. I felt guilty, but I had missed him so much. He was great in bed and I enjoyed talking with him, especially since my ex-husband had not been good in bed and hadn't talked with me.

I spent my time looking for a job, bowling, and dancing. My sister, Betty, had purchased a red convertible Mercedes back in July, so we drove around in that and had a great time. On July 24, Betty and I went to Baltimore, where you collect your lottery winnings. She said we were going there on faith. She didn't check the numbers on the lottery ticket until we entered the room. There wasn't one right number, but we had a great time eating out and taking pictures. It was so much fun doing something spontaneous, but when I told the Knight, he told me that I was weird and was just like his wife, who lived in a dream world.

On Aug 23, I went up to Berkeley Springs to stay for four days. On the way, I stopped at a palm reader and he told me to drop the Knight because he was just a boy and I needed a man. Unfortunately (or fortunately), I did not listen.

I meditated, read self-help books that included *How To Have More In A Have —Not World*, by Terry Cole-Whittaker, went on a nature hike, ate at many different restaurants, swam at Capon State Park, had a massage at Coolfont, and got tires for my car.

It was rejuvenating and then I came home. Bob, the president of NESI, called to find out if I was coming in the next day. I had suspected that he might close the office down that week, so when I saw Bob the next day, he asked if we could close the office by Thursday, August 31. I said, "Sure." I was okay with it and very calm. Bob paid me three weeks severance pay. *Great!*

Mom, Mary, Jeanelle & Catfish Landing sign

September 1989 through August 1991

I went to the unemployment office on September 5 but didn't end up collecting since I found a job before the three weeks were up. On Friday, I received a call from a CPA firm, Keller, Brunner and Zanger, and had an interview on Monday with two partners. When I went bowling on Saturday, the Knight did not speak to me. On Tuesday, the CPA firm called and said the position that I interviewed for had been filled, but would I come in on Thursday for an interview with two more partners for another position?

One of the partners asked whether I knew how I had gotten the interview. It turned out that the owner of the store where I had bought the white horse for the Knight had given my name to the owner of the firm. I landed the job, thanks to Bob's recommendation, and started a week later. I also interviewed on Wednesday with a temporary service and was offered a job through them. *Positive thinking does pay off.*

I went bowling on the Sunday night league and the Knight's wife was there. He said that he would introduce her to me, but she left before I finished practicing. On Monday, I went to the store where I bought the white horse and thanked the owner for passing my resumé on. He suggested that I read *The Richest Man in Babylon,* by George S. Clason.

In September of 1989, my divorce was final. I was happy, but not ecstatic since we still had to do a settlement, which would take place almost two years later.

Betty had just returned from two weeks in Hawaii and we took off to Boston to take a Werner Erhart's Communication II class. On our return flight, the flight attendant offered us a drink but we both said we couldn't drink since we both had to drive home. We told her that we were burned out from the class we had just taken and she gave us both a bottle of wine to drink when we got home.

I was supposed to do a project and Federal Express it to Werner Erhart, but I didn't. I felt LifeSpring and Werner Erhart were too controlling and I stopped putting energy in either of them. But I am very glad I took the classes because they encouraged me to think outside of my box.

I had already begun at the CPA firm before I took the class. After I returned they had an image consultant come in and I discovered that I am a summer person. After reading all the manuals and procedures, I began to like it there. I had a variety of financials and tax forms to do. I learned a lot and they offered in-house training and paid for classes outside the office. I liked the professionalism there.

In October I decided to sign up for a dating service, but I never got a date. *Was that because my heart and energy was with the Knight?* His wife had surgery and actually had to go back in the hospital after she came home.

The Knight came over on a Friday night and said he had missed me. His wife wouldn't be able to have sex for seven months. The Knight looked at my bulletin board that had a picture of us at my 25th class reunion. He began to hug and kiss me. He cried. Then he picked me up and carried me to the bedroom. He told me he loved me.

I purchased a bottle opener and we drank the wine the next night. I had written an affirmation when the Knight and I first started dating: "The Knight and I, Mary Reed, will be in an enriching, empowering, and happy, honest, passionate, prosperous, rewarding committed relationship by August 11, 1989. We are one."

August 11th was the day I told him we could only be friends, but that statement was not true for long.

If I were writing an affirmation today, I would not put a date on it. I would also not put someone's name on it, because I am responsible only for me and don't need to control someone else. Furthermore I would not use the word "will" because it implies in the future never to be in the present. More powerful to use "am." Today I would write: "I, Mary B. Reed, am in an enriching, empowering, happy, honest, passionate, prosperous, committed, and fun, intimate relationship."

Let God provide the "Who" in the relationship. I'll supply the energy for it and so it is.

On November 29, 1989, my friend, Terry, took me to the doctor's. I had to leave work because every five minutes I had to run to the bathroom to change my Kotex and tampon because I was bleeding excessively. I had to put newspapers under me on the drive home and to the doctor's.

At the doctor's office I told him I had passed a blood clot the size of a softball and had almost passed out. When I had to run to the bathroom in the examining room, my doctor told me not to shut the door. I almost passed out and he came in with the smelling salt. When he pricked my finger, the blood was translucent orange. He called an ambulance.

I was given two pints of blood at the hospital and put in a bed where the foot of the bed was elevated. After a pint was given, I passed a quarter-sized clot, and the nurse exclaimed, "My God what a big clot." If she only knew that I had passed the softball size one earlier in the day! I said that was the first one I had passed since I left my doctor's office. She said, "That's because you had no blood. How could you pass a clot?"

After a day in the hospital, another doctor gave me a DNC. Betty came and did Reiki on me in the morning. I meditated before the procedure and when the anesthesiologist talked with me, I asked him not to use too much on me. He said I looked like I already had a pill to calm me down. When I went back to my family doctor for the follow-up visit, the receptionist said there was so much laughing going on in the examining room that she thought a party was going on and was completely surprised when the ambulance came to take me to the hospital.

When my mom brought me home from the hospital, there were unsavory characters outside of the apartment. I told the Knight about it and he gave me his hatchet for protection after we chopped down a

Christmas tree for the apartment. My girls, my son-in-law, Mom, the Knight, Betty, and her boyfriend came over for Christmas dinner. I kept the Christmas tree up until the end of February.

Being the mistress gave me a depressed feeling; it didn't ring true with my belief or values. Even though the Knight had said his relationship with his wife was just out of convenience. He had told me that she had bought a wedding dress and said that she was going to commit suicide if he didn't marry her, so he married her. I did a lot of soul searching and questioned the relationship I had with the Knight. *Happiness is within -- not outside of you.*

The Knight had told me he would leave his wife by spring. One day his wife called saying she was with UPS and had a package for me and needed to know how to get to my apartment. I knew I did not order anything so I hung up.

The Knight was there and asked if he could move in with me. I said "Yes," but there was some anxiety going on in the pit of my stomach. That day in February the Knight left his wife and moved in with me. He had kept his word about leaving his wife by spring.

A couple of weeks later after I got home the Knight called and asked if his wife was walking the street with a large butcher knife. She had been out there earlier, evidently looking for my apartment. I looked but didn't see anyone on the street carrying a butcher knife. But why didn't the Knight call me at work and tell me? He went to his father's and called me from there so it was safe for him. What about me?

Angels must have been looking after me that afternoon. I usually left work right at 5:00 p.m., but an employee in the cubicle beside me came in and we talked for a while. Then I went to the copier room where a bookkeeper started talking with me. So I arrived home much later than usual. *Thank you, angels.*

In late April I started throwing up just before it was time for us to go catch a bus to Florida to bowl in the National Bowling tournament. I ended up flying down to meet up with the Knight and the rest of the bowlers. I had a terrible odor coming from me, but the Knight was very loving anyway. When I got back from Florida, I went to the doctor and found out that I had not removed a Tampax. Ick. Eeewe.

One night when the Knight and I were sleeping, I turned over on my side and saw a pair of hands come out of my left side and push him out of bed. He rolled out of bed and then climbed back in. I was afraid he would be mad at me for pushing him out, but my real hands were not near him when he rolled off the bed.

He told me that he had rolled off the bed because he saw something on the ceiling coming down at him. One of my psychic friends said that on another dimension he was supposed to move and my soul agreed. Joy (Betty's psychic friend) also told me the first time that I met her that the Knight and I had come together so I could confirm to him that the messages he was getting were not in his mind.

There were many dreams and sounds of music from the Civil War era at that apartment. The Knight and I had many experiences of unlocking the door and it would open on its own.

In August of 1990, the Knight and I went to Ocean City, Maryland. That was the first time I had been there. The Knight and I had a great time riding bicycles, riding the boogie boards, taking walks, riding the rides, etc. This was worth the relationship with the Knight. We had fun every time we went, although the Knight always wore himself out and there was very little intimacy between us when we went to bed. To this day I still go there to take my continuing education credits for CPA or massage therapy.

The Knight's father was at the V.A. Center in Martinsburg. When we went to see him, the Knight told his father to stop repeating his stories. His father said he wanted the Knight to learn from his mistakes. His father said the most important thing in life is that when you go home, that you want to go home.

In September of 1990, I didn't want to go home. I could recall being in a hurry to go home, but not any longer. There was a lot to learn and I was struggling with the relationship. It was good, but then it was bad in my eyes. Perhaps I wanted more than the Knight could give. Was I like my mom who expected Dad to make her happy? Or was the Knight's self-fulfilling prophecy coming true? He had said earlier that I would leave. "They all do."

I had learned about self-fulfilling prophecy in a history class. *Do we make a statement then consciously or unconsciously make it come true? Where we put our energy is what we will create every time.*

While at Keller, Brunner, and Zanger, I didn't have enough to do so I was studying IRS publications. Then one of the partners called me in and told me he was sorry, but they did not have enough work for me. He said that this was the first time he had to let someone go that was doing their job.

Here I go again, I thought. I wrote down: "I choose to be happy."

I started my own business and the Knight was wonderful. He handed out cards and had a sign made which he put up in the lot at the apartment. Then the City of Ranson said he had to take it down, and the landlord wanted to double my rent and require that I carry insurance. The Knight pulled up the sign. He told me that the night before he had dreamt he was pulling the sign up.

The Knight bought a trailer and asked my mom if he could park it down on her river lot so he could rent it out. They would share the income from it. I had a sign made up that said: "Catfish Landing" and I put an ad in *The Washington Post*. In May, we borrowed money from Mom to buy a truck (Big Green) to haul the trailer out when floods happened. The Knight was supposed to pay my mom, but I was the one who ended up paying her. The idea did not take off.

In August we found a house in Leetown, West Virginia, which I put a deposit down on. But I didn't like the feel of the garage, so I spent the night looking through a lot of real estate books. I then looked in the *Buyer's Guide* and found a house that had just been put on the market.

The real estate agent was a member of my church so I called him on Sunday and asked if he had given the deposit to the other agent. He hadn't, so I ask him to hold it because I wanted to see this other house.

I had prayed and asked, "God, please help me find the house I am supposed to live in." The house in the *Buyer's Guide* was it. I have lived in it since August of 1991.

Trying to settle with my husband was basically just making our lawyers rich. There were court hearings that were constantly postponed and so I decided to take charge and I gave my lawyer three options to offer my husband for settlement. I knew he would take the cheapest option, but I gave him a date in which the check would have to be in my hand, after which the options were no longer valid. The check was in my hand on a Friday and I settled on my house on a Monday.

Spunky

September 1991 through March 1993

I felt a little queasy and nervous when the Knight and I signed the loan papers for our house. I didn't know why, but I just didn't have a warm and fuzzy feeling.

The following month after buying the house, the Knight bought a tiny dog that was a mix of Lhasa Apso and Chihuahua. This was my first experience with a house dog. In Feng Shui, a pet inside of the house is good. Pets are good in that they go places we don't; such as under beds which moves the energy there.

The Knight called her Spunky and she would sing for him. After Spunky dug up my lilac several times, I went after her with a broom and had her cornered in a bathroom. She almost came after me, but fortunate for me she didn't. Did Spunky know that I had learned the lesson of treating animals with respect?

No, I did not hit her, she was more important to me than the lilac. I decided never to go after her again though, after seeing the terror in her eyes. Funny thing is, she never bothered any plant that I planted after that.

I was collecting unemployment at the time we bought the house and right after that the Knight became unemployed too. Keller, Brunner, and Zanger gave me a client for my business that kept me busy, but not enough.

In November of 1991, my first grandson was born at Fort Bragg in North Carolina. The Knight and I went to see him and arrived that night. Of course, he was beautiful and special. Words cannot explain the feeling you have when you are holding your first grandchild.

Four months later, Jeanelle and her family moved to Germany where they would be living for two years. (She wrote me in March of 1993 that a friend told her that it looked like Casey Jr. had a halo on his head. I agree that he has such compassion and does not seem to be bothered about possessions but rather about humanity. Is he taking after his Great Granddaddy Frazier?)

One of the partners of Keller, Brunner, and Zanger recommended me for a job at another company that she did the taxes for. I started to work there in February of 1992, and the president wanted me to go through the books in search of embezzlement while the other bookkeeper was still there, and to get the information back into the computer that had been lost during a crash of the system.

He was then going to fire the other bookkeeper because she had written herself a loan check, even though she had paid it back. The president hired a consultant to fire her. She knew she was going to be fired, but worked diligently to get the work done. It was sad to see the impersonal firing of her by a stranger.

In April of 1992, I received a court summons from the Knight's wife's attorney to appear at the divorce proceedings. At the presentation of the court summons, I asked for a witness fee, otherwise I would not have been entitled to one.

The Knight was very upset since he knew I would tell the truth but I just surrounded myself with white golden light and stayed calm. The Knight's lawyer was surprised that the wife's lawyer did not ask me questions he thought she would.

After the Knight and I moved into our house, he informed me he had only gone back with his wife because she had promised to put his name on the title to her house. This upset me greatly, since after we moved into our house, the Knight treated me differently. It was as if he was only concerned about our house and the intimacy greatly dropped off.

After the Knight told me this, I put a letter to the angels in my Bible. It said, "Please make the divorce settlement fair and equitable between the Knight and his wife." I also prayed and asked God to make it fair and equitable. His wife kept the house.

At work I was experiencing challenges of an ethical nature. I had been told to do something that I disagreed with and it put me in a quandary. I was having very disturbing dreams and I finally decided I would not do as told. The Knight was worried that I would be fired. My decision was to stand my ground for what I thought was right.

The stand never took place because I was offered a job at SES.

Did the decision to stand up for what I thought was right create energy for a new job offer? I had been looking for another job and when I was interviewed at SES, I felt that I had the job. Interesting was the fact that the president and the estimator went by my middle-maiden name.

Photo by Robert Kane Chan

March 1993 through May 23, 1999

I knew when I worked at Keller, Brunner, and Zanger that I was going to work at SES. I almost delivered a printer cartridge to them, but someone else did. They told me they were looking for a bookkeeper or an accountant, and I thought, "Wow that would be close to where I live. I am going to get that job." So, two years later I did.

Two weeks after I started working for SES, I pulled my sacroiliac out. I was reaching for the phone to call Betty when I got a great pain in my hip and fell down on the floor, screaming. The Knight helped me get in bed. When I had to go to the bathroom I would get dizzy, nauseous, and hot. The Knight let me hold onto him while I relieved myself and then he helped me back into bed.

Spunky got into bed with me on Sunday and Monday. She normally wouldn't come to me unless there was a thunderstorm and then she wanted to be on my lap. But both days she got up on the bed and kept licking me. She truly, like many animals, had the ability to heal.

I meditated most of the day and read books. I also looked up "hip" in Louise L. Hay's book *You Can Heal Your Life*. The book gives a list of problems, the probable cause and then a new thought pattern. I started saying the new thought pattern for my hip and for hip problems to aid me in my healing. I refer to the book when I have a health issue to get the thought pattern that will help me.

The Knight's parents picked me up and took me to the chiropractor on Monday. *Thank God for chiropractors*. He was surprised that I didn't want to run to the bathroom right away like all his other patients whose sacroiliac goes out. Most people who pull their sacroiliac out cannot sit down without a lot of pain until it is put back in place. I was still sore, and stayed in bed a few more days.

A palm reader best described my experiences at SES. She asked, "You experienced a lot of abuse at your job, didn't you?"

I thought back and said, "Yes." But people only do to you what you allow them to do. So, I was just like my mom, I allowed abuse.

The first secretary, when verbally abused by a man in the office, would stew for two or three weeks and then he would win her over. It sounds like Mom and Dad, and the Knight and me. I often wondered why the secretary would not say anything to the man.

One day this man verbally abused me over the intercom system so that the entire office could hear. He wanted everyone to hear because he was mad at people answering the phone and not getting the person's name right.

The new secretary told me to just excuse him and said that he was under pressure. I thought that wasn't right, so I wrote a letter about my feelings and stated the reasons why we didn't always get the name right, and gave it to him the next morning. He gave me a letter the next day apologizing. I learned from watching the first secretary and giving her advice that I ended up taking myself. Unfortunately, I would have to learn again. In massage school, we were taught to set our boundaries as to what we want to experience, but I still hadn't learned to do so. The victimhood was engrained in me.

My relationship with the Knight certainly was one of being a victim. After reading in my journal about our relationship before we lived together, I had actually written that he was verbally abusing me. This was very disturbing to me while I was writing this book. So why did I get into the relationship with the Knight?

The Knight was intelligent and a conversationalist; we would talk about different issues, unlike my ex-husband who very seldom said anything. He also was a good listener and once actually missed three turns when he was driving because he was listening to what I was saying. Another thing I liked was that he wanted to have fun, and most importantly he liked to take walks, which my former husband would never do. He took care of the lawn and fixed things around the house.

The Knight was also very spiritual and psychic which helped him to be good in bed. He was very kind, gentle, and loving to animals. In addition, he was clean, neat, and handsome. He would also praise me when I decorated the house and designed the Peace Gardens.

During 1993, I was looking at the similarities between Mom and Dad's relationship and the Knight's and my relationship. Dad never kept promises to my mom and the Knight never kept his promises to me. Some of these promises he wrote down because I asked him to.

Mom would do anything for Dad. He would come home drunk at midnight and ask Mom to fix him something to eat and she would run and do it. If he were pounding on the bedroom floor upstairs, she would run up to him. I did not quite do just anything for the Knight because I saw him ridiculing a wife of a friend of his. The Knight laughed at her because she did anything that his friend asked of her. But I too, loved too much, just like my mom.

I wanted the relationship to work out and I was searching for a solution. Dad gambled and so did the Knight. The Knight liked to manipulate and get reactions out of women. I knew this because one day when we went to dinner, before we bought the house, I saw him flirting with a woman at the next table.

The search for a solution was disturbing, and I knew it had to do with me. To say it was the Knight's fault was to give my power to him. But in reality, I still blamed him for not being what I wanted. I was questioning what the lesson I was to learn from the Knight. My mom provoked most of the beatings. How was I provoking the verbal abuse?

In February, 1994, a doctor did an office procedure on me to help me to stop bleeding so badly during my period. I had made the decision not to have my uterus removed, even though it had some fibroid tumors on it. Just before the decision I had a prophetic dream.

In the dream, I was cleaning a linoleum floor and there was a rug in the corner. I said it had to go because there was no reason for it to be cleaned or left there. An Oriental man with a bare chest removed the rug. His brow was sweating so I wiped his forehead with a white rag. The rag turned black. So I went to get a clean washcloth and I went into an empty room that had five or six hair dryers lying on a hardwood floor in a curved row. When I went into another room in search of the washcloth, my Aunt Ruth told me that there was a white one with a big red heart in middle of it. I thought, "Kiss of Death." I did not choose that one but I chose a light blue washcloth.

In the dream, I take the light blue washcloth into the bathroom where the Oriental man is standing there in the nude. He is standing six to eight feet away from the commode and he is urinating in it and hitting it perfect. That was the end of my dream.

A bowling friend had told me about a procedure where the doctor removes the fibroids from the uterus, so I went to a doctor that the Knight's mother had gone to. The doctor advised me not to do the procedure, but said that he would refer me to a doctor at John Hopkins if I really wanted to try. His consulting room was a light blue like the washcloth.

I then went to my regular doctor and he told me that maybe I could just take iron pills. He also said that maybe I was just going through menopause and would be all right since I did not want to have my uterus taken out. The room was a light blue like the washcloth so I decided not to do anything. It was the right decision and my doctor was right. The hairdryers were the number of years before I would stop having periods.

My son was married in June, 1994. He hadn't spoken to me for years; probably since the Knight and I had gotten together. Two weeks before the wedding my son sent me an invitation and I did not respond. He called me a week before the wedding and asked whether I was coming. I said, "You haven't talked to me in years, but yes I will come."

In August of 1994, my second grandson was born. I had a dream the morning he was born. In the dream, Jeanelle and her husband were asking me to deliver their son. I was given a bedpan to catch him in and I was taken aback. Why had they given me a bedpan to deliver the baby?

When Jeanelle called to tell me that my grandson was born, she told me that he was in intensive care because he had had a bowel movement before he was born. The Knight would not go to Fort Bragg, North Carolina with me. So I went by myself because I knew I had to be there. I arrived later that day and Jeanelle took me down to see my grandson. He was on oxygen and all of his vital signs were unstable. Jeanelle returned to her room while I stayed with my grandson.

I talked to him and I told him, "Welcome to our world." I also told him how wonderful it was to have him here, how much I looked forward to seeing him, and how much I loved him. I also worked on his feet very lightly, lightly rubbed his back, and stroked his hands gently. The nurses told me I could hold him so I did. When Jeanelle came back down, she told me all his vital signs looked better and were stable.

After I told Jeanelle what I had done, she said she would do the same thing after I left to go to her house to spend the night. The next day my grandson was out of intensive care and they were going to let him go home the following day.

I began to design gardens in 1994. I started with a circle with a six-pointed star inside of it with a small cherry tree planted in the center of it. I trim this tree every spring after it blooms so it will not block the energy coming into the front door. This garden was expanded after studying Feng Shui to have an oval-like shape. The oval shape would represent an open sack to bring in the wealth since my lot was not square or rectangle but pie shape and the small part of the pie shape was in the front yard.

I had also purchased an owl birdbath when we first moved there in September of 1991 that I moved from the front right garden into this garden beside the circle with a star in it. Some Feng Shui books say a water ornament to the right of the front door invites one of the couple to be unfaithful. Sorry to say, I moved it too late.

But the energy was already there because the couple who lived in the house before me had split due to infidelity. This may be in part due to the love and marriage section of the house being missing (after an addition was added to the back of the house) according to the form school of Feng Shui. Every time I did something to correct this, the Knight became disturbed and our relationship seemed to drift further apart.

Sometimes a correction will do this if you are in the wrong relationship. The love and marriage section also has to do with loving yourself as well as others. This part certainly did come true after the corrections. One of the corrections I did was to put a concrete pedestal with two turtledoves kissing at the point to complete the corner missing on the house. I later made concrete bricks that said, "We are one" and placed them in front of the turtledoves.

While writing this book, I placed a white marble stone under the bricks, which has increased the loving of me even more. I was being verbally abused at a meditation circle by the leader, but I didn't want to quit the circle because I liked the people in it. But I wrote to the leader and gave thanks for teaching me that I want to put myself in a loving and supportive environment. I quit the meditation group and I am so grateful for the leader's lesson. If I truly love myself, then accepting abuse is a thing of the past. *I hope!*

The next garden after the Star garden (# 1 on map in appendix) was the Spiral garden. It has stepping stones that make a spiral with flowers planted on each side as you walk into the spiral. This idea I got from my friend, Joyce Gedeon, who had planted corn in a big spiral which had a path to go into the center where you could meditate. Mine is not this big, perhaps 17 to 18 feet in diameter. An angel reader suggested that I put words in my gardens so I made bricks with the Irish proverb: "Dance as if no one were watching, sing as if no one were listening, and live every day as if it were your last." These were placed on the perimeter of the spiral.

After the creating the Spiral garden, I made a step-up Swan (#6) garden that was eight feet by 16 feet with an outline of two swans facing each other. A few years later I placed two swan topiaries that are a little over two feet tall in place of the outlined swans. I made a brick heart with the word, "Love" engraved on it along with a cross that was placed in front of the swan topiaries.

A few years later a friend added an extension to the left of the Swan garden that reached beyond the river birch tree that is called the Solar (#5) garden for a friend of hers that had passed away. It has an angel, a sunflower stepping stone, yellow flowers, a duck with a fairy, and a sunflower flag in the garden.

I also did an extension on the other side that is the Lunar (#7) garden that has a small pagoda, tall lavender phlox, a black marble in shape of a pond that has a pair of koi fish on it, a dark purple iris, and an apple tree.

After the original Swan garden, I made a Hexagon Water Fountain (#14) garden. The water fountain was a lady with a jug on her shoulder that stood on a pedestal. That sat on a hexagon stepping stone that was supported by cinder blocks that were hid by tan castle buff bricks that had been placed in a tight circle three bricks tall. Chipped, white marble was put on top between the stepping stone and the bricks.

After the circle, another hexagon was made of four scallop bricks on each side. Mulch was placed between the circle and the hexagon. Then a circle of edging was placed around the bricks where white marble was placed between the hexagon and the edging. After the edging, ten feet cedar boards formed the last hexagon that had pea gravel between the edging and the last hexagon.

In October of 1994, the Knight told me to get out of the house. I was shocked since he had always said the house was really mine because I made the down payment and paid most of the monthly bills. He would say he was just renting. It just showed how much our relationship had deteriorated.

In March and April of 1995, I added a Wealth (#8) garden, a Secret (#24) garden, a Turtle (#15) garden, a Redbud (#16) garden, a Faith (#20) vegetable garden, and a Gratitude (#20 heart-shaped) garden. When Betty saw the Star, Spiral, Swan, Hexagon and other gardens, she suggested that I dedicate my gardens to peace.

I said, "Not yet. I want a 64-foot garden by the split rail fence with each eight-foot section colored a different color of the rainbow before I dedicate my gardens to Peace." I figured I'd be done in a year.

God had different plans. On May 25, 1995, a storm came through and uprooted a beautiful large apple tree just beside the Swan garden. To my surprise, the Swan garden was not damaged. On the other side of the backyard near the split rail fence, another large apple tree was uprooted, but that only knocked one of the split rails off. When Butts Tree Service came to cut up the trees and take them away, I told them I wanted to do a rainbow peace garden along the fence. The owner of Butts Tree Service said he would till it for $25.

I said go ahead and I used the apple tree trunks and large limbs to outline the shape of the 64-foot Rainbow Peace (#18) garden. The owner of Butts Tree Service gave me some mulch to mulch the whole garden with. When I went to Lowe's to get some additives for the soil, one of the managers sold me six torn bags of peat mulch at half off. I also got other torn bags half off. I then knew that the Universe was supporting this Peace garden.

I planned the first Peace Gathering for July 1, 1995. On the invitation, I asked each person to bring a specific color of flower for different sections of the garden. The first eight-foot section was a black or dark section. The dark sedum that was planted is still there. There is also a black knight butterfly bush along with some black stones and a maroon one that looks like a person's head.

The next section is the red section, which still has the first red daylilies and claire bells that my daughter April gave to the Peace garden. It also has red hexagon brick stepping stones in it. Beside the red section is an eight-foot section of orange flowers, which also includes some orange-toned stepping stones, which are natural.

The yellow section has the same yellow daylilies that Mike of SES gave at the first Peace Gathering. The yellow section also has some yellow-toned stones and calendula that still reseeds every year.

The Lady's Mantle that was given by the president and his wife of SES is still growing in the green section along with bells of Ireland and other herbs. Green Caroline lace rocks give you a place to step on in the green section.

In the blue section, the blue sage given by the Knight's mother is, in spite of everything, growing along the fence where it was first planted with some blue slate rocks for stepping stones. The purple section even now has the lavender given by Aunt Esther growing from the first Peace Gathering along with the lavender sparkle rocks to step on.

Last but not least, the white section is flourishing with the Shasta daisies and the White Blazing Star (Liatris Alba) I planted at the first gathering and it has reseeded to the heart garden. There are white brick stepping stones in the white section along with a crystal. A large white marble stone was added a couple of years ago.

The word "Peace" was written in medium-sized white marble at the path around the Blue Cedar Atlas that was planted before the gathering where the apple tree was before; the garden reaches out to surround the Atlas tree. A few years later a path of green concrete stepping stones with evergreen leaves embossed in them was placed at the Atlas tree. Also three-to-four-inch cubes of granite were used to spell out "PEACE" along the path of stones just in front of the lion and lamb that were placed under the tree's branches.

On the other side of the yard, a River Birch was planted where the other apple tree was pulled up by its roots. I planted the River Birch in memory of my dad because he lived along the Potomac River.

Guests planted their flowers, had thoughts of peace and put a marker in front of their gift to peace with their names on it. There were over 40 guests from all walks of life. We prayed, sang, meditated, shared a meal, and everyone left with a sense of peace. Running Deer did a Native American opening and closing for the dedication.

The Knight was mad when I told him that I had invited his parents. Funny, when his dad came up to me after the dedication he said, "This is really me."

His mom said, "I am so peaceful. I don't remember ever being this peaceful."

My mother has attended several of the Peace Gatherings also, which is surprising since she avoids social functions.

Peace is what I got from the gathering and dedication of my gardens to Peace. That is the reason I have continued to have at least one or more a year. If everyone could experience that peace within themselves, then it could be carried out to the Universe and we would experience Universal peace. *Think, feel, and visualize Peace and you shall have it. Peace starts with you. Peace be with you.*

In the spring of 1995, my son and an electrician put an electrical line to the lights of my Hexagon Water Fountain garden and to the pump for the fountain. When he installed it, I noticed he banged on the pipe that had the wire coming up to hook to the outlet box. Later the box was not working.

He would not fix it after several calls so I wrote him a letter over a year later and complained about it. Unfortunately, in the letter I made a comparison to his father and him about never listening. That was a very big mistake on my part, and Larry has not talked to me since, except to tell me not to call him. If he wants to talk to me, he will call me.

I have not seen him since the Christmas of 1995, when Jeanelle and her family came for Christmas dinner since they had moved to Fredericksburg, Virginia, in August of 1995. He has two sons I have never met, but I say a prayer for him and his family every night as well as for my girls and their families. *A mother's love is forever and so is God's.*

In January of 1996, we had a big snowstorm and a few days later six more inches of snow. Then it got very warm which caused the flood of 1996. That is when Mom lost everything she had in the trailers.

Kitchen Before and After Pictures

I redecorated the kitchen with new wallpaper, sanded down cabinets, painted them and the walls. We also put up new curtains, and put in a new floor, stove, hot water heater, dishwasher, and refrigerator. New carpet was put in the family room (which is now the massage room) and I laid tile down at the doors.

I was also working part-time in the evenings and weekends for Ed Rude Carriers, helping them to get a new system running. The gardens were rededicated to Peace. In July, our dog, Spunky died. Kids from the neighborhood were throwing firecrackers at her and she dug under the opposite fence. She got in the road where she was hit twice by two trucks.

That was so very hard on the Knight and me. We cried together on the swing that we had put in the backyard. A few days later the Knight brought Timber (Fluffy) home. She is a Bischon Frishee and as of this day she is alive but having some aging problems. She is the best dog and my companion. Unconditional love is the lesson dogs teach us. Of course, Spunky trained me so I am a better master. Fluffy trained me to play fetch and after an hour I would call the Knight to hurry up and get done preparing for the next day so Fluffy could wear him out playing fetch.

In January of 1997, a young student named Monica came to work for SES. She was a joy to have around. She was the person who introduced me to Feng Shui. One day she came into my office and said, "You have the best Feng Shui in here."

Since I had no idea what she was talking about, I signed up for a class on Feng Shui that was being offered at the Jefferson High Adult program and have since taken another class. I also have more than 12 books on Feng Shui, which I now know is the study of placement of furniture and objects with the emphasis on where the energy is moving.

April played the French maid in "Private Lives" and Loretta graduated from college with a Bachelor of Arts degree. *Yea!* I also bought the swan topiaries for the step-up Swan garden.

In June, the Knight bought a wooden speedboat in Fredericksburg and left it there for Jeanelle and my son-in-law to strip and repaint. I also went down a couple of times to help them. They used the boat after they refinished it, and the girls enjoyed it along with the grandsons at Mom's new place up in Hedgesville, West Virginia. Having a boat was so much fun.

Before and After of Boat

I took my first foot reflexology course from my massage therapist. I had injured my arm and drove the hour to see her because I knew she could fix me. When I arrived, I could not lay on the massage table because I was in too much pain. Alice suggested that I try sitting on the platform rocker and she would do foot reflexology on me there. To my surprise, I could then lie on the massage table after the reflexology, so I decided to take the two-evening course from her.

A student in the introductory course told me I should do this as a profession. When I went home, the Knight had to grit his teeth to sit in his platform rocker. I worked on him and to his surprise when he got up, he did not have to grit his teeth. His back was better. In March of 1998 I started to do foot reflexology.

I wrote a note on July 1998 about my feelings concerning my relationship with the Knight. I said that the relationship had two different individuals leading separate lives, but together sometimes. I said that I felt as though I was last in the relationship, that I didn't feel secure and loved unconditionally, and that I felt as though I had to protect my feelings.

"Every once in a while a touch of love, like a small thread to keep me there. I am scared the Knight does not have the same compassion I have for him. The Knight tosses me a crumb every now and then to fuel my love, but it is not fulfilling. The only time the Knight is affectionate is when he wants me to do or give him something."

One of my foot reflexology clients encouraged me to learn more, so on September 22, 1998 I went to the Virginia School of Massage. I had been looking for a massage school closer than Baltimore or Washington, D.C. When I went to Joyce's in Afton, Virginia, I saw an advertisement in the newspaper for the Basic Massage class in Winchester, Virginia. I called on Monday and started the very next night.

At massage school you chose a partner to practice with and I was fortunate to have a young lady named Nikki. One day we were doing backs in class and Nikki and I had different people we were working on. I had my back to Nikki while I was working on someone else when I heard her saying, "Mary, give me a massage. Help me." I almost turned around to tell her I couldn't because I was massaging someone else.

On the way home, Nikki told me the woman massaging her back at the time did not take her watch off and she had long fingernails. She said that she was thinking, "Mary, give me a massage. Help me." There certainly was a connection with the two of us and it was one of the cognitive times that I received a message via mental telepathy.

While in Basic, I experienced seeing two people's aura. The first one was John who became my intermediate partner. He had a white aura completely around him that extended two feet out from his body.

The second aura I saw was around a teacher's assistant during practice. She was surrounded from her head to her waist with a beautiful purple aura that was one foot in diameter. A few weeks later she told me that she thought I had seen an angel around her because she was in an accident the day after I had seen the aura. The policeman told her he could not believe that the only thing wrong with her was one injured arm.

On August 2, 1998, I gave a Create Universal Peace party, and I asked the guests to bring stepping stones. Some of the stones given were natural, some were painted, and some were in different shapes. Most are on the pathway of the Rainbow Peace garden.

In January of 1999, I went to Shenandoah College to view cadavers. I almost did not go, but at the last minute I decided to and I am so glad I did. It gave me a very different perspective of the human body. We were fortunate that classes were not in session when we went so the smell of formaldehyde was not very strong, but I still changed into clean clothes and washed the ones I had on immediately after I got home.

In March, I purchased carpet for our bedrooms and living room. I also painted all the rooms before the carpet was put down.

We were studying deep tissue work in the Intermediate Massage class. Deep tissue work on the body brings up deep issues that have been stored in the body. On a scale of one to ten, a massage therapist should not go above a seven for pain on the client. One night in April of 1999, I let my partner go above a seven. On the scale it was a nine–ten, but I knew it would get to the heart of the matter. I could feel my heart beating when he rubbed up my back. The next morning I had a profound and vivid dream.

During the dream, I was holding my mother who was gray and the size of a large (two-foot-long) rag doll and she had just died. I told my mom if she had told me I could have saved her. Then I realized that all I had to do was breathe life back into her and started to do so. But in the dream, I pulled back and told her, "I honor your decision to die." She immediately shrunk up and died.

Since my mother was controlling, I felt that I needed to let go of controlling in my life and to stop mothering others. *Treat others as equals.* In view of the fact that in the dream my mother was doll-like, it signified to me that this is a game I have played for a long time. Perhaps the game (control) will lessen.

I had been questioning for over two years what game the Knight and I were playing. It takes two, so that included me. I had been playing the game less and less, so therefore the Knight was there less and less. He liked the game.

After the dream, I concluded that I had been mothering the Knight and it was time to end the relationship. I was going to a weekend course in Charlottesville, Virginia and had asked the Knight to take me to Martinsburg, which was a five-minute drive. He acted like it would be a big chore.

The day I was leaving I decided not to go into work. I was looking for the camera that I had given the Knight because he had told me he didn't know where it was. I searched in his dresser drawer and lo and behold I found a box of Trojans. That put the final nail in the coffin. The Knight happened to come home, saw me, and left right away. I did not say anything to him. I figured that when I came home from the weekend class I would talk to him.

The Knight returned and took me to catch my ride. After he put my luggage in the trunk of my ride's Jeep, he thought I would hug him good-by like I had always done. But I just told him very loudly and sarcastically, "Thank you for taking time out of *your busy schedule* to bring me here. *Goodbye.*"

I told everybody in the van about the events and we all laughed on the way there. Massages and friends got me through this crisis with flying colors. When I got home on Sunday night, I kept my mouth shut. I was tired and didn't want to talk then, so I waited until Monday evening on May 17 to tell him we were through.

The Knight tried to tell me that his father bought the Trojans from a yard sale and gave them to him. I had a great laugh about that story. A week later he told me he had three married girl friends and three single girl friends. I wasn't surprised.

Jeanelle had told me at least three years before that the Knight was running around on me. I had made the decision that I would not follow him like my mom had done with Dad and try to catch him in the act.

One night, when I was young, Mom and I had gone down to the river and poled a flat-bottomed boat over to an island. We walked down to the end of the island and sat in the dark to see if she could catch Dad with someone. I decided then and there that I would not be checking on my mate. If the relationship was over, then it was over. I would not need evidence, though it was fortunate for me that the Universe supplied the evidence after I made the decision.

When I went to work the next day (Wednesday), the president of SES asked me to meet with him on Saturday. He wanted to talk with me.

Work during this time was very stressful because the president had taken over three companies and it was my job to merge them. The exam I took and failed in college was on merging companies. How ironic was that?

I had asked to hire another accountant to do the additional work, but the president had said no. I refused to work more than eight hours a day because I wanted to pursue other interests and I was going to massage school.

The meeting stripped me of my protective shield. I was exposed and I sat there and heard the president telling me things I already knew. He wanted me to talk less in the office. He said I influenced the rest of the office. He wanted me to work more hours and he would pay me more.

I went home; cried and wailed to my soul. All of a sudden it was too much for me to endure. One good thing was I still had a job and the president said he wished he had two of me.

Graduating from Virginia School of Massage
Photo by Ruth Hatcher

Aftermath of May 23, 1999 through 2000

The week after the meeting with the president, I did a lot of soul searching and asked him if he would meet with me on Saturday. That Saturday, before the meeting, I went to have my hair done in Falls Church, Virginia at Phantacee. I told Luis, the owner, about my experiences and he said let me tell you who you are. Luis' description of me, like the man at the gas station when lightning struck the first time, raised my vibration and gave me an awareness of how strong the little things we do in life for others are so powerful. After having my hair done, I had the meeting with the president of SES.

I asked the president if he remembered when he came into the office one day and I was talking and the other lady ran back to her room, but I continued to talk. He said he remembered. I told him I wasn't going to pretend that I was not talking since it would have been a lie and I believed in being truthful and honest. *Did I get this honesty from my Granddaddy Frazier?*

I brought up the incident because at the time it happened I knew it ticked him off that I hadn't stopped talking and run back to my room. I could tell from the moment it happened that it did not set well with him and our relationship had been strained ever since. But this finally cleared the air between us.

I also told him I was willing to give up asking for a raise if he would allow me to hire an accountant and he said that I could. *Wow, I should have cleared the air sooner!* I also told him that I wouldn't work additional hours because I was going to massage school and that one of the reasons I had accepted the job at a lower rate of pay was so that I could do other things in my life and only work eight hours a day.

The secretary and I were also battling during this time. She would say something then I would put my two cents in. The president called me into his office once again and said she was leaving because of me. He wanted me to talk with her and convince her to stay. I went to her desk, and asked her why she was leaving.

She hollered back, "I tried to change you, but you wouldn't change."

I was shocked. How dare she try to change me! I wrote a letter to her and suggested that if she had wanted me to change, she could have told me what was bothering her and I could have made a decision to change or not to change. She tried to manipulate me with kindness. *Was she mirroring the way I had dealt with the Knight? Oh yes. She certainly did mirror me.*

When I would watch my mom bitch and complain to Dad, I would think that it was no wonder he didn't want to be there. I didn't want to be at home either. So with the Knight I gave him plenty of freedom and every time I got mad at him, I would think of all the good things I loved about him. The Knight always knew when I had shifted my energy from negative to positive.

You know the old saying, give him enough rope and he'll hang himself. That is exactly what the Knight did. He had actually told me about giving advice to other male friends that they shouldn't run around on their wives and girlfriends. The Knight should have listened to his own advice! It just goes to show that the advice you give to others is the advice that you need yourself.

He would also tell me throughout our relationship how all these women were coming on to him. Just a few months before we broke up, I asked him, "What are you doing to encourage them to do so?"

He said, "Nothing."

I insisted that it had to be something, because it takes two. He stopped telling me about the women until after we broke up.

I actually tape recorded the communicating sessions between the Knight and myself during the month after we broke up. Years later, I could hear the pent up anger I had about him. Or was the anger for me? Of course there were things said by the Knight that would have embarrassed him if other people heard it. Worse than that, I sounded like a very, very angry person. I didn't like the sound of my voice. I destroyed the tapes for they had served the purpose (though not exactly what I had in mind) when I recorded them.

It would actually be years later before I would completely get over my anger. The Knight would appear in my dreams and I would tell him in my dream, "Get the f---k out of here." Then one night we made love in a dream and I knew I had finally healed in my heart, although in my mind I thought I had healed soon after I broke off with him.

After the Knight and I broke up I started to write a book, which actually helped me to write this one. It also helped me in my healing process. Walking a lot in the gardens helped to put me at ease, since the Knight continued to live at the house until March of 2000.

The Knight tried to be at the house more until I told him that the sight of him made me sick to my stomach. He stopped spending nights at the house in January of 2000 right after I replaced the tan stuffed dog and the blue bunny that were on my bed with two red hearts.

The Knight had given me the tan stuffed dog when I almost bled to death, and I always thought it represented him. When he gave it to me he told me he would always be with me. He gave me the blue bunny when we spent our first Easter together and I felt it represented me. The Knight must have thought so too, since he stopped sleeping at the house after I took them off the bed.

I was going to massage school, which helped, because I had to give and receive massages with a partner. I placed a prayer in the Bible in

November and asked God and the angels to take care of it. I wrote down the amount I was willing to pay the Knight for his share of the house and to take over the loan. I asked in the prayer that the settlement be fair to the Knight and me. *Let go and let God.* I decided to focus on finishing massage school and not worry about a settlement with the Knight.

Six days before massage school was over, the Knight gave me an amount that he wanted for settlement. I told him no. He backed out of the driveway and said he would see me in court.

I said, "Yes, and then you will pay me."

He drove back into the driveway and agreed to sign the settlement I had typed up.

In March, the Knight and I settled. I signed a loan for the house and he received a check. I felt absolutely wonderful when I signed the papers this time. There was none of the nervous apprehension that I had felt when we had signed the papers to buy the house together. It felt good. That was an important lesson. *If it doesn't feel good don't do it.*

After writing the letter to the secretary to convince her to stay, I made a great effort to not voice my opinion whenever she gave her point of view. But she left a couple of months later because she had asked for more money and was turned down.

Abuse at work continued. Sometimes we use excuses for the other person because we understand what is going on with them. This I did for almost ten months with a third secretary, until I changed the energy in my house by adding a blue tablecloth to the knowledge section of the massage room. She had been in a different position at the company before the second secretary left, and she had loved the second secretary and thought I was the reason she left. She verbally abused me, along with another accountant, until one day I looked her in the eyes and almost cried.

That night I made the decision that I would not pretend it was okay, because I was not taking any more verbal abuse from her. The next day, the third secretary was concerned that I would have her fired. I had asked everyone in the office to go to lunch to celebrate her birthday and she asked me if I was going. When I said that I wasn't, she went off the deep end.

I took her to my house where we had a discussion and then I went to lunch with the office personnel. Later that night, I felt as though I hadn't told her everything, so I wrote her a letter, but in the morning I decided not to give it to her since we all have perfect knowledge.

I had concluded that when she first took the secretary position, she and her boyfriend had been in a fight the night before, and everyone was calling – her mom, her grandmother, her boyfriend, etc. During the whole goings on, I didn't place any judgment on anyone involved. I kept repeating to myself, "She has perfect knowledge. She has perfect knowledge."

After an hour or so, she came to my desk and said, "I don't know why, but I feel like doing cartwheels."

I knew at that moment that God was speaking through her. He was saying to me, Mary, you finally get it. She will never remember saying this. It wasn't in sync with what was going on at the moment she said it. We all have perfect knowledge. It is easier to observe someone else making mistakes, and give an advice on the situation than to look at one's self.

I have found it absolutely true. When I give advice to someone, I think about it afterwards, because the advice I give, is the advice I need for myself. What is the message for me in the advice or opinion I have about someone else's situation? They are mirroring me or I need the advice I have given.

After reading the *Destiny* path of the accountant, I knew she was here to learn not to be so abrasive in her communication. And even though she always said she would not do something I asked her to give me, I knew she would do it. I ignored her abuse. I was only concerned that everybody does the job they were hired to do. Get the job done.

Another clerk was very nasty when I would ask for her to give me something, and she was rude when she asked for information, both of which were very seldom. I decided to send her pink light for love, surround myself with white, golden light for protection and kept saying to myself, "She has perfect knowledge. We are one." One day I happened to notice that she was being nice to me. When I asked for information or if she asked me for something, she did it with a smile and a friendly tone. *Hurray*!

I cannot change another person. What I did do by sending love and thinking she had perfect knowledge was to raise my vibration. And in doing so, I did not attract the negativity from her any more. This happened around a year before I left SES.

While writing this book, I realized that by allowing the verbal abuse from the Knight, my body's personal vibration was that of abuse, so I in turn attracted the verbal abuse at my job at SES. Thank God I was going to massage school to give and receive massages and I was working on the Peace Gardens, which helped to raise my vibration.

A month after the Knight and I broke up, I asked his mother to come over. I told her that the Knight and I were through. It was also in June that the Knight's father found out he had a dime-size cancer on his throat. I went to see him when he went into the V. A. Center for testing. He was shaking, so I held his shoulders and gave him energy. He then was very calm when he went into the room to be tested.

I did some touch for health techniques on him a week before he died. When I came in a few days before he died, I asked him if he wanted some energy work. He nodded yes, but the next day he refused and I knew he was ready to die. He died a day later in August.

It was also in June of 1999 that I called my Aunt Alvernon and asked her if I could talk with Uncle Buck about my dad and their childhood. I told her I wanted to write a book. She called Aunt Daisy, Aunt Margaret, and Aunt Carrie and they were all there for the interview on the very next day. I am so glad that I taped part of the interview and took notes because Aunt Daisy has a hard time talking now.

Also in June of 1999, Jeanelle and her family moved to Texas. Loretta, April and I helped them pack up a big moving van. Jeanelle came up the week before and I gave her a massage and energy work. After the massage, she said, "I want to do what you do."

I said, "What is that?"

She said, "Connect people to their souls."

When she called a couple of hours later, Jeanelle did not remember saying that.

In massage school, you are required to do clinic during intermediate and advanced massage classes. The clinic was open to people in the community. My first client, in July, was an 11 or 12 years old boy from New York. He had been in a school bus accident a few years before and had done a cannon ball in the pool that afternoon and hurt his neck and head. But he hadn't put that on his intake sheet. I was glad that I had prayed before I started the massage on him.

He told me that God has a purpose for everyone, like Christopher Reeves. I wanted to impart my wisdom, but decided to ask him, "What do you think is Christopher Reeves' purpose?"

He answered, "To show love and fun."

Out of the mouths of babes we get truths and pearls of wisdom. I was astounded at how precise he spoke the truth and had much admiration for him. I also told him that I wouldn't heal him, that he would heal himself.

He said, "I know I do."

His grandmother, who was there during the massage, told me that she would have given me a tip if it had been allowed because I had given her grandson more than a massage.

He gave me my worst review. I think it was because I didn't answer his question about whether his knuckles would get bigger if he cracked them.

The next client was a regular and asked me why there were so many new faces. I said, "This is the first day that the intermediate class is allowed to give massages."

He said, "I hope you learned your lessons well. I hope you listened to your teacher. I've gotten good massages before and I am sure you will do well."

While he was getting on the table, I made the decision that I would do my best and if it were not good enough, it would be his problem. I then prayed and asked Mother Mary to help me.

It was very unusual from the moment I touched the client. I said a prayer of protection for him and me and asked that only good come out of the session. My hands seemed to have a mind of their own and I was not doing the routine I had been taught for the face. (I usually start on the feet.) Within minutes the client said, "If I was a cat, I would be purring now." He told me after the session that I didn't have to ask about the pressure as much as I had done. On my comment card he wrote, "Only intermediate. Wow."

In July a friend confessed her sins to me. She said that by doing so, she felt that she was healing her past relationships. In August, I finished intermediate massage and I gave a Create Universal Peace Gathering.

In September, Mom had a stroke at my house. She did not want to go to the hospital. I asked her, "If it were me would you take me?" Of course she said yes. So I got her to the hospital.

Although, while I was checking her in, she kept saying, "I want to see my lawyer." They did tests on her and found out she had had many small strokes and several heart attacks. She was fortunate that only her speech and her right hand were affected, but she was very depressed. I am so thankful that my sister Marie took care of her.

It was also in September that I learned that my friend Cheryl Johnson had cancer. When I came back from visiting Jeanelle and her family in Texas in November, I was going to call her after work, but got a telephone call at work telling me she had passed away the night before. Her boss read the poem I wrote in the bathtub the night before the burial.

All of the events: breaking up with the Knight; talking to the president of SES; telling the Knight's mom that the Knight and I were finished; giving energy to the Knight's dying father; helping my daughter move to Texas; seeing my mom have a stroke and observing her reactions; and hearing about my friend dying were almost more than I could bear over this seven-month period.

I was very depressed at different times and I was questioning the purpose of life. At these times, someone would always call me. Receiving massages and having my classmates to talk to also supported and nurtured me.

During an advanced massage class, I learned the Jin Shin Central Channel Release, which clears and balances the chakras in the body. When my partner (John) was holding my third eye position and my crown, I felt like a mass of energy popped from my crown and then a small energy popping; after which I experienced a release by roaring with laughter. I also felt like my head was making a figure eight (which is the symbol for eternity) when he held my crown and occipital groove (where the head meets the neck.) At one point, I felt like John was levitating me. I was mad the teacher didn't teach me to levitate John.

When I used the Channel Release on a client, I felt that energetically my hand had gone to the middle of her heart on the hold with the crown chakra and the heart. The client told me after the session that she felt like her heart had opened up and she saw a bright light that continued to get brighter. I felt she was ready to receive and give love.

Because I was completely calm after the Jin Shin Central Channel Release, I use this procedure when I do emotional releases using essential oils on my clients. I also do reflexology after the emotional release to bring the internal organs into balance. Just before I finished massage school, I learned about essential oils.

Essential oils are essentially to the plant what blood is to us. They also work faster than anything I have ever used, especially for headaches. I have found peppermint and eucalyptus oils are good for headaches as well as lavender.

In addition to the emotional release there is a raindrop therapy, where certain medicinal oils are dropped along the spine and then heat is added afterwards to help with avoiding viral infections. I personally have someone do this once a month for me.

On February 26, I talked to the Knight's father who had passed away. I conversed with him for over four hours. When I went to bed and couldn't sleep, I opened my eyes and hovering over the foot of the bed was a hooded spirit. Needless to say, this frightened me, but I closed my eyes and asked God to protect me and when I opened my eyes the spirit was no longer there. I have never since conversed with someone who has passed over.

My final day of massage class was on February 29, 2000. I wrote a poem, which I read at the graduating ceremony which was held with another massage class on June 24.

Massage School, What an Experience

Starting massage school was an exciting and anxiety experience.
Wanting to facilitate healing was exciting
Having to memorize was agonizing.

Testing was the pits.
In basic, the final hands on with Neva left me in a tizzy
My hands were steady to my surprise
Because deep inside were butterflies.

While observing Mary demonstrating deep tissue massage,
I glanced around the class to sleepy eyes.
Balika was reading, "Go v-e-r-y s—l—o—w—l—y."
And I burst into laughter uncontrollably.

Mary Furgeson said, "Mary would you
like to go get a drink of water?"
"No." For I didn't want to miss any knowledge.
Neva Clayton, Mary Furgeson and Joey Clayes taught me much.
While Sabrina, Balika Rozzi and Dave Waddell refined my touch.

If there was snoring in our class,
We all knew it was George completely in a trance.
But in practice if you heard a machine gun fire,
It was me passing gas.

Poor John Miller. Pam and Jessica accused him of the deed,
When he backed away and flew open his arms.
The whole practice room was laughing
In alarm.

P.D. shared his experiences of color
While I was doing myofascia on his crown chakra.
And Jose healed her shoulder
The day I noticed surrounding her a green aura.

Sue's nurturing hands put me to sleep
And Heidi shared her energy stories.
John Sponaugle with fantastic hands
Would often respond, "Tee Hee, Tee Hee."

I learned much from my classmates.
Lynn taught me to shut my eyes and feel.
I learned to set my boundaries from Tammy.
And Nan and Lore taught me sensitivity.

Growth was tremendous during the course.
Kendra the quiet one
Volunteered to be critiqued before the class,
While Ralph allowed drawings upon his gluteus maximus.

Clinic was quite a unique experience.
My first was a young boy with his grandmother present.
Then a regular who hoped I had learned my lessons well
For he had received good massages before and expected me to excel.

Then there was the client,
Who peeked at me from under the sheet,
Who during the next massage
Was willing to expose herself before my eyes.

It's been over three months since I left here,
And the gifts and experiences I took have served me well.
The aching necks, sore arms, stiff muscles have been eased
With the knowledge I have received.

Thank you very much for teaching and sharing with me,
For Oh what an experience at the Virginia School of Massage.
By Mary B. Reed

I practiced and practiced reading the poem so I would have the right delivery, and during the ceremony I was very calm and collected. When I was called on stage, I calmly went up, but all through the reading of the poem, my voice shook. One of the other ladies told me that my delivery was perfect and many people laughed where it was funny.

One of my sisters came up to me and said, "Mary, it just goes to show you are human."

The surprise to me was that a teacher, who I thought would love it, didn't say anything. And the teacher who I thought wouldn't like it, told me it was wonderful and exactly described what massage school was all about. *Never judge someone.* My classmates were glad I had written and read the poem because the graduating ceremony had seemed to be all about the other class until I read it.

My mom came with my sister, Betty, to the graduating ceremony. I was very thankful to Betty and much honored that my mom came, since she did not like going to ceremonies and hadn't gone to any of our high school graduations. She had a wonderful time and enjoyed meeting my classmates and John's (my massage partner) girlfriend, Ruth. My youngest sister, Ruth, came with her daughters.

Just after I finished massage school, my youngest daughter April got married in March to a wonderful man. When she suggested that she would try to lose weight so her wedding dress would fit, her husband-to-be told her to just get the dress altered to fit her. I loved it when she told me that, because the Knight had complained about my weight and told me that when I reached 200 pounds, we were through. I weighed 202 pounds when we broke up. *Did the Knight mirror what I felt about my excess weight?*

After the Knight moved out, I sanded down the spikes on the ceiling of the massage room since I felt the spikes were like knives that would be poking at any client who would be in there. The Knight had also smoked in that room and I wanted to get rid of that energy. As I did the sanding, I asked God for easy lessons and that I would process the lessons fast. My friend, Julie, helped me to prime and paint the wood paneled walls.

After I had stated what my intentions were: To let people know I was in the massage business; to let people know the benefits of massage so all the local massage therapists would benefit; and to get someone at the newspaper to experience some of my work, I called *The Journal*.

When I talked to the editor, I told her I was a CPA employed as a controller at SES and that I was also nationally certified in Therapeutic Massage and Bodywork. I asked if there was a reporter who would like to come and receive a massage. She said she had the perfect reporter who was always stressed.

When Sherree Casper called me, she said a photographer would come to SES to take my picture and she would call back later. I sent her information on my massages and she called back and asked if I would do the interview over the phone and I said no. She said she wouldn't be able to put the story in the newspaper that day. I said that was fine, since the photographer never took pictures. I then agreed to meet her at my house on Friday, April 28, 2000, for an interview.

A photographer came to my office and I had cleared off my desk of all my papers. The picture was not used because a clean desk didn't really represent a CPA. Then another photographer came and took a picture of me giving my friend, Milly Shepherd, owner of Beautyland Hairstyles, a massage.

Sherree Casper came for the interview at my house. She had been in the service and was very detail oriented. She said that she was not going to have a massage. I told her about working on an accountant who worked for me in Bethesda, Maryland. The accountant had brought her children when she came to visit the week before and I had worked on their feet. After they raved about how they felt, the accountant let me work on her hands.

When I told this to Sherree, she asked if I would do reflexology on her hands. I did, and when she called me a few days later, she told me the swelling in her hands had gone down. She also got on the table where I gave her a partial massage before her beeper went off. I had given her a brief history of my life and told her about the Peace Gathering I was having in three weeks. She was there for over two hours and said the article wouldn't get in the paper that weekend because she was past the deadline.

After talking with her on her follow-up call, she said the article might only be an inch or two. So surprised I was, when April called and told me there was a small picture on the front of the Sunday paper which referred to another section that had a large picture of Milly and me. The title on the front page said, "Balancing the mind CPA doubles as masseuse –D1" and the section D front page said, "Balancing Body, Mind and Spirit Martinsburg CPA knows all too well the stresses of everyday life: with new talent, she hopes to give others comfort as massage therapist. By Sherree Casper, *Journal* staff writer." The article was about 21 inches long, not counting the photo taken by Jason Turner.

My neighbor saw me outside and said that he had seen my picture and the story. He also quoted some of the benefits of massage, such as deep relaxation, increased blood circulation, energy, restful and deeper sleep, relief from tense muscles, lessening of pain, sense of well-being, nurturing, and a healthier state of being. *Wow! It sounded like the article was all that I intended it to be.*

The wife of the president of SES had had an article written on her for making flower arrangements for the Peace conference held in Shepherdstown. When she saw my article, she called and told me that my article was more of a human-interest story than the article that *The Journal* had done on her.

Stating your intention before you do something gives power to your intention. It also showed that by being relaxed, staying in my own power, and not being fearful of the newspaper not doing the article that I got the results I wanted.

The newspaper also ran a four-inch article on the Peace Gathering on the front page of section C on May 17, 2000. "Local peace party planned for May 28." I am so grateful because when strangers meet me they will say, "I've read about you and the Peace Gatherings in *The Journal.*"

The more we envision peace; the more energy we give to peace, thereby creating it.

In August of 2000, I took Reiki levels I and II. Reiki is a form of Japanese energy where attunements are given to the practitioner. When the practitioner gives Reiki, the client becomes very relaxed and therefore can heal their body. The body is amazing and a Reiki practitioner can facilitate the client's healing.

When I do Reiki, I say a prayer of protection, ask that only good come of the session, and allow the light of God to pass through my body to the person on the table. Whenever my ego gets in the way, I just let go and ask God to do his work through me. It is amazing what happens when I do this. The person's energy blockage moves almost instantly.

During the first Reiki I level attunement, I felt as though my crown chakra was being peeled back like a lotus blossom blooming as the Master attuned the very first person. When I received my Masters, I learned that the Master does open the crown chakra of the person they are attuning.

I also experienced my spirit guide (angel) for the first time. I felt this huge energy standing before me. Cindi Wallace had described my guide as a Native American Indian who was big and savage looking with long black hair.

While exchanging Reiki energy in the class, the client I had was very right brained. When I did her head I felt no energy on her top left side, so I double cupped my hand and to my surprise the energy release felt like a dolphin coming out of her head and going back in.

As I worked on her back, I noticed no energy coming from the right lower section. I again double cupped my hand over the area and to my amazement, when the energy blockage released, it felt as though someone had poked me in the middle of my palm with a finger. When we shared our experiences, the client said that she was about to knock my hand away from her back because it got so hot that she thought I was burning her.

During Reiki II, we did a meditation before we learned the Reiki symbols and during that meditation my left side of my head felt like it was being peeled back. *Was that because I was going to have to memorize the symbols? The left brain is more rational while the right is more intuitive.*

I learned the symbols to increase the power, to work on emotional issues and to do long-distance work. I didn't do too many long distance sessions until I designed and created the Healing (#13) garden in October of 2003.

On August 25, 2000, Fluffy had an operation to remove stones from her bladder. I tried feeding her a diet that the homeopathic veterinarian gave me, but she would have to have an operation again in a couple of years. The next day after her operation, I had another Peace Gathering.

One of my major lessons learned in November was to listen to your gut. It is always right. Two other massage therapists and I were giving seated massages at the IRS. I was giving the oral presentation and we had two groups we were doing at different times.

In between the groups, one of the massage therapists sat on her massage chair and said, "I need a massage." My gut said no, but my heart went out to her so I gave her a one. Some people for the next presentation were already seated when I was gently pulling her arm like I had done many times before. She hollered out, "You are hurting me." You can imagine what the people seated thought, not just about me, but about getting a massage. I will always try to listen to my intuition from this day forward.

I learned a second lesson (which I already knew) but it was reinforced that day. The clients heal themselves. The massage therapist that hollered had heard my many stories about the results my clients were receiving.

She also had received good results until after this demonstration. She was no longer getting results and I knew it had to do with her not wanting to heal. Yes, I think she was jealous, which led to the third lesson. Keep my mouth shut about the results I was getting with my clients to other massage therapists. It is the client who heals themselves, not me. I only facilitate. I happened to be fortunate to have many clients who wanted to heal. I am so grateful to her for the three lessons I learned.

On December 9, 2000, I was working on a fellow massage therapist who was diagnosed with MS. I did a lot of energy work, used crystals, and did massage on her. While working on her, I sensed a child jumping up and down on the massage table. I almost said out loud, "No more jumping on the bed."

She had wanted a baby, but when she was diagnosed with MS she put it out of her mind. I told her about wanting to tell the child, "No more jumping on the bed." She thought it might have been her nephew who was not born yet. Not so, in seven months, she was pregnant with her son even though she was told not to have children. Her son has been a joy and he is as cute as a button.

**Children's Universal garden,
photo by Robert Kane Chan**

2001

This year a large amethyst wanted to come home with me; a pair of persistent cardinals came to visit; I started going to singles' dances; practiced and learned more Feng Shui; and learned Shiatsu. A trimmer attacked me and I was also involved in a car accident. There were two Peace Gatherings and spit in my eye.

On February 3, I went to the On the Wings of Dreams shop in Shepherdstown, West Virginia. This is where I met my friend who was working there in a shop that sells crystals. I had become very interested in crystals since the stones put off healing energy when you hold them. There was an amethyst geode that was almost a foot high with flower-like clusters. I feel the stones that I want to buy; if the stone zings me with energy, I will buy it.

This amethyst was too heavy for me to get the zing, so I put it back up on the wooden shelf. I turned my back on the amethyst and waited for my friend to finish with a customer. I heard this grinding against wood and thought oh no; the amethyst might fall off the shelf. I picked it up and moved it back approximately a half of an inch, or less. A piece of the amethyst fell off in my hand.

I told my friend that I was going to keep the piece that fell off. The cost of the amethyst was $220 so I told my friend I would think about buying it. I went home and sat down and thought, "The amethyst moved toward me and it gave a piece of itself to me. Maybe I should buy it." I went back to the store the next day and gave my friend the piece that had fallen in my hand and bought the amethyst.

Amethyst aids with spiritual growth and finding inner peace. It is also a healing stone for the mind, body and spirit. It helps one cope with addictions, insomnia, and mental stress. It is also a stone of wisdom. A client who is a seer said the stone wraps its energy around me and helps me when I do body and energy work on clients.

During the winter and spring, a pair of red cardinals kept coming to my bedroom window and one of my massage windows. They kept flying at the window and walking on the air conditioner and pecking at the window. My friend gave me a stuffed red cardinal because of this.

After painting a mountain on canvas and hanging it behind my bed, I asked for a large raise and got it. The reason I painted the mountain and put it behind my bed was to receive support since it was in the right compass direction according to the compass school of Feng Shui. I also put one behind my desk at work. I feel that the results after I have placed or moved things has a lot to do with the intention behind my action.

I started to go to single dances in March. The very first dance I went with another lady and when a fast dance was being played, I told her I was going to dance. When she turned around to find me, she was surprised I was dancing by myself. My husband would never dance fast dances and one New Year's Eve the Knight sat through most fast dances. That night I decided I would never sit and blame some man or woman for the reason I was not dancing.

It was surprising over the next two years how many men and women would ask if they could dance with me while I was dancing alone on the dance floor because they wanted to dance too. *Your happiness is dependent upon you. Be happy.*

Since reviewing my relationship with the Knight, I realized I knew everything about him before we started living together. I knew about him because he told me.

Before I bowled on his team, a man asked me how I had bowled in a tournament with the Knight. I said, "I bowled my average or better."

He said the Knight had told him that I bowled badly while he bowled well. That was funny since the Knight had not bowled his average. Knowledge number one, the Knight doesn't always tell the truth.

The Knight bragged about going on vacation with his wife and her family and meeting his girlfriend at the same time. Knowledge number two, he didn't respect his wife or women. The way he treated his wife would be the way he would treat me.

"You'll leave, they all do," said the Knight.

Knowledge number three, he would make sure his self-fulfilling prophecy would come true. It is funny because I listened, but didn't think he would treat me the way he treated his other relationships. *Wrong!*

Therefore, when I went dancing and met men, I listened very carefully. Usually within minutes, the men told me all I needed to know. It is amazing what you learn when you really listen to what someone is saying.

Another healing modality I learned in March was Shiatsu, which has helped me in my practice and in my personal healing. Shiatsu, along with color therapy, diet, and Reiki helped me when I got poison ivy followed by eczema. Shiatsu works on the meridian patterns, which go through the body.

Poison ivy was something I never had before. I was pulling some out of a flowering bush and had a short sleeve shirt on in over 90-degree temperatures. I just picked the ivy up and carried it to a garbage bag where I inserted it. My arms and chest broke out in poison ivy. I must have scratched my lower leg for it became inflamed and I could push my finger down about one inch on the swollen area.

When I went to the doctor, he could not see my leg since I was wearing a long skirt, but he could see the eczema on my arm and a little on my chest. I told my doctor what diet changes I had made and what holistic things I was doing. He said I was doing all the right things. He suggested a salve, which made it very itchy, and an over-the-counter drug which made me hyper. When I pulled up my skirt to show him my lower leg, he gasped. I only went to the doctor because I was concerned I might lose my leg.

Because I knew that each major meridian goes through a particular organ and that each organ works at its height at a particular time of day, I checked when the itching was at it peaks. After finding out that it was the lung and large intestines and the spleen and stomach meridians, I worked on them and also the two meridians before, and the two meridians after, to bring my body back into balance. I also added color therapy by using a lamp with colored film to decrease the itching during its high points. I used turquoise and blue because they can calm the body. It took awhile, but using all the modalities and changing my diet helped me.

I had a client whose legs were swollen and I worked on the bladder and kidney meridians on him. When I was done, he said, "I don't know what you did, but I have to go to the bathroom." It helped him to release the excess water his body was holding. Shiatsu also helped another client who had to go to the bathroom, but could not urinate. After the session, the client could urinate. The client knew that the bladder problem stemmed from the fact that she was pissed off at someone.

At Lowe's in April, I was looking at a trimmer box for more information and a Black & Decker trimmer fell on my nose. It was instinct, as soon as it hit my nose that caused me to swing my arms and knock the trimmer away before the heavy motor could hit me. Thanks to a man that heard the trimmer hit the floor, I received a settlement from the insurance company that handles Lowe's claims.

The man told me to go to the service desk to report it. The bridge to my glasses had been hit and driven down against my nose. My nose was scraped open, but most of the pain was where the trimmer had smashed the eyeglass pads into my nose at the impact point.

I wrote to Lowe's and was glad that the next year most of the trimmers were on more stable holders. It is funny that every time I looked at the trimmers before this I got the feeling one might fall.

Later in April, I was on my way to see a friend at Red Lobster in Hagerstown. There was a van in front of me in the fast lane that all of a sudden was getting closer to me. I hit my brake, but I still hit the van and did $200 in damages to it. I got out and prayed to God to have someone help me.

Sam, the driver of one of the cars in front of me, came up to me and said, "Don't worry, I saw everything."

This woman in front of Sam crossed the fast lane, got in the middle strip, and took off in the other direction. Another man took after her in his car and got the license number. Both men told the officer what happened and the only thing I had to do was sign the report. God does answer prayers.

Love of gardening was something that I got from both sets of grandparents, and both Grandmas loved to plant flowers just like me. Grandma Burkhart always showed us her beautiful flower garden when we visited and Grandma Frazier was known for her plate-sized dahlias.

The Peace Gardens grew. I laid a patio in front of the gate beside the Japanese Lantern (# 3)garden, working on it while it was raining in the spring. I also added a Quan Yin (#1a) garden, a Unity (# 12) garden, a Hummingbird (#19) garden, an Eagle (#23) garden and a Laughing Buddha (#25) garden. I had two gatherings in 2001, on August 11th was Create Universal Peace and the one following 911 was, Walk in Peace.

After 911, a Children's Universal (# 21) garden was designed. My neighbor's son, Robert Chan said he wanted it between the Rainbow Peace garden and the Gratitude (#22) garden. He also wanted a universal being in the center so I used a large stone for the head, a heart-shaped stepping stone for the chest, a large round sun stone for the abdomen, and used granite stones to form the arms and legs on the universal being. The arms are raised out wide as if in praise to God.

The Children's garden was dedicated on a sunny warm November 4, 2001. Robert directed the dedication ceremony, and he and Ashley Green wrote a poem. When Robert showed me the poem, it stated what they did not want. I asked Robert to change the statements to what they did want. Stating what you don't want only gives energy to what you don't want. It is better to create what you really want by stating it in positive terms. Here is the poem that Ashley Green read:

Universal Peace
By Ashley Green and Robert Chan

Have you ever wondered about a world with Universal Peace?
A place where everyone's free!
A place where there is harmony.
A place where we are safe from harm.
A place where everyone welcomes with wide-open arms.
As we stand on the ledges of tomorrow's upbringing,
We wonder where the world is hanging.
We soon hope this day will come fore that war will be no more.
A movement of Peace is taking its setting and
a new way of life is just beginning.
You too my friend can look deep within and
see all the Peace that will begin.
Last but not least a closing without a doubt.
We want to say,
We pray to God that everything will turn out.

The dedication included four-year-old Dede Anthony, who played "Twinkle, Twinkle Little Star" and "O Come, Little Children" on her violin. Of course, she was wonderful. I was amazed at her professionalism. When Fluffy went up to her just before she was to perform, Dede shooed her away. But when her father started the music, she ignored Fluffy completely and started playing where she was supposed to.

The Cub Scout Pack 83 from Harpers Ferry was the Color Guard and led the guests in the Pledge of Allegiance. The Cub Scouts brought blue hyacinths and yellow daffodils and planted them in the Children's Universal Peace garden. Blue and gold are the Cub Scout colors. I was so proud to see the Cub Scouts perform, especially since I had been a den leader for Pack 83 over 20 years ago.

Kristin Hiser a 14 year old from Hagerstown, Maryland, wrote the following poem after 911 and read it during the ceremony:

America United
By Kristin Hiser, 9/23/01

Waking up and going to school
Was just another day
Only to find out an hour later
Things would not go our way.

Parents came to get their kids
Teachers didn't know what to do.
Everyone was worried…
But nobody actually knew.

They didn't know who got killed
Or who was still alive.
They didn't know who actually did it,
Until the news report had arrived.

The Trade Centers had fallen
Thousands had been lost…
We started to cry and pray,
Keeping our fingers crossed.

Then we heard another story,
The Pentagon had been hit.
The plane crashed into the side,
Crumbling it bit by bit.

Back up in New York
People were still missing.
We asked what we could do to help,
As we were still reminiscing.

Firefighters and police
Worked as hard as they could.
Even though they tried their hardest,
Some of it didn't do any good.

Thousand were still missing,
Donations were still needed.
A lot needed to be done,
But our lives still proceeded.

We don't know what will happen next,
Or if this is a war.
All I know for sure is,
We will not take this anymore.

Now we stand together,
United as a whole.
To defeat this terrible tragedy,
Is our ultimate goal.

God Bless America.

Joyce Gedeon channeled as the Fairy God Bunny and gave words of calm and peace, along with laughter, for the ceremony. Peace is just a thought away, especially in a garden. Joyce has performed at all of my Peace Gatherings; she is an artist, poet, sound healer and more. Following is a poem she wrote that was very appropriate for the occasion.

Peace in the Garden
By Joyce Gedeon

Gather around me and a story I will tell.
Of times gone by are they times yet to come?
Famine and plague war and upheaval.
Bodies piled high blood running between them.
Not a pretty sight do we see as this story unfolds of the times of old.

All want to leave there, all are unhappy.
Grieving and sorrow surrounds every hamlet.
Not one soul is untouched by the hand of grim reaper.
All are distraught no hope can be found except for those dwelling

deep under the ground. In caves lined with crystal, moss and web of
the spider do dwell the souls who have survived this.

We tell you this story not to scare or to shock.
It is of a time far behind you.
This is a fear that is carried within.
We say release this one for it does not serve as souls are creating
whatever souls hold.
Instead hold the vision of peace and of union, a picture of gardens
lined with beautiful visions.

See souls gathered in numbers to celebrate new times when
memories of old no longer reside within them. Singing and feasting,
joy and great laughter in every heart celebration not disaster.
Every color each hew, every size shape and form, all creatures
from the great to the small. The young and
the old and the in between too
remember only the peace that is in each and in all of the one.

We hope you remember this story we've told in the dawn of new
days for all to behold. We caution you creators, when weaving your
webs of days in the future stay present but never forget. You create in
the moment what is held deep within. Hold nothing that's fear based
and all you will find is a garden of pleasure for all coming time.

The announcement about the Twin Towers came over the radio
while I was at work. Because I could not get any stations clearly on
my TV, I went to my friend's house to watch the coverage of 911. My
gut reaction when I saw the towers go down was that it looked like a
demolition job to me. When I went to a meeting the following Saturday
in Afton, Virginia, most of the over 40 people gathered there were
highly intuitive. There was a mixed bag of reactions. For the most part,
people were there to express their feelings and comfort one another.

The most important thing that came out of 911 was seeing how
people came together to help and support one another. Also, the
outpouring of money to aid the victims was astonishing. Differences did
not matter. Compassion and love came across. *We are one.*

Around Christmas time, I got an eye infection that would not get better. My doctor referred me to an eye doctor the day after Christmas who told me to get a prescription and put it in my eye every half an hour and to come back the next day. I then had to come back the day after that. Then for every week and then every month, and then it tapered down to every two months, then every six months.

The eye doctor said I could have gone blind from the virus leaving scars on my eye. I was fortunate the scar was not in my field of vision. I feel I got this virus when a dancing partner accidentally spit in my eye when he was talking to me. This is just a warning for you to be cautious if you get an eye infection.

I have met two people who have had a virus in their eyes. One of them had an iris implant because she went blind in one of her eyes. Basically my eyeball was very sore.

I ended this interesting year dancing in Hagerstown, Maryland at the singles New Year's Eve Party. *Have a great one.*

New Water Fountain, Mary B. Reed and Geraldine Weaver.
Photo John R. Baker

2002

In 2002 I am still going to the Eye Center; Joyce's house burns down; I fall asleep at the wheel; the water fountain breaks; mourning; "I am perfect."

Joyce wanted her house to be paid off. And even though she understood how powerful her words were, she sang a mantra while exercising: "Debt free by 2003 and with my perfect mate."

On March 1, 2002 she was on her way to attend her mother-in-law's funeral with her two sons. When she arrived in Ohio, she was told that her house had burned to the ground while she was on the road.

So her wish that her house be paid off came true nine months later (by 2003) when she got the insurance check, but unfortunately she lost one of her dogs (Zimba), art creations, photos, and other things that could not be replaced. *Be careful what you ask for, you just might get it.*

She was also in a relationship that left her wiser and stronger after it was over. She finally loved herself more than the man. When Joyce called me crying, she often compared her relationship to the relationship that the Knight and I had had. The part about loving yourself more than your mate certainly mirrored my lesson.

I went down to visit her in the beginning of April 2002 to help support her. The devastation of the fire was worse than the flood damage that happened to my dad. There was next to nothing to salvage, but Joyce was not attached to the material things and was thankful that a neighbor's son happened to come by and got one of her dogs, Star, out of the burning house.

A friend that had farmland took Molly and Star, but Molly (a wolf that was not in the house but ran around the house barking while it was burning.) would not eat. The friend brought Molly to me to do an emotional release using essential oils. I did not know if it would work on a wolf, but did the release anyway. Molly ate immediately after.

On my way back from Joyce's, I woke up to see the bridge pillars I was heading towards while in the interstate medium. I jerked my wheel to the right, ended up crossing the northbound lane, and hitting the guardrail. Bouncing off the guardrail, my car turned and I was facing west on a northbound lane.

A trucker came up to my car and said, "You do not have to worry about being hit. I have parked behind you with my flashers on." He also told me that he had fallen asleep at the wheel, too. When the ambulance came, the driver and medic told me that they both had fallen asleep at the wheel. Then the sheriff also told me that he had fallen asleep at the wheel.

The tow truck driver said that he had also fallen asleep while driving. *Wow!* It is kind of scary when I think about it. It was broad daylight and I was tired, but I never thought I would fall asleep. If it had been dark, I would have stopped and had a Coke to keep me awake. Now if I am tired, day or night, I'll stop and take a rest or get a Coke. Caffeine will keep me awake for five to six hours, especially Coke.

My sister, Betty, came to my rescue since I still had two more hours to get home. She even took me to pick out another car. It is great to have a sister that will drive an hour to pick you up, take you back to her house, and then drive you home the next day. I am so fortunate to have her as my sister.

Six days after the accident, I had a Create Peace gathering. I was still going to see the eye doctor and April graduated with high honors with an associate's degree in May.

Also in May, I took the water fountain apart because it was not working right. I took the lady with the pitcher off and as I swished the water around the bowl, all of a sudden a piece fell to my right side, then another piece of concrete fell to the left with the largest piece of the concrete bowl falling off the other side of the base in front of me.

I was not injured at all. I felt that I was protected and very thankful to God that none of the concrete pieces of the bowl had fallen on me. The lady with the pitcher was put between the two forsythia bushes as a beautiful lawn ornament.

In October, I went to a Feng Shui class. It was great to get a new perspective on energy. The instructor gave me a new insight, and with this new insight, I went home to find a box of family photos that Loretta had given me a few years after I had divorced her dad. I had hidden this box as far back in the closet as I could and it had several boxes on top and in front of it.

The instructor had said to put something you want to create in the creative section according to the form school of Feng Shui. This section is to the right middle third section of a room or house. I wanted to put a picture of my son and me hugging since he did not communicate with me.

I had hidden the box because it made me sad, even though there were many happy pictures of all my children. I didn't know why I was so emotional about the box, but while looking for the picture of Larry and me hugging, I decided to cry and asked myself why I always got upset when I just saw the box.

It was during this process that I realized why the box upset me. I had spent years with my husband so my children would have both parents together while they grew up. What I grasped was that I had never mourned the breakup of the family unit that I had spent over 27 years keeping together.

After I finally mourned the breakup of the family unit 14 years after the divorce, I now laugh and smile when I see the pictures that I have since placed in albums. How amazing that process was and I am so grateful that I took the class.

In December, I went to San Angelo, Texas to see Jeanelle and her family.

One day her husband said, "I am perfect."

I laughed and said that I was going to go home and tell people that I met God in Texas.

He said, "God made me in His image and He doesn't make mistakes."

When I arrived home from Texas, I painted a picture that says, "I am Perfect" and it hangs in my massage room. *We are all part of God.*

Healing Garden,
Photo by Mary B. Reed

2003

In 2003 I continue dancing with Sim; a Mother's day letter arrives from my rebel daughter; I have a client in pain after massage; Jeanelle and her family visit; the Peace Gardens article is in *The Journal*; the Healing Garden is designed; I meet Tony; swan visits; mysterious message; hospital; and a poem.

I am still going dancing but with a new friend, Sim. She and I are taking turns driving to different dances on weekends. Sim is from a very rich family in Korea. After she divorced her husband she cleaned houses and barely survived. She said that she decided her family was rich, so she asked for her share and she got it.

Despite being rich, Sim continued to be a cook at the Jefferson High School because she loved both the children and cooking. Her boss said that Sim was really the boss. Sim said even though she was the youngest in her family, everyone listened to her. Sim said when she was young she was spoilt rotten. When the cook gave her food and she didn't like it, she would throw it on the floor and tell the cook to cook something else.

Sim was just the opposite when I met her. She would make 500 egg rolls and give them away. She also would make large pots of soup and then give it to people she thought needed food. She had endless energy and even though she couldn't speak English very well, she was very money and people smart.

Massage was out of the question for Sim because she was hyper. She told me she wouldn't be able to lie still long enough for a massage, but one day she invited me over to dinner and she was wearing a back brace. I asked her if she would like some Reiki and she consented. To my surprise, I had to hold her up because she almost instantly relaxed completely while sitting in the chair.

On Mother's Day, my rebel daughter Loretta sent me a letter. Loretta talked back to me and tried my patience from the age of one through her high school days. As a toddler, she would lie on the floor and scream and kick when she wanted her way. Her older softball teammate told her once that she shouldn't talk back to me the way she did. That is why this letter means so much to me and, also shows, more importantly, the wonderful woman she has become.

> "Dear Momma,
>
> I just wanted to add a short note to say how much I do appreciate the things you did for us kids. I know I never showed it before, as I took it for granted and never realized how much you did. Now that I have a child and also grandkids I see things better. One grandchild was with us for two months and I saw myself doing things you had done.
>
> I realize you gave me so much to grow and learn on. You always took us places and we learned things. So many kids just stay at home and do nothing with the parents. I was doing things with Cyndi and teaching her. Thank you so much for all you did and sacrificed and didn't get any credit or acknowledgment for.
>
> I love you. Loretta"

In May, I also had a lesson from a friend that has helped me in my massage practice. She came to me for a massage, which surprised me because she had said she would never get one. She told me that she had been in pain for over two years and had gone to doctors, physical therapist, and tried different drugs, but was still in pain.

As a last resort she came to me for a massage. Afterwards she made another appointment, which she did not keep. I heard from a mutual friend that she was in a lot of pain the next two days, but after that, she felt better than she had in two years, but was afraid to come back to me.

After I heard this I began to warn my clients that they might experience pain for a day or two if they have gone a long time in pain before they come to me. I tell them to put ice on the sore spot for 15 minutes, then off for 45 minutes.

I also advise them to drink plenty of water. One time I massaged a fellow body worker who was going on a trip alone. She did not drink water because she didn't want to stop and go to the bathroom. The next day she began to get nauseous and realized she had not had enough water to flush out the toxins I had loosened during the massage. She began to immediately drink as much water as she could. The nauseous feeling went away and she enjoyed the rest of her trip.

Soaking in the bathtub with one cup of apple cider vinegar added to the bath water is something I also suggest to my clients. You feel silky and you don't smell like vinegar after the bath. The vinegar bath was advised in massage school to help detoxify the body.

When I have done this after being worked on all day while in massage school, I have not experienced any pain or sickness.

In June, I did a Rock (#2) garden with a subliminal figure eight (that stands for eternity) at the side of the garage. I also laid down pavers to extend the sidewalk up to the end of the corner of the house.

While doing this, I wondered what would happen if I took round stepping stones, put one in the middle, and put the other stones around it. It took exactly six stones on the outside of the circle. I liked it and decided to get larger stepping stones that had leaf imprints on them to make the second part of the subliminal figure eight. The first part was a round garden with smooth stones encircling it.

A visit from Jeanelle and her family in June was rewarding in many ways. The first reward was just to spend time with Jeanelle and her family, who drove from Texas to see the whole family (Loretta, Larry, April, her dad and their families) who all live within a half an hour of me. As soon as they drove up and saw me spreading gravel on the driveway, right away her husband started helping me.

My son-in-law, along with April's husband, replaced the boards on the side of the garage and some of the siding where the wall meets the back stoop. Jeanelle and her husband helped to paint the new boards and siding.

When I came home one day, my son-in-law took me to the shed behind the garage and showed me the two shelves he had put in and how he had arranged the tools as well. He also suggested I break up the concrete sidewalk that was tilting towards the house. I was concerned that during heavy rains the water was being directed under the garage. He also suggested that I replace it with pavers. He showed me how to break up the concrete with a sledgehammer.

While they were out for the evening, I surprised myself by entirely breaking up the concrete sidewalk, which then my son-in-law took to the landfill to dispose of the next day. *Yea! What a wonderful son-in-law.* A few weeks later, I laid down the pavers in preparation for the August Peace Gathering.

When I sent the notice to *The Journal,* I had made a request for them to cover the Peace Gathering. Lisa Montgomery, a reporter, left a message on my answer machine four days before the gathering. I heard the message when I came home for lunch and I called her and she said she would be over shortly to interview me and see the gardens.

I rushed outside to mow around the Rainbow Peace garden, the Gratitude garden, and the Children's Universal garden. I managed to get half of the backyard mowed and wished that I could have finished the rest so that Lisa could take a long-shot photo.

After the interview, Lisa went outside to take some photos of the gardens and her camera would not work. She asked if she could come back since her camera was not working.

I said of course, and while she was gone, I quickly mowed the rest of the backyard, which I finished as she was taking photos of the Children's Universal garden. I had a flowerpot sitting on the entrance into the garden with a small sunflower that had just bloomed. I thought that getting behind the sunflower and taking a long-shot photo of the yard with the sunflower in front would make a great picture.

I did not say anything to Lisa, but at the end she did take that long-shot picture behind the sunflower that ended up on the front page corner of *The Journal* with the caption "A piece of peace." A large photo of St. Anthony in the Universal Children's garden was also put on the front page of section C along with the sunflower picture.

When Lisa got back to her office her camera worked. It is amazing how the Universe worked out all the details!

Lisa did an exceptional job. I received phone calls and several guests as a result of the article. Most importantly, the message of peace was being given energy. The facilitators for the gathering were Joyce Gedeon, who recited her poems, Dale Scully who led a drumming meditation, a singer who sang inspirational songs, Pat as the Leprechaun, and someone who played the guitar and sang.

There was also a group angel reading by Sharon Cunningham. During the reading she told me I would be doing another garden. I thought to myself, no way. But after the party, I found that a guest had left a myrtle tree, thyme, and other herbs. So I designed a Healing garden that helped to hide the gutter hoses that led from my house.

I met Tony at this time. He and several other veterans had started a non-profit company to establish original, contemplative, monumental shrines. The shrines were to be dedicated on behalf of all veterans of all wars who died for peace, in order to help comfort their survivors with pride. I loved his idea, but felt that those veterans who survived needed comfort.

Tony was a Vietnam veteran who had been a prisoner of war. They made him put a revolver in his mouth and pull the trigger (Russian roulette). That night he killed the guard with his bare hands. He was very psychic and could see spirits. The doctors gave him pills to get rid of his visions, but he didn't take them because he knew he saw what others could not.

At the Rocky Ridge Garden Center in Martinsburg, I saw this purplish brown stone slab that I fell in love with and decided to make a bench with it for the Healing garden. Tony helped me get the slab to my house and to put it in place. I planned a dedication for the Healing garden on October 26.

I decided to do some long distance work using Reiki since I had not done so before, and on September 29, 2003, I did long-distance Reiki on a lady near Charlottesville. The next morning when I got up there was a swan in the Japanese Lantern garden. The lady whom I had worked on had told me she was known as the Bird Woman. Interesting?

I called Lisa Montgomery of *The Journal* about the swan because it had a red band on its left leg. I shared with her that my business cards had two swans facing each other. The newspaper sent out a photographer the next day and it appeared in *The Journal* on October 2, 2003. I was in a continuing education class all day and when I arrived home, I saw the owners of the swan in my development trying to find it. The secretary at work said they had called there, crying.

Needless to say they were very happy to get their swan back, and so was Fluffy. The swan had been at my house for three days. One of the reasons it stayed was because two of my neighbors fed him bread every day. They both thought the swan looked like he belonged in my yard. The swan would sleep on the stoop, and when Fluffy wanted to go outside the swan would hiss at her.

The swan also fertilized the gardens and the porch so I was ready to see him go, but I used the feathers he left behind and the story of the swan for the healing garden dedication.

Besides working on the Bird Woman, I also did long-distance Reiki on a friend in Pennsylvania. I asked her to notice what she was feeling while I did the session and I would call her back. When she called me back, she told me she felt energy in her legs first, which is where I started. She then said she felt energy in her shoulder and then her head, which is the order I did them in.

I asked her if she had any problems in her left shoulder and arm because I felt a lot of erratic energy there and she said that she had. I asked her if she had any problems in her abdomen and she said her network chiropractor told her she had some intestinal discord that was causing her hip problems. *Wow! This was the first time I was getting confirmation about what I was feeling using long-distance Reiki.*

She came to me the next week for a massage, and normally if someone is having a problem with their shoulder I would have to do energy work first, but I did not have to with her since I had done the Reiki a few days before.

When I told Jeanelle, who was living in Texas, about this and another incident, she asked me to work on her. I asked her why and she told me that she was experiencing back pain. After I worked on her, I called her and she said the pain was gone.

On October 12, while I was working on a client a woman called three times and left a message on my phone each time. I continued to work on my client, but I wondered who felt as though they had to call back three times and leave a message within minutes of each. After I was finished, I checked my answering machine and there was no message.

My client came out and asked who left the three messages. I asked the client if she heard the woman leave the messages.

She said, "Yes, someone must need your help."

I thought I knew who it might be. When doing Reiki without permission, I pray and ask God to send it to the person. I also ask that if they don't want it, to please send it to someone who needs it. In addition I ask for protection for the client and me.

While doing the Reiki, I was surprised that a vision of a man I knew who had high blood pressure and heart problems came to me. The person I was working on definitely had a heart problem and excess energy in the head. When I asked the person I thought I had worked on, she responded that she was going through trauma of the heart and that she got better. *Did God direct Reiki to both of them?*

The Healing garden dedication created itself in that a woman sat on the bench and sang an Indian song. After that a man sat on the bench and shared his anguish about not getting a project he wanted to do off the ground. At that instant, a guest arrived with a garden stone that was upright and facing forward so you could see the words. Almost instantly several guests said there is your answer. The stone had engraved on it "Faith." *We all could use faith in the future and now.*

On December 5, I was shoveling snow in the dark and I was almost finished, when all of a sudden near my mailbox I stepped down and sliced my ankle on the culvert pipe. When I pulled my foot up, I sliced it again about three-eights-of-an-inch from the other incision. My foot was numb from being cold.

Mom was staying with me at the time and when I took off my boot, I could tell I would need stitches. Mom went to get my neighbor and while she was gone, I put some Young Living essential oil blends called PanAway and Purification on my incisions.

My neighbor and his wife took me to the emergency room and his wife stayed with me in the waiting room. We were there a total of four hours since the room was completely filled.

When the nurse looked at my incisions, she asked me, "How much pain are you in?"

I said, "Nothing if my foot were propped up on my pocketbook."

The nurse asked, "Well what is it if your foot is on the floor?"

I said, "About a two."

She said, "I'll use that number." She asked another nurse to look at the incisions and told her how many centimeters she thought they were. The nurse told me not to leave because I did need stitches. I then went back and sat in the emergency waiting room until they called me back.

The nurse who took me back asked me what was wrong. I said, "I stepped in a culvert pipe and sliced my ankle."

She replied, "Oh, you are the one."

I asked her, "What do you mean by that?"

She responded, "You are the one that should be in pain and aren't."

I guess the PanAway worked.

When the doctor was about to give me a shot to numb my incision sites, I told her I did not want anything put on it, that I wanted to use my PanAway essential oil blend. She told me she could not use anything from outside of the hospital, so when she went to get the sutures, I put some PanAway on the spot. She came back and told me she got the smallest needle she could find.

While she stitched I did deep breathing and only two stitches hurt when she pulled the thread across the anklebone. After she put the eight stitches in, she told me that my deep breathing and the smell of the essential oil put her at ease. *Funny, I wouldn't think that the doctor would be upset about putting stitches in.*

The shot I received for tetanus flared up and I caught a cold from sitting in the waiting room while I had an open wound with people who had the flu. The essential oil blend of Thieves would have been good to put on, since it is a blend of oils from herbs used by thieves when they robbed dead bodies that had the plague.

If I had the equipment, I would have stitched it up myself. I also could not wear the stretchy bandage around my ankle because it inflamed the area. I evidently was allergic to it.

I wrote a poem in December that I sent in my Christmas cards entitled "A Year Gone Away." It described some of the above events and it listed a lesson I learned, which was that *you* create your day. The example was that I wanted to enjoy the Peace Gathering on Sunday and Lisa Montgomery from *The Journal* came and I mowed on a Thursday, which freed me to enjoy the day and not be tired from mowing on Saturday.

Another example of creating is how I wanted the sunflower picture taken and the backyard completely mowed, and because Lisa's camera did not work during her first visit, this happened.

Our thoughts do create our reality. So have pleasant thoughts and thoughts of what you want because you are creating your reality.

**Model of Bahlahnsay,
Photo by John R. Baker, both inside & outside**

2004

2004 was a year that felt like I was in one of the books written by James Redfield, author of *The Celestine Prophecy*. I learned more body mechanics; continued with the women's group, came up with a design for a center; took a BOCA code class; built a three-foot model of Bahlahnsay that took me four months to construct; went to a wedding in D.C.; attended three funerals; visited an Islamic Temple, and received a wonderful, unique Christmas gift.

I took an Alexander Technique course at Shenandoah Valley School of Therapeutic Massage in Edinburg, Virginia given by Emily Clark. I had some experience with the Alexander Technique when I went to massage school, but I wanted a refresher course. The course teaches you how to use your body to avoid complications from bad body mechanics.

Some times while giving a massage, I will notice what I am doing with my body and where I am feeling stress. This is important to me and to my client since I would be transferring my stress to them. After taking this course, I attracted a client who learned the Alexander Technique to help his back and he said it worked for him.

During this time my daughter, grandsons, and son-in-law would call me for sessions if they hurt themselves or were sick. One time my daughter called when a group of women had met at my home for meditation. She said my grandson had a high fever and that he was hallucinating. The whole group of five or six women sent energy to him. I used a teddy bear that has hearts on it to represent my grandson while I was working on him.

During the session my hand sunk half way into his heart. After the session, I asked the women what they were sending my grandson. I don't remember the words but they all were definitely forms of love. I was overwhelmed by the love. No wonder my grandson's heart opened. Yes, he got better.

There was a group of women meeting at my house on every other Sunday morning. We would meditate, read quotes, belly dance, say prayers, do readings and share. It was very informal and off the cuff. Sometimes we would just talk. This group gathering helped me to relax and get through the week at SES.

One day I asked the group members what they would do if they had a million dollars. After their responses, I asked them what they would do for mankind. That night after the meeting, I designed a center using their ideas and mine. After I finished it, I thought, I need to take a building code class.

Two days later I received a flyer in the mail that offered a BOCA code class through the school. Two days after that I was at SES working and a vision came to me of a bridge. I realized that there would be a bridge at the center. When I went home for lunch, in my mailbox was a poem, "Past Sorrows" that my friend, Joyce Gedeon had channeled from Sitting Bull.

Past Sorrows
Copyright Joyce Gedeon 2004

Like arrows shot through the heart and never removed
The past may haunt you
Tweaked by memories the pain arises
Only to fall once again into the darkness of silent separation.

Nations struggle blood flows loved ones perish
All seems lost the past is always present in the prison of mind.
With no body tears may not flow
The past has nowhere to go remaining ever present.

Only the living can build the rainbow bridge
Uniting nations that once were linked only by flowing blood
Past sorrows must be healed now
Rainbow warriors must be found.

Fallen ones in spirit alone have no voices to speak
You shed their tears without knowing
We may guide and hold you dear
Only in body can the rainbow warrior build the bridges
Of all colors
Of all nations
It is time to bury the arrows of past sorrows
I am Sitting Bull.

When I read this poem to a group of about 20 people who were interested in the center, tears flowed from my eyes. I was surprised. A lady offered to finish reading it, but I knew I was crying for those who could not and so I finished reading the poem.

This was not the first time I had burst into tears. My sister facilitated a group about 10 years ago and she had each person say their name and tell what they did. Before each person could say their name and what they did, they had to say the names of all the previous people and what they did.

I hate memorization, and guess what. I was the very last person to give their name and there were approximately 25 people there and I only knew one person. Well, when I got up I was prepared to name everyone, but when my mouth opened, I began to cry uncontrollably.

I feel I was again crying for the group and me. This is because the first time I met Joy Melchezidek and shook her hand I began to cry uncontrollably. She told me that I was crying because I was sensing her pain. Joy is a psychic who endured a lot of physical abuse as a child, such as an uncle who stuck her hand in a boiling pot of water and held it there as one example of many tortures she endured. (She is writing her story which includes the healing of her hands from that damage that took place that night when she was two years old.)

On April 6, 2004, I started the BOCA code class. When I entered the classroom the teacher was writing on the board, so I introduced myself to seven men in the class. There would be another woman and her son auditing the class as well. When the teacher turned around he said, "You all were in the Philadelphia Experiment and you have come together in this class." Then the professor began to teach the class.

I was stunned because while I was doing an emotional release on a client, she had told me that she could see herself melting into the hull of the ship that was in the experiment. The government was trying to time travel and/or have ships become invisible to German radar during World War II.

My sister happened to come to my house when this client was there and she told the client that she had been in the Philadelphia Experiment too. My sister also met a man who had jumped overboard when the ship arrived in Baltimore from Philadelphia. His whole energy field was messed up.

I knew when my sister said that she was in the experiment that there was a good chance that I had been in it too. From what I have read, souls who reincarnate usually come together with the same souls. They are in the same soul group.

So you can imagine how I felt when the professor said we had all been in the Philadelphia Experiment. When I questioned him, he told me that not everyone heard what he said. Only the ones who were suppose to hear, heard. He was right because when I mentioned it to another student, the student said, "I didn't hear him say that."

After the professor made that statement to the class, he asked the students to write about themselves. He also asked us to write why we were taking the class. I was shaking so badly that I could hardly write. Another psychic friend thought I was moving my vibration up to his. It took me an hour and a half to stop shaking. I then volunteered to talk about myself and the Center of Gratitude.

The professor and I had one thing in common; most watches stop working when we wear them. He also cannot work on a computer too long or it will stop working. The class was very valuable to me. I learned a lot, but quite frankly I was in a tizzy most of the time. My desire to be perfect and know everything was just blown away in this class.

The class required a lot of work and met two days a week for three hours each night for ten weeks. There were a lot of subjects where I just found myself lost. The guys would laugh at me and tell me not to get so upset, because I always came through in the end.

The second day of class a student stopped me during break and told me he had seen my center. I asked him where.

He said, "I think I dreamed it."

At the end of the class when I brought a simple model of Bahlahnsay (the dance hall/ meeting hall), the professor asked me how much land did I want. I said between 400 and 600-acres. The other lady in the class said that the same man who thought he dreamed about the center had 600 acres.

I took a vacation day so I could get the first model of Bahlahnsay done. Bahlahnsay is the phonic spelling of "balance" spoken in Spanish. If you look at the photo, located at the beginning of this chapter, you will see that it is six-sided with two levels of roof. I had just about finished the model when the first level of roof would not sit on the model right. I decided to stop and lie down and relax before trying to solve the problem. Within a few minutes, the solution came to me and I finished the roof, and it fit perfectly. *Stay calm and things come to you.*

The Professor was impressed, asked me to bring in certain paints, and he showed me how to make the roof look natural. I used this technique on my final model.

The mission statement for the Center of Gratitude is to unify mankind by offering a variety of modalities by which the individual may choose to become self-empowered with a heart full of gratitude. It will consist of a dance/meeting hall which will be called Bahlahnsay, a restaurant, a healing center, a co-op, health food store, gift shop, information and counseling building, day care, chapel, Peace gardens, and a Pathway of Peace.

Bahlahnsay will have a kitchen, offices, gift shop, restrooms, stage (for plays, speakers, and bands), chair room, mechanic room, all purpose room, health store, coatroom, storage rooms, and entrance way (with information & ticket booths). As Bahlahnsay grows then the other buildings will be built.

While attending the BOCA code class, my friend John got married in Washington, D.C. The president of SES offered to take me, but I knew he was usually late and Tony had offered to take me.

Tony and I arrived at the church a half an hour early, but Tony said we were going to get a parking space in front of St. John's Episcopal Church. I didn't think so, but since Tony is psychic I didn't say anything. Tony drove around the area for 25 minutes before I said, "Don't you think we should find a parking garage?"

Tony agreed, but when we came to the first garage, he said the next one was cheaper. So we went up the street and sure enough it was two dollars less. Tony then had to put his suit coat and tie on. Then we had to find an elevator. He opened a door and said it wasn't the right one.

I remembered that in parking garages there are sometimes two doors, so I went back and opened the second door. When we got to the parking lot lobby, he asked the attendant if there was a bathroom. You can imagine I was getting a little exasperated! I said, "I will go to the one at the church."

When we got to the church, a lady showed me a bathroom, but it was already being used so she took me to one where we had to go through where the ceremony was going to take place. I met John with his minister and the lady showed me the bathroom off from the altar. She said, "Come back and we will seat you."

I saw that the president of SES and his wife were sitting in the front row; he told me later he got there a half an hour early.

After I got back, the usher took my arm and we walked down the aisle. I felt as though I was floating down the aisle. It was a great feeling. When he stopped me at the row of seats, he said, "Madam, you are going to sit in the row of seats where all of the Presidents of the United States have sat in."

Wow! So that is why Tony was being guided by his angels to keep driving around the block for 25 minutes.

Tony said the acoustics were great in our seats and that is why the Presidents sit there. I agreed, for when the singer sang I felt like I was in Heaven. On the way home, Tony told me that Sim and he were dating and that Sim was concerned that I might get mad at her.

When we got home, I teased Sim on the telephone and Tony got upset, but I started laughing and she knew I was kidding. She was so happy with Tony that they took me out to dinner because I was the reason they met. She also was upset with me because I was not going dancing anymore. I told her it had nothing to do with her, but that I was busy doing homework and building my model.

She called one Sunday and asked if I was going to the singles' dance in Frederick, and I said that I was too busy. Then another person called and asked if I was going and I said no. Then a third person called and asked me to go. Since three people called, I felt I was supposed to go and I am so grateful that I did. It was the last time I saw Sim alive.

Sim died two days later in a single car accident. A friend called and asked whether I had heard about Sim. I felt as though I had been hit by a truck and I couldn't believe that she was dead. It was surreal.

My friend then asked, "Does Tony know?"

I called Tony and when I told him, he said that he had seen a vision of her Explorer crashing, Sim going through the windshield, and hitting her head on the pavement. When she hit the pavement, Tony saw a flash of light and knew she had died, but he didn't want to believe that his vision was true. The casket was closed because of the damage to her beautiful face.

Sim was about to inherit another million or two, but she didn't care about the money. Her sister wanted the money and she was telling her other siblings to give it to her. She was supposed to go to Korea the week before, but postponed it to the next week.

She and Tony were planning to get married and they were having a ring re-sized. I truly know that Sim died happy and felt fulfilled. She gave so much of herself to so many. The Jefferson High School band played and the Jefferson High School choir sang. It was so touching to see the teenagers give tribute to her. When someone came through the lunch line hungry, she would pile the plate high. I am sure she was smiling in Heaven that day.

On Mother's day a client's only son passed away. It was very hard on her. She had prepared her son for her death, but she was not prepared for his. I had seen the whole back of my massage room light up with this golden glow a little over a year before his death, while I was working on this client. The client also saw this brilliant glow. *Was it an angel or her uncle?*

The client told me a year after her son's death that she had been given a warning in that she had a re-occurring dream a little more than a year before her son passed. In the dream, an uncle who had died from a heart attack at the age of 36 kept appearing. Her son died when he was 36; she said she has not dreamed of her uncle since her son's death. This client said she would fight the devil because there is nothing worse than losing her son and she did not fear anything.

Her son was about to get married and she was looking forward to having grandchildren. They called each other every weekend and discussed books they were reading, so you can imagine the void his death left.

I admire her because she did not take any medication to get over her loss, but read several books about grieving and allowed herself to feel the pain and heal slowly. It has taken approximately five years, but she is finally looking at the beauty in the world. She is an amazing woman.

Her good-looking son must have been amazing too. A year after his death she traveled to the other side of the United States to attend a memorial service for him. She was shocked and proud to see approximately 3,000 people there to honor him.

On May 25, I went to visit another old friend who had decided to marry his long-time girlfriend on February 7. He had lost one of his lungs to cancer and was hoping they would be married long enough so she could get some of his benefits, but unfortunately he did not live long enough.

While at the hospital, I did some Reiki to help him to cross over. When he had enough, he asked me to stop. His wife, Sandy, is an angel. She had helped many people to cross over and was present for him and did not leave his side. He died two days later.

I loved how Sandy did the funeral service. She gave the eulogy and her daughter-in-law also gave one. There were other people that spoke and it was so personal. It was a wonderful tribute to a man who had helped many people to bowl better – including me.

In September, John Baker, a photographer friend took pictures of the model of Bahlahnsay. He even blocked out the background on the two photos that are on the flyer about the center. I am so grateful for the time and professionalism he showed. I displayed the photos and the model of Bahlahnsay at the October Imagine and Create Universal Peace Gathering.

The professor suggested that I go down Route 7 in Loudoun County, Virginia, and find a Hindu or Islamic temple. He said that there would be a gate and a guard, but that I should go alone and try to get inside.

On November 7, I went on my adventure. I traveled down Route 7 and saw a gate that was half open, but since it wasn't near McLean I continued to another gate and stopped there.

I stood outside the gate for 15 minutes and thought to myself that this wasn't the place, so I went to Meadows Farm Nursery, which I had already passed, because I needed some green granite stones for the Laughing Buddha garden. I went in and asked the young lady at the counter if she knew where a Hindu or Islamic temple was. She did not, but suggested I ask the other lady or young man.

The other lady did not know, but the young man told me to, "Go through two lights, go approximately 300 feet, and it is on the right. There is a guard at the gate."

I went out to where the green stones were and came back in with five of them. I asked the girl how much they were, but she said she didn't know. The young man said to give them to me for $.49 a piece. I went out and got five more since they were usually five dollars a stone.

After parking outside of the gate, I went up to the guard at the Islamic temple and he told me that they only allow visitors on Sunday from 11:00 a.m. to 1:00 p.m., but he kept calling up to the temple to see if a lady would allow me to come in even though he thought she was teaching a class and wouldn't hear the phone. The guard told me about the Islamic religion. They believed in God and that they respected and revered Jesus as a prophet and await his second coming. They also consider Mother Mary to be the purest woman. They additionally believe that Muhammad is the Messenger of God.

After awhile, another good looking man who was in charge of the outside work came to the gate and told me that no one was allowed in the temple. Then I remembered that the directive from the professor was to get inside of the gate, so I asked the man if I could just walk around the outside and I would not go into the temple.

He said, "Okay."

On my way up the hill, I saw a man in a wheelchair at the end of the parking lot. I said hello to him and continued up the hill to the temple. While I was walking around, the man in charge of the grounds came up to me. I gave him two of my business cards and he gave me one back with a phone number to call about the temple.

He also pointed to the azalea bushes, some of which had died. He said it was much like people that come here on the earth. Some flourish and others don't, even though they are given the same good soil to grow.

I then returned to the gate where the man in the wheelchair waited on the left, with the guard. He said, "Hello, my name is Frank. I took an American name when I came here. Black and white is the same. Voting is a privilege. I voted for Bush."

I told him that I had voted for the other one. We hugged because it doesn't matter who you vote for, just as long as everyone uses their right to vote.

As soon as he said, "Hello, my name is Frank," I experienced déjà vu. On my way home, I kept trying to remember where I had met Frank. It came to me that 20 – 24 years ago I had gone to the Grotto at Mount Saint Mary's in Emmitsburg, Maryland. My sister-in-law Celie had taken me there and when we were coming down the path, I saw this man in a wheelchair to the left of the path and sensed he was waiting to see me.

Frank said almost the same thing the first time I saw him, except for the part about voting for Bush. Therefore I felt I needed to go to the Grotto. I could not remember anything about the Grotto, but seeing

Frank waiting for me at the end of the path and knowing he wanted to speak to me. On November 13, I planned to meet my friend up there.

At work, the lady who took care of water customers took off early. So when a couple came in to sign up for water service six weeks before they needed to, I took care of them. I told the couple that I was going up to the Grotto the next day and they told me I needed to go to the Immaculate Conception Chapel at St. Mary's. The couple was from the Emmitsburg area. *Surprising!*

Saturday I went to the Immaculate Conception Chapel first. When I went in, there was no one there. I was asked to put two names on the prayer list. I didn't know at the time but I put the names in this book that actually was the right place. I also put a sticky note on the podium with the names of the people.

When I went up to stand under the dome where Mother Mary is painted in the clouds, my knees buckled. Since my knees have never buckled before, I sensed that I was to kneel and pray, which I did at all of the altars. I sat in a pew and meditated. I heard the door open, but no one came in.

Since it was almost time for me to meet my friend at the Grotto, I left. I arrived early and there was only one parking spot, which was the out path, but at the time I thought it was the beginning. There is a golden statue of Mother Mary and she chimes every 15 minutes.

I walked up the path, read the plaques, and looked at the awesome tile work that displays the events of Christ's life. When I got to the large pond with a statue of Mother Mary in the middle, I decided I would circle it three times. The first time I circled one way, the second time I circled the other way; and the third time I twirled one way to the spring (holy) water, drank some holy water, and then twirled the other way.

When I finished, the golden statue chimed and I knew it was time to meet my friend and her son so I went back down the way I came. My friend was not in the parking lot. I saw the priest to the Grotto and asked him if he would put the names given me on a prayer list.

Another young man with short, dark, curly hair joined us and the priest said that since there were three of us, we could pray then. After the prayer, I gave the priest an offering and he said he had to go.

An older man joined us. The young man told him that someone had stolen around $100,000 from his church and a few weeks after the church burned. He also said he was going to be celibate.

The older man said that when he got the money out of the chest at the cave, that someone else had to be present and that they were mixing the money from the chapel with Mount St. Mary's. He also told the young man that he had been drawn to come to the Grotto.

That's funny, because 20–24 years ago I heard the same stories and both the old man and the young man looked exactly like the men that were telling the stories back then. *Does history repeat itself? It gave me chills. Was I in some time warp? Or was the young man the son of the man from 20–24 years ago?*

I then saw my friend and we walked up the right path with her son. When we got to where we were across from the pond, a squirrel came up the path and stopped directly in front of me and looked up at me. The squirrel then went directly in front of my friend and looked up at her and then off to the wooded area he went. The squirrel never looked at her son who was standing beside of her.

My friend told me that the land was sacred American Indian land and that often the Catholic Church chose Indian sacred land to build on. We proceeded up the path to the cave where the candles are and a statue of Mother Mary is in an alcove over the cave.

My friend commented that they position Mother Mary so that the sunlight always shines directly on her face. I looked around and thought, no. It was because the leaves were off the trees that the sunlight shone directly on Mary's face.

This was only the second time that my friend had been to the Grotto.

I lit a candle for the two people I put on the prayer list and we sat in front of the waterfall that falls into a small pond to the left of the cave. Then we went up to the bridge that leads to the Crucifixion of Christ with Mother Mary and Mary Magdalene at his feet. My friend and I decided to state our intentions for the Center I wanted to build before crossing the bridge.

When we got to the statues, there were seven homemade natural crosses on the shelves. My friend said that someone had left a message, but she was not getting what the message was. We left and went to the wonderful Shamrock restaurant on the way home where my friend had ordered some homemade pies.

The next day I went to the Islamic temple. I had called the two phone numbers that the groundskeeper gave me. The BOCA code professor had asked me to go to a Friday evening prayer call, but no one called me back. When I got to the temple, I was going to park outside of the gate like I had done the previous week, but the guard motioned me to park in the parking lot.

The temple was awesome and clean. There was an attended coatroom where you took off your shoes and could leave your pocketbook if you wanted. The guard had already told the lady at the entrance that I was there and she greeted me. When I mentioned about the prayer call, she said that they no longer had it. I also mentioned that no one had called back. (When I arrived back home, I had a message from the one that I originally called.)

The greeter gave me earphones so I could hear the lecture in English and said if I needed anything to just ask. Another lady escorted me into where the sermon was being given in Arabic via a large screen. The lady asked if I wanted a chair but I said no and she said to motion her if I changed my mind. Almost everyone was in white, and this was the second time that I was in a situation where I was wearing purple and almost everyone else was wearing white.

I sat up against a wall beside an elderly lady. The professor had given me a directive to find someone at the prayer call, but since there was no prayer call, I decided the person would be here today.

He had me repeat the word 20 times. He said, "You will know who to say it to." I sensed it was this elderly lady who appeared to be upset. I didn't know if it was for one specific person or for her people. Near the end of the service, the elderly lady tapped me on the knee and I knew she was the one.

When I said the word, she started talking to me in Arabic and I raised my hands, shook my head sideways, and said, "I don't speak Arabic." We hugged and I helped her out of the room. I then asked the lady who greeted me, "Do you have a tape recording of the mantra they were singing during the service?" I felt like I was swirling up to heaven when they were singing. I am sure that the fact that underneath the dome the floor descended in steps where people sat had something to do with the acoustics as well as the dome.

The sermon was on the sweetness of life and afterward they passed hot tea in glasses and cubes of sugar. I dropped the cube of sugar in the glass and realized it wasn't going to dissolve fast enough and I didn't have anything to stir it with. The lady who escorted me in promptly came over and gave me another sugar cube which I put between my teeth and sipped the tea through it.

I picked up my shoes and coat and upon leaving, they gave me a delicious Arabic dessert, along with a small bag of fruit. It was such a wonderful, enlightening experience that was full of love and respect.

At Christmas time, April gave me a framed picture of when I graduated from Shepherd College. The picture is the moment I received my diploma. She said it took her five years to research and get permission to turn the negative into a photo. I had forgotten that I wanted the picture. What a treasure!

To end the year, I went to Colorado for Christmas and delivered a book to Focus on the Family, in Colorado Springs. The tour of Focus on the Family was so warm and friendly with positive energy. The tours were also very informative and the children's section was filled with happy children playing.

We also visited the Garden of the Gods, which has fabulous red rock formations and there was a great gift shop. After that we saw the Christmas lights at Seven Falls where my fear of heights crept up at the overlook. I was getting as close to the wall and as far away from the railing that I could get.

Bumble Bee one of my totems.
Photo by John R. Baker

2005

This year was about looking for land; meditating and meeting with the group. I also did a return visit to the Grotto, the Knight called, and came to visit.

Over the next three years I would look for land for the Center. In May, I went to Fort Valley, Virginia; there was a property for sale that had two houses, a well-kept barn and a stream going through it. The large house would work to start the Center and the guesthouse could have been my home. It felt so right – as though I belonged there – and it felt solid.

There was an open field as you entered the property where I could picture Bahlahnsay standing. When I took my psychic friend Dale, who is very sensitive to energy, to see the property, she said she felt as though she was floating and the hair on her arm stood up when we drove into the driveway by the barn. She did not get to see the two houses or the stream since I did not have an agent with me. Pictures that I took in the big house had orbs in them.

Two months later I met a gentleman at the single's dance in Martinsburg who said he was from Fort Valley. When I mentioned the property, he told me he had had lunch with the owner of that property that day. He also told me the tile in the bathroom had been imported and that there was another property across from him that was for sale.

I visited the Grotto in July. When I went to the cave where the candles are, I lit a candle for the Center of Gratitude, but I only had a 20 dollar bill. After lighting the candle, I was headed up to sit on the bleachers when I saw a two-foot lizard running on the concrete backdrop.

While I sat on the bleachers I decided that I should put two more dollars in the drawer to make the number 22 – which means master builder. I decided to wait until the sun was shinning directly in Mother Mary's face, but I didn't think that was going to happen because of the foliage of the trees.

A bumblebee flew in front of my face and I moved down closer to the front of the bleachers. I then moved over to the benches in front of the cave. A bumblebee also came up to me while I was sitting there and I decided the next time a bumblebee came to me I would put another two dollars in the drawer. I felt something crawling on the middle of my arm, which was making a bracelet with its path.

When I turned my arm over it was a bumblebee crawling on my arm. I saw in a vision that the bumblebee would just shake and fly off if I flicked it. Therefore, I flicked the bumblebee off of my arm. It shook and flew off in the opposite direction of me just like I saw in the vision. I then put the extra two dollars in the drawer.

The bumblebee is one of my totems. A totem is an animal or insect that you study and learn its habits and you, in turn, can learn from it. They are here to help you, according to Ted Andrews in *Animal – Speak*. If a certain animal has bitten you, it could be one of your totems. When I stayed at Granddaddy Frazier's house, a bumblebee just came along and stung me in the palm of my hand. I also, without knowing, made the Water Fountain garden in a hexagon shape, which is the shape of the beehive cells. When writing this book, during an interview with my Aunt Carrie a bumblebee was on my skirt and I shook it to get it off and it did not go.

Aunt Carrie said, "Mary I don't think the bee wants to leave you."

I went to the edge of the porch and flicked it off with my finger.

My next stop at the Grotto was at the crucifixion statue, which had 40 natural crosses placed on it. I made four more to make the master number 44. I put some holy water on the flowers near a statue that were drooping. I also put some holy water inside of the model of Bahlahnsay to bless it.

In August, I went to look at land in Lovingston, Virginia which had a spring coming down the mountain. I liked it very much. Part of the land up on the knoll had a field of wildflowers that was covered with butterflies. The agent wasn't sure if it was part of the land being sold. There was a small house with no running water. Where the trees met the mountain at the top of the hill, I took pictures that also had orbs in them.

I liked the agent very much because she had spunk. We walked the cow field and avoided the cow pies when the temperature was almost 100 degrees. Her husband stayed back at his car. When waiting to meet them at a store, I saw and purchased a hexagon-shaped stepping stone made out of concrete with a honeycomb design on it with two bees. It is in the Rainbow Peace garden's path.

In September, the White Knight called and asked if he could come over to see me. He arrived on Saturday and he apologized for all he had done to me. He had tears in his eyes. I felt compassion for him and wanted to hug him, but I did not. I wanted to stay in my own power and I wanted him to stay in his own power. So I listened instead.

He said it had all come back to him what he had done to me. The Knight had not paid me his share of the expenses for the house, even though he lived there for nine months after we split up. I had had to beg him for his share of the house payment. He had a house that he rented out, twice tenants did not pay, and it took him three months to get each of them evicted. *So what you put out does come back to you.*

I told the Knight I was going to have a yard sale to get some seed money for the Center and he said that he would bring a couple of bags of clothes over for me to sell. I said, "You are only as good as your word."

He said, "I will bring them tomorrow."

And he did. The clothes were still in the plastic garbage bags I had put them in when he moved out. I suspected they had never been opened.

In November, land around Clarksburg was drawing me to it. The house on this land could have definitely been the start of the Center. It had land that the owner used to sell cattle that were not given antibiotics and no pesticides were used on the land. There was also rich fertile land for growing a garden and a six-acre lake, which was stocked with fish. I used the knowledge I had gained from the BOCA class to make a topography map of the land since it had many hills and valleys.

A psychic friend told me that I was to walk around any land that I was interested in. I was so enthused about the land because I saw a hawk, turkeys, and deer while I was walking it. But unfortunately, when we were almost finished the tour, I felt near this deep drop off beside the road that something was trying to pull me into the hole.

Two of my psychic friends told me that there was a very angry energy on the land that was not happy with what had been done to it. I can only guess that it has to do with the three gas wells that were put on the land along with the gas rights. *I am so glad I walked the land.*

Limahuli Garden in Kauai,
Photo by Mary B. Reed

2006

2006 is a magical year: Betty offers a place to stay in Hawaii; I teach Jeanelle and my grandson Reiki; I get to witness a birth; give a talk to a leadership class; take an EFT course; go to a regression seminar, take the first level of Medical Intuitive; continue my search for land; and quit my job. I also meet Jesse in June and will devote the next chapter and part of 2007 to him.

Betty was going to Hawaii to stay on the island of Kauai and since she had a timeshare with two bedrooms and two bathrooms, she invited me to stay. Betty had lived on the island off and on for several years so she knew where everything was. She was a wonderful tour guide.

I found tickets on the Internet for $899 to stop in Denver for three days, then on to Hawaii for eight days, then back to Denver and on to

Dulles International, but had not made up my mind to go. The next day the cheapest I could find was $1,200. I then said a prayer and said, "God, if I am supposed to go to Hawaii, let me find tickets for $900 or less." I then found tickets for $889 and off to Hawaii I went.

My first stop was in Colorado to see Jeanelle and her family. While there, I taught and gave Reiki I attunements to Jeanelle and my grandson; and on the return trip, I gave them their Reiki II instructions. Jeanelle has used her Reiki in various situations, including when she has been at ballgames where the parents from both teams were getting angry and when she has seen an accident.

Kauai was wonderful and the temperature was between 69 and 82 degrees the whole time I was there. I met a Vietnamese chiropractor, a lady who worked with her, and a writer and her husband. The first meeting was on the beach and the second meeting was at the Hindu Temple. The gardens at the temple were spectacular and in the temple is a large quartz crystal that came from Arkansas. I attended one of the ceremonies to experience it. The participants were very humble.

Water scene in Limahuli Garden

I was also much honored to meet a writer and friend, Jeannie Madelyn Ruman, who wrote *As They Walk Among Us – An Amazing*

Look at Nature-within-Nature. She took me on a spiritual tour of the Limahuli Garden. A picture I took appeared to my psychic friend, Dale Scully, as if it were taken in another time period. I had the picture enlarged for her.

When we went to feed Jeannie's horse, we met a native who was meditating, and from the conversation Jeannie had with him, she felt he was a Kahuna (spiritual leader). Jeannie also took me to the many sacred sites on this island.

On the morning of our helicopter ride, Betty's friend said he was not going with us because of the safety issue of helicopters. When he was in the Air Force, he was never allowed to ride a helicopter due to the importance of his position. He also said that there was a story in the newspaper about a helicopter crash that happened the day before. I asked him whether anyone was killed and he said no. I said, "Good. Betty and I are going on a helicopter ride."

Before we got on the helicopter, we were under a tent and were given instructions about what to do if we crashed. A lady said, "If it is my time to go, it is my time to go."

I said, "It is not time for me to go. The pilot and I are having a safe trip up, around and will arrive safely back."

Betty said, "Me too."

I truly believe in stating what you want.

On the last day I was there, Betty asked if I wanted to go see the lighthouse on the island and I agreed. The lighthouse was not open, but from the shore we could see the whales swimming. There was a mother whale with her baby and one of the whales flipped its tail. We watched for about an hour.

My daughter April said to me afterwards, "When my husband and I went to San Diego, we paid to go on a whale watch and didn't see any whales. You stand on the shore of Hawaii and see whales!"

Betty said that of all the times she had been in Hawaii over the past five years that was only the second time she had seen whales from the shore. Indeed, I felt blessed.

My dear young friend, Ali, asked me if I would be present for her son's natural birth. I had been put asleep for all of my children so I was excited about seeing her son come into the world. It was my honor to be present at such a sacred event.

Her husband was wonderful and stood by her the whole time. Her water broke and they gave her 12 hours to go into labor before she would be given drugs to force the labor. They gave her the drugs around two in the afternoon and I got there around 5:00 p.m., but she didn't have her son until almost seven the next morning. One of her biggest concerns was that her husband and I would fall asleep. She never had to worry about that.

Her son looked just like his good-looking father. It was amazing to see him come out so fast; after his head came out, his left shoulder came out quickly and he was born. He looked a purplish blue at first but quickly turned to normal color. I then went and got Ali's mother who could not stand to see her daughter in pain because she felt her pain. All of us that were present for the birth felt her pain as Ali was trying to give birth to her son. I feel we all were pushing with her and all were empathic for her.

Ali said during the labor that she was not having any more babies, but the moment her son was put on her abdomen, she said she wanted another baby. We all shared her joy and exuberance.

A couple of weeks later I was in a Leadership Class and gave a talk about my life and showed the model of Bahlahnsay. I felt it was one of the most important things I had ever been asked to do. Robert Chan, my neighbor's son, asked if I would come to his class to give the speech. It was important the messages I wanted to convey, since these were the leaders of tomorrow.

One of the points I wanted to make was that our parents do the best they can with the knowledge they have. A second point was made by a demonstration that I had seen part of at a seminar near Baltimore, which I had never done before the speech, but I knew it would work.

A ROTC student volunteered to be the guinea pig for the second and third points. He stood before the class and I asked him to hold his arm out and resist the pressure I was applying to his arm. He was very strong and could resist it easily. Then I asked the class to think negative thoughts about him, and when I applied pressure to his arm, it was considerably weaker. I then asked the class to think positive thoughts about the student, and when I applied pressure to his arm, it was strong again.

The demonstration was to show the second point of how powerful our thoughts are. *We have a choice as to what we want to put out to the world. What do you want to give to the world?* I did something else that I had not seen done, but knew it would work. I asked the class to think positive thoughts toward the student and I showed a card to him with the words "I am weak," written on it. I then asked him to repeat to himself the words that were on the card. Even though the class was thinking positive thoughts, when the ROTC student was thinking, "I am weak," his arm could not resist the pressure I put on it. His arm was weak just as he was thinking.

Next I asked the class to think negative thoughts about the ROTC student, but gave him another card to read to himself. When I applied pressure to his arm, he was very powerfully strong. Even though the class was thinking negative, he was saying to himself, "I am powerful." And so he was.

The third point is that it is more important what we think of ourselves than what other people are thinking of us.

I also gave them a fourth point, that they could use when people became jealous or were abusing them, which was to put a white golden light of protection around themselves and send pink light of love to the other person. (I later learned that this works because you raise your vibration when sending pink light of love to the other person.) Love, being the highest vibration, attracts love and not the lower vibration of abuse and jealousy.

I also discussed the Peace gardens and told them they each had the power to create peace. They were the future and they could bring in the 1,000 years of peace that is written in the Bible and has been predicted by their choice of thoughts. By their choice of thoughts and actions, they could leave the world a better place than when they came into it.

The students stood up and surrounded the model of Bahlahnsay. I had prayed and asked God to help me say that which I needed to convey and was delighted when a student asked a question about why the building was six-sided. I told her it was for the symbol of love and community and that it also had Mother Mary energy. Most of the students hugged me and I was later to learn that they felt that I was a lady of peace.

The search for land continued in March with an agent who took me to see a very expensive piece of property that did not feel good to me. The house on the property felt even worse.

We also went to see another piece of property, and the agent was worried that the other real estate agent would want to see proof of financial backing to buy it. I told my agent not to worry, if the other agent insisted on papers, then the property was not for the Center. The other agent did not ask anything about finances. This property had better energy, and I would later meet the lady who purchased the houses, but not all of the adjoining property.

In February, I came across an issue at SES that I wanted corrected. Fortunately, after several attempts by me, the issue did not get corrected, so I resigned my position at SES in March of 2006.

As I look back I realize that I created this situation. Back in 2005, I had thought to myself, "I have enough in my 401K to live off of until I am ready for early retirement if I were to quit my job when I am 59 ½ years old." In February of 2006, I was exactly 59 ½. Interesting how I created that for myself by my thoughts and the Universe supplied the way.

In April, I took a home study course on the Emotional Freedom Technique. It is a tapping procedure which premise is that when there is an emotional issue, one or more meridians get clogged or blocked and by tapping the meridian points you open it up again. It also has a procedure called the setup to erase blockages on a mental level. I used EFT to help me with my fear of heights.

When my children were young, I took them to Washington, D.C. to see the museums, we went up on the second floor and there was a balcony around so you could see the first floor. I wanted to crawl on my stomach and get my children away from the balcony, but of course, I did not. I had a fear of falling and a fear of being pushed.

After doing the EFT tapping procedure for my fears, I went with several friends to an A-frame house that had a porch that overlooked a steep slope. The porch was just unpainted plywood that had been laid over the beams and they shook as you walked on them. I walked on them and looked out over the slope and felt nothing.

We went inside where the steps to the top loft were made out of a large log suspended from the ceiling along a wall. My friend, Joyce suggested, that I see if I could walk up the log to see if heights bothered me. I preceded up the steps in my two-and-a-half inch heels and was going to go further, but the owner suggested that I stop because he had not leveled the upper steps.

The next day I had a Peace Gathering and taught the EFT at one of the classes being given that day. While I was explaining to the class about my own experience and mentioned the log steps, Joyce added that she could not believe I went up the stairs that were suspended and only had a rail against the wall and nothing on the other side of the log. She told the others that she would not have gone up them. *Isn't that interesting?*

Joyce did the tapping for pain in her knee and was surprised that it went away. Another student tapped for anxiety. When asked on a scale of one to ten, what his anxiety was, the student replied 20. After doing the whole procedure twice, he said his anxiety was zero.

You can learn more about the procedure and can down load a free booklet by going to www.emofree.com.

In late April I was treated to a Hypnosis and Regression seminar at the Fairfax Unity Church. The class was taught by Henry Bolduc and I was surprised when I went back to a past life during the regression exercise.

With your eyes closed, you were to look at your feet and notice what kind of shoes you had on. I saw leather sandals and as I moved up my body I saw canvas clothing and then I saw a shepherd's cane in my right hand and a lamb in my left arm. I then saw myself in a colored robe of three-inch stripes that were in the colors green, red and gold. On the table were one-inch cubes of gold and gold coins. I had curly black hair and was a very handsome man. Beside me stood a tall bearded man who had a dagger in his hand and was going to kill me.

I felt no fear or pain. It just was. The fascinating thing is that I had been wondering if I had been killed for being wealthy in any of my previous lifetimes and if that was the block to being wealthy in this lifetime.

It was in the middle of June that Joyce and I took the first level of Medical Intuitive from Kim Seer. This class taught me to trust my intuition and the information I get when asking questions about a client's condition. I have to be in a neutral state when I do this. It includes a look at many different things going on in the fields of energy around the client. There is a chart that can be checked for different issues that need to be cleared or brought back to balance and harmony. These include physical, mental, emotional, spiritual, memories, etc.

One of the procedures I use most from this class is the endocrine system reconnection. This helped a recent client who I noticed all of a sudden had sweaty feet and hands. Someone had emailed me that sweaty hands and feet could come from thyroid imbalances. The week after I did the endocrine system reconnection her feet and hands were not sweaty like the week before. Another is the brain synapse, which I have used with some success on an autistic boy and when someone's mental field is erratic.

It was during this class that a fellow student told me that she saw a large owl and a spider on my body. She also told me that I am a teacher, healer, old crone and a survivor. I agree with survivor and all the students were facilitators of healing. When I worked in Bethesda, Maryland, a fellow worker gave me an owl pin that had glasses on it because she thought I was very wise.

In the *Animal–Speak* book by Ted Andrews, he says that your totems could be any animal or insect that you dreamed a lot about. When I was young, I often saw spiders in my dreams. Sometimes the spider would be bigger than the bed and I would wake up sweating. When the student saw a spider on me, it made a lot of sense to me. The book says that the spider's keynote is creativity and the weaving of fate. It also asked, "Do you need to write?"

In June my friends Sandy and Dave came to stay for a few days and I met Jesse.

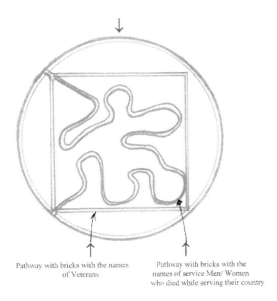

Pathway that will have bricks with the names of People who support Peace.

Pathway with bricks with the names of Veterans

Pathway with bricks with the names of service Men/ Women who died while serving their country

Pathway of Peace-I drew

Jesse

Sandy and Dave took me out to dinner at the Market Place and then Sandy wanted to go for homemade ice cream afterwards. The owner suggested the Ice Creamery a few blocks down the street, and even though I wasn't really interested in ice cream, we walked until it poured down raining (and then we ran) to the Creamery.

We were waiting for our ice cream when Jesse came in and stood by me at the counter. He spoke and I replied, but then he quickly jerked his head in the opposite direction and began to talk to the lady on the other side of him. Sandy came between us and talked to the both of us because Jesse had such beautiful sparkly, blue eyes; she wanted the conversation to continue.

Jesse and I talked until Sandy said that she was getting the car and would come back and pick me up. Jesse and I could not remember what we said at that first meeting, but he did tell me that when he turned and first spoke to me he saw this aura and glow around me and he knew he was in trouble, so he immediately looked the other way. He said it felt like someone had hit him over his head with a baseball bat.

Jesse was given up to a foster home when he was two and a half years old, sent to another foster home at seven, was drafted in the army, and served in Vietnam and the Panama Canal. He worked for the government, met his wife-to-be in college, fathered two children, became a drug addict, went to a post-traumatic class, met me, and then died two months before his sixtieth birthday.

Jesse had one sister and three brothers, and some stepsisters. He and his two older brothers were put in a foster home, which turned out to be a brother and sister posing as husband and wife in Maryland. His sister and other brother were put in a different foster home.

He said he was beaten to near unconsciousness and they would tease him with chicken bones while he was in a cage. Jesse said that one of his brothers and he learned to communicate by mental telepathy since they were not allowed to talk to each other.

One time after a beating, he was placed on a stool and the foster mother allowed Jesse to prop his head on a cabinet that had lead paint on it. Jesse's wounded head absorbed the lead and it swelled up, but the foster mother did not take him to the doctor so the social service sent someone to interview him.

During the first interview, Jesse told the interviewer that he was being treated okay, since he was their pet and he didn't know any better because he was so young when he was put in the home. His older brothers told Jesse that they were being treated badly so when the social worker came again, Jesse told her that they were being abused.

Because of the interview, the boys were put in another foster home that Jesse absolutely appreciated. The foster father was a gardener, which Jesse loved to do. He said that his foster father grew pineapple trees in Maryland and had been written up in magazines for his experiments. At this home, he was taught values which he treasured, but different ones would be drilled into him in preparation for war.

I write about Jesse's experience in Vietnam to provide an understanding – not pity – for those who served in the war. Hearing about Jesse's experiences has made a difference in that I now want a

Pathway of Peace in the Center. The Pathway will honor those who died during war, as well as those who fought for Peace and did not die in the war – because they suffer the most. It will give an opportunity for those who support Peace to contribute to the pathway. (A description is at the appendix at the end of the book.)

Jesse and the Vietnam War

After orientation to camp, Jesse dropped to the ground on a rope out of a helicopter. At the age of 20 and 145 pounds, he found himself hugging the ground, terrified, with gunfire all around him.

"What do I do?"

It didn't take long for him to realize it was kill or be killed. He was expected to be on duty 12 hours or more, seven days a week and not get an R & R until after six months. Then it was back on duty.

Jesse said drugs, alcohol and cigarettes were free and rampant at camp and that most young soldiers woke up saying they were going to die that day. A lot of them did. Men that were drafted had to take an oath that they were willing to die for their country.

At night Jesse would sleep with his gun to his chest and only got about two hours of sleep a night. When he would get in the helicopter, he would fall asleep and the pilot would holler, "It is time to jump." Another friend told me that two hours of sleep was about what he got each night because he was too wired up and alert. The soldiers were under 24-hour stress from the fear of dying and trying to be alert to danger. *Could you sleep?*

Not only were the soldiers worried about the enemy, but they also had to deal with the elements. During the raining season (it rained for three months straight), Jesse would wake up and pull leaches off of his body almost every morning. One time he said one was in his ear sucking out his brain. When one would be in his crotch, he would get another man to take a lit cigarette and burn the leach until it dropped off. The weather was always hot and humid.

When out in the jungle, Jesse couldn't see two feet in front of him, but his sense of smell heightened and he could smell where the enemy was. My friend said he could also smell a Vietnamese. Jesse said when the government sprayed Agent Orange, he could wipe it off his shirt and arms because it was so thick. When he had to crap in the jungle, he did not stop for fear of being shot.

Jesse was sent on a mission to get two bodies. He knew it was a suicide mission since the Vietcong would be ready to ambush them. Unfortunately, he was right and everyone was killed but him. His best friend's limbs were shot off and when Jesse tried to push his friend's lung back into his chest, the man's heart fell into Jesse's hand.

The friend said to Jesse, "I lied to my parents. I am not coming home."

He tried to match the body parts of the men and when he returned to camp, they stripped his clothes off of him and burned them. Jesse said they offered him a medal, but he didn't want it. He said he chopped an enemy's head off and carried it around with him for months.

After going through a village several times, and losing men every time, Jesse gave the order to burn a village down. A friend of mine was in the Air Force and when he entered a village, he told his men that he would do to them what they did to anyone in that village. Was that because he only entered a town once?

When I went to visit Jesse at the V. A. Center, another patient said he had talked to a sergeant of a command boat. The sergeant had to choose what man would be radioing out. Because the boat was so well armored, in order to get a signal out the radioman had to stick his head up and was usually shot. After losing several radiomen, the sergeant gave the order to shoot at a village. *Would you have wanted to choose?*

A friend told me that he saw many barbaric things that he thought he would never see in his lifetime during the war.

As a combat soldier, Jesse saw many comrades disintegrate before his eyes. He survived to hear fellow soldiers crying and screaming in pain from wounds and hollering, "Help me, help me."

One soldier told a friend when he went back home, "They only train a combat soldier to die." So he went back to Vietnam and died fighting.

Johnny Cash gave a show in Vietnam. Jesse said they took them off the field and they sat in the front rows while others hissed and booed at them. But right after the show they were put back down in the combat zone.

Jesse was in a helicopter crash and was told he was all right. He was put back in combat without an examination. After all, combat soldiers were expendable. Jesse would years later find out that he had broken a bone in his shoulder.

Because Jesse was so small he had to crawl into tunnels that the Vietnamese had dug out. He said he could hear his heart beating and there was barely room to crawl. Later he found out that these tunnels sometimes led to an underground cave where the Vietnamese set up hospitals.

Jesse, after the War

When Jesse came home to Los Angeles, he said the war protesters spit, cursed, booed, and threw bags of dog shit on him. They also beat and robbed him.

I met another veteran at the Veteran Center in Martinsburg who told me, "I will never forget the horror of coming home to L. A."

Did the war protesters become what they had fought? When you give energy against something, you actually give energy to what you are protesting.

At his foster home, Jesse climbed a very high tree with a rope and jumped down. His foster mother fainted and his foster father told him he was not his son anymore because Jesse had become an animal. Jesse said he was only trying to show them what he did in the war, but he had become very barbaric.

In the Native American culture, they know a warrior needs to be deprogrammed to be able to return to the tribe. Jesse re-enlisted to go to the Panama Canal since he didn't fit into civilian life.

He went to college after leaving the service and met his wife. Jesse said she was beautiful and a very talented singer, but he did not love her. They had two children whom Jesse loved very much. His brother found him a job with the government and he rose from a GS3 to a GS12 in a short period of time. He built a large house and by most standards was very successful.

But the war memories would return. One day Jesse was in a grocery store, he dropped his wallet, and his family pictures came out. The memories of all the wallets he had taken off of the dead Vietnamese with photos of their family in them came back to him.

"They had families too," he said. "The pictures of the dead Vietnamese families stare at me and I do not sleep."

He would question: Why were we fighting? What values did other cultures teach their children? If he was a Vietnamese, he would have defended his country just the way they did. Why did the government brainwash him into doing things against his values? Who really profited from the war? *We are all one.* His search was a soulful one.

To get away from the war memories, Jesse turned to drugs and alcohol and he lived on the streets of Baltimore. He left his family because he knew it was not good what he was doing to them while on drugs and alcohol. His sister would try to help him, but to no avail. Her husband would also help Jesse with his legal problems and Jesse had a very high regard for him.

Jesse said he was not afraid to sleep on the streets of Baltimore for 12 years since it was better than when he was in Vietnam. I am sure if someone tried to bother him that they found out that they had made a big mistake. Jesse had no fear except of enclosed places because of crawling into holes in Vietnam.

After many attempts, Jesse was finally admitted to a program for PTSD at the Veteran Administration Center in Martinsburg, West Virginia. While there he was placed in an intensive post-traumatic stress program in Perry Point, Maryland where he went through a transformation, thanks to Alan Breck and his staff.

It was during this program that he visited the Wall in Washington, D. C. He also went through a sweat lodge with Tom Pender that he said helped him a great deal. Jesse finished the program in March of 2006 and I met him that June. He said I would not have liked him before the program because he would have growled and snapped at anyone trying to get close to him.

**Peace Path with Lamb & Lion,
Photo by John R. Baker**

After Jesse and I Met

On our first date, we met for lunch. Jesse interrogated me, and halfway through the conversation I decided that he didn't need to know everything about me.

"Why aren't you answering all my questions?" he asked me.

I replied, "You don't need to know everything."

He said, "I know enough."

At the end of lunch, he asked me, "Where are we going now?"

I was caught off guard and called my mom to see if she wanted company. She said to give her an hour or two. Now what was I to do with Jesse? I ended up taking him to my house to see the Peace gardens. He was ecstatic when he saw them because he loved gardening and he had been praying in church and asking God for a woman of God, a woman who liked sex, and he wanted to experience peace. *God does answer prayers.*

That evening I looked up his numerology to give me an insight into what type of man he was. Amazingly enough, being born on the 29th set him up for one of the heaviest karma of all. He would have the same path of Job and would have to have the great faith in goodness and the power of self.

His name came up to a nine in Chaldean-Hebrew Kabla numerology in *Linda Goodman's Star Signs*. One of the things about a nine person is that they are very direct and they demand what they want, which catches people off guard. The nine usually gets what he wants. Hmm. That happened to me yesterday when he asked me, "Where are we going now?" Nines also have a Mars' temper.

The next day he made a statement that was to set the tone of our relationship and the lessons I was to learn.

He sat at the kitchen table and said, "Don't try to fix me. I will fix myself."

Well, I had certainly learned that you can't change anyone during my relationship with the Knight. *Just accept people the way they are.* So I thought to myself, okay, I wonder what I am in for now.

In July, I attended a stone massage class and was impressed with the deep relaxation that resulted. When I gave one to Jesse, he said he went back to a lifetime as an Indian and was in a sweat lodge ceremony like the one he attended at Perry Point. Jesse was very psychic and knew we had met in a previous lifetime but he couldn't remember the lifetime.

In the middle of July, I went to a court hearing in Maryland with Jesse where his brother-in-law represented him. The hearing had to do with him taking off with a vehicle owned by a chauffeuring service. He said he blacked out and ended up in North Carolina. After the hearing, Jesse took me to the Perry Point VAMC so I could meet Alan, Sarah and the others that had helped him. It was a pleasure meeting them. I had read the book that Sarah Hansel Ph.D. co-edited with Ron Zaczek and was co-authored by Ann Steidle and Grace Zaczek, titled a *Soldier's Heart, Survivors' Views of Combat Trauma*.

Jesse shared the book with me, which is a compilation of stories, poems, and paintings that soldiers have used to express their feelings of war. You can see a progression of healing in some of their writings as you go through the book. It also opened my eyes to what nurses endured. It is quite compelling and I would highly recommend it for anyone wanting to understand a veteran or for a veteran who wants to heal.

Jesse gave me a lot of material about post-traumatic stress so that I would understand what he was going through. One of these explained that before the Vietnam war, whole companies would return together which allowed a sharing of their experiences. The Knight's father had gone to his World War II company reunion every two years. Unfortunately in Vietnam, only one or two vets would go home at a time, so the bonding and support was not there for them.

Also, veterans from World War I and II were greeted and honored, whereas the Vietnam veterans were treated badly by protesters. As I said before, the veterans were greeted with bags of dog shit, booed, spit at, beaten, robbed and cussed. *Home sweet home?*

We visited many parks in the area. While at Cacapon State Park, we went up one of the trails and he became on edge because it was wooded and reminded him of Vietnam. We also attended St. John's Lutheran church in Harpers Ferry, West Virginia, and afterwards went to the Grotto, which he enjoyed immensely.

After the visit to the Grotto, we went to the Shamrock and I had to exchange seats with him because he did not want his back to the door. He had to be able to survey the whole room, which is how a lot of veterans feel.

On my birthday, my daughter took Jesse and me out to dinner. She seemed very standoffish to him. We sat at a table with a friend, her husband, and her daughter who had just gotten back from Iraq. My friend's daughter was constantly surveying the room and never did rest and relax.

Jesse said, "Look at her. She already has the searching eyes."

My daughter called me a few days later and didn't leave a message so I called her back and I asked her why she called.

She said, "I am warning you. I had a dream before you met Jesse. In the dream, you are dating a Vietnam veteran and he kills you."

I told her okay I could take care of myself.

She said, "If you die, I warned you."

A year later she would tell me she had a dream of the airplane flying into the Twin Towers. It is probably good that I didn't know this fact.

Jesse called me after my daughter gave me this warning and told me that he had thought of some horrible things that he would do to me. He also prayed and asked God to forgive him for those terrible thoughts. I did not ask him what he was thinking because I didn't want to give any energy to it. Surely God was warning me through my daughter.

One of my psychic friends also warned me; however, I felt she was projecting her past experience on me. I only focused on Jesse's light. Another psychic friend told me that she had been a drug addict and alcoholic and to be careful. After being locked up for two years, she has been dry for more than 25 years, but said the only thing a drug addict wants is the next drug or the next drink. She said not to fool myself. *These forewarnings served me well. God always gives you what you need.*

Besides the stone massage, I did an emotional release using essential oils on Jesse. He was awed with the results. It gave him a sense of peace. But that peaceful feeling did not stay long. The war haunted Jesse.

Jesse had not chosen to go to war. He was drafted. He was threatened with prison and a deep dark pit. He was brainwashed to commit acts that he felt were against his upbringing, his values and his beliefs. He had much guilt and torment about the terrible things he did in Vietnam. *Would God forgive him?*

The war veterans who survived are suffering. A young friend, whose father was in Vietnam, said, "One day after it had snowed, my father was driving down the road and the snow on top of the car roof fell on the front windshield of our car. My father let go of the steering wheel and ducked under the car dash."

Another friend's wife told about her husband waking up in the middle of the night crying, "I killed the babies. I killed the babies."

Most veterans do not talk about the war the way Jesse did.

Still another friend says that about 12–15 years after the war ended, three different times she was almost choked to death by three different war veterans who were experiencing flashbacks. The first time she woke up in the middle of the night and knew in a moment her neck would be snapped. She hollered his name and said you don't want to do this and her husband let go and apologized to her.

The second time was with a prospective mate who had his hands around her throat when she woke up and she said, "You don't want to do this." And he let go.

The last time was a friend who had asked her to do some energy work on him. He wanted relief from emotional pain and she was unaware of how much pain and what the cause was. As she started the energy work, a voice came from him yelling, "Do not do this. Why are you doing this to us?"

She began to say the Lord's Prayer. He leapt at her and started choking her.

She said, "You don't want to do this."

And he exclaimed, "No, I don't!" He proceeded to tell her about his war experience and how his three friends had been killed and he felt he was to blame. He would pull his finger and toenails out for physical pain to relieve the emotional pain. She sent him to his pastor to get counseling and put him on a suicide watch.

Jesse had several flashbacks every day. I could tell when he was staring off in space that he was having another horrible war memory. Most of the time Jesse could not get to sleep unless he had medication, and even then he woke up in the middle of the night, back in Vietnam.

Near the beginning of August, I was noticing that Jesse was more agitated when sitting outside on the swing talking. I would sometimes go inside of the house at that point. I knew I didn't have to be abused verbally by him. During this time a spider bit him while he was clearing out the shed by the fence and he was having side effects. The bite site swelled to two inches wide and was hard. He was also having stomach problems. A week later we went to the river to celebrate Mom's birthday.

In the middle of August, I went with Jesse to City Hospital to check to see if he had a blockage in his artery. A few days later, I was taking a Medical Intuitive Level II class in which I learned to do energetic surgery on a knee and how to do quantum healing with the help of a chart. I would use this chart to help Jesse clear part of his family time line.

In September, we went to Perry Point for an Intensive PTSD picnic. When I saw one of the instructors, I noticed he, too, would leave the present time and go back to Vietnam. When an airplane flew over, I saw several veterans going into the motion of ducking and some actually fell to the ground. Almost 40 years have passed, but the veterans still have this reaction.

We participated in a sweat lodge facilitated by Tom Pender and his wife before the picnic. It was the first one that I had attended and was told to bring another set of clothes since the ones I had on would be soaked. One of the things I said was, "I want to give up control." That opportunity would come all too quickly.

Betty took several of us to Hershey Park to spend two nights. Jesse did not want me to go since he had a trial to go to in Maryland. When I got back, I called the V. A. Center and he was not there. I called his brother-in-law and asked if he knew where Jesse was. He had left Jesse earlier and thought he should be at my house by now.

He told me the trial had gone pretty good and that Jesse would have to pay damages. After paying damages, Jesse would still be left with some of his settlement for getting 70 percent disability.

I did not hear from Jesse for four days. He had gone off on a drunk and his friend Rich insisted that he call me. Jesse was in a program at the V. A. Center, but he got kicked out because he hadn't returned on Thursday.

When Jesse came to see me, he got mad when he saw his clothes out in the garage, because he knew we were through.

He said, "Why didn't you tell me that you had made a decision before I wasted my time trying to convince you?"

Since Jesse was very demanding, I often had to visualize my feet going into the center of the earth before I would give an answer to his questions. He had been trying to move his things into my house a little at a time. In fact, I had let him put his TV out in the garage, but had said no to making the garage a room. I sensed from the beginning that his alcohol problem was not under control.

Jesse said he drank to forget the war. "I am not an alcoholic," he said.

But starting in September he would not arrive at my house until after 6:30 p.m. Before that he had come over my house not too long after he finished the work program at the library at 5:00 p.m. I figured he was visiting one of his friends so he could drink before he came to my house. Whenever we went to see his friends, the first thing he did was get a drink, and if they didn't have any, he would go out and buy beer for them.

We did not see each other until after he called me on October 19 and told me he had fourth-stage pancreatic cancer and had been given three to six months to live. He asked me to go with him to the V. A. Center to see the oncologist, because they treated veterans differently if someone was with them. The oncologist was unemotional, stared at his computer screen and barely looked at Jesse while he confirmed that it was fourth-stage cancer. Jesse was admitted to palliative care at the end of October.

Jesse would later get to the oncologist's heart. I saw tears running down his face as he fought not to cry when Jesse asked, ten days before he died, "Will you be testing my blood in two weeks to see if I can have chemotherapy?"

A few days after Jesse and I went to see the oncologist, I went to a seminar at Fairfax Unity Church where Charles Cayce gave a seminar. Charles is the grandson of the famous Edward Cayce who made many predictions that came true. Edward Cayce could also go to sleep laying his head on a book and when he woke up he knew the information in the book.

Charles gave out a meditation that I use during the Energy Circle at the Centre for Positive Living in Martinsburg. I also read this meditation several times to Jesse to help him heal and relax himself.

In November, Jesse crawled under the house to fix my bathtub even though he hated doing so since it reminded him of crawling in the holes in Vietnam. A week later I found his turquoise ring that had been missing since the beginning of August, which he thought someone had stolen.

I did not tell him, but that day I had decided I would go buy him a ring since he was so fond of the other one. But just before I was going to go, I found it on the floor near the sliding glass doors to my massage room, which I pass many times each day to let my dog out.

The ring had never been there before or I would have seen it. Also, the weekly cleaning person would have seen it. It was quite a mysterious reappearance of the ring. Jesse was so thankful to have it returned. *Did an angel put it there?*

Jesse spent the night at my house before Thanksgiving and had a pass for four days. This meant he had medication from the hospital for four days. When it was near lunchtime, Jesse said he wanted to watch a football game.

I said, "If you want to, go." (I can't get any TV stations since I do not have my TV hooked up to cable and only watch DVDs on it.) My sense was that he wanted to drink and knew I wouldn't approve since drinking with pancreatic cancer is like a death sentence.

When Jesse came back to my house, I could tell he had had plenty of alcohol. He said he was going back to the V. A. Center but he was leaving his medication at my house since they told him not to bring any back with him. I felt like he was using me to get drugs, and I called him and told him that. He said he wasn't and we'd talk about it later, but we never talked and he never asked if he could spend the night again.

Jesse went to Washington, D.C. at the end of November and decided to start getting chemotherapy instead of just waiting to die. I took money out of my savings to purchase glyconutrients and other products that had helped some cancer patients. Taking these products had stopped the ringing I was having in my ears, so just maybe they would help Jesse.

On December 21, I was supposed to go to Denver, but the airport was closed because Denver had 30 inches of snow. I had this sense I was still going, even though there were no tickets available until December 27. I kept seeing myself at my daughter's on Christmas Day. On December 22, I called Delta at 7:40 a.m. and the line was busy so I redialed immediately.

The Delta lady told me that there was only one airport open. When I called Jeanelle on my cell phone, she said it was six hours away from Denver. She also was on the other line with Delta trying to get a ticket for me and they couldn't get in the account. So I made reservations for December 27, but I was told that if there was a cancellation when I called, then I could exchange the tickets. What were the chances of calling and someone canceling at the same time?

The Delta lady asked me to hold on while she confirmed my reservations. She came back on the line and was confirming the reservation when she said, "A ticket just became available for the December 24. Do you want it?"

I replied that I did and I was there in time for Christmas.

My daughter gave me a beautiful round puzzle with an Indian maiden on it with a black and a white wolf. We put it together and it now hangs on my kitchen wall and I remember this story of faith when I see it.

**Rock Garden with Angel,
Photo by Ruth Hatcher**

2007

I am still looking for land, went to Medical Intuitive III, watched Jesse's health deteriorate, and made a list during the first few months of 2007.

When I realized I was putting more energy into Jesse being healed than Jesse was, I told him that I was done unless he put some in as well. He got mad, but I let go and let Jesse fix himself. I let go of control and honored his decisions.

He was a chain smoker and every time I went to see him he would go down to the smoke room and I would wait in his room until he came back, then he would tell me, "It is time for you to go."

Even though it was only a couple of minutes from my home, I decided I was wasting my time, so the next time I went to visit and he said he was going down to smoke, I told him I was leaving. I asked him, "Why should I come just for you to go smoke then come back here and tell me it is time for me to leave?" Jesse got mad, but I stood my ground and told him I was going home.

Jesse would then call me every day and ask, "How are you?"

I'd say, "Fine. How are you?"

He'd say he was doing as well as could be expected and then say goodbye.

On January 8, I got a call from the V. A. Center wanting to know if Jesse was at my house. Then his sister called and asked if Jesse was there. The next call was from his brother.

"Well I guess Jesse has gone off for his last hurrah. If you hear from him, let me know."

I called the librarian who was over the work program Jesse was in and she said she just knew he was missing. When I asked repeatedly over the next month if I should call Jesse on his cell phone, I got a no. I felt that maybe he needed to work something out and needed to be left alone. It was not only him that needed to change.

On February 16–19, I was taking another level of Medical Intuitive. The instructor, who can see inside of your body and actually see your organs working and blood flowing through your veins, was also going through a similar situation with her father. She knew she could help her father, but he refused her help. He was ready to die.

As a facilitator of healing, the most important lesson is to honor a soul's decision to die. During the class we learned techniques that could be used on cancer, fibromyalgia, arthritis and the spine. One of the exercises we did during the class was to talk to another student about an emotional issue until the teacher said to stop. The other student was only to listen until the teacher said to stop.

I let the other student go first because I wasn't sure what I wanted to discuss. When it was my turn, I started with my mom, but I really didn't have much to say. I then talked about the wall that comes up between people when you don't agree with a decision or action by another person. You disagree with the way they are living their life. It is the wall of judgment and disapproval of another. The wall was there between my dad and me. The wall was there between Jesse and me.

I asked, "What do you do when the wall comes up? What do you do?" I sat there in complete silence, which seemed like an eternity when all of a sudden a voice came to me. It simply said, "Open your heart." My heart opened and I started to cry.

On February 25, when I asked about calling Jesse on his cell phone, I got a yes. When I saw him, the whites of his eyes looked like someone had taken a fluorescent yellow magic marker and covered them. His skin was also yellow-toned from his liver not functioning properly. Jesse told me he had gone off to drink himself to death, but when he called a taxi, he was bent over in so much pain that the taxi driver drove him to the V. A. Center.

He told me that the reason he had not called me was because he knew that I did not approve of what he was doing. Another reason was to let me go so I could go on with the rest of my life. *True love is just that, when you love enough to let go of the other person.* That is why I sat beside Jesse while he passed over. I loved him and didn't want him to be alone.

When they did another MRI on him, they found the cancer had metastasized to two sites in his liver and Jesse was readmitted on February 10th to palliative care. He was given 30 days to live. On March 3, Jesse told me his life was "a wasted life."

"No life is wasted," I responded.

A friend of mine who is also a recovering alcoholic said her therapist tells her, "There are no bad people just people who do bad things." *That is food for thought.*

The next day I brought him a list of things I loved about him. It said: God centered, intelligent, beautiful sparkling blue eyes, worldly, kind, generous, giving, humorous, loving, educated, thoughtful, respectful of me, spiritual, dancer, singer, spontaneous, gentle lover, supportive, cook, leader-take charge person, conversationalist, handsome, protective of me, love of nature, gentleman, positive expressed appreciation to waitresses and cooks. In addition, I wrote him a letter that listed the many things he had done to help me.

Expansive Mandalla (by Mary)

Jesse's Passing

On March 21, Jesse called and he was mumbling. I called him several times that day and didn't get an answer on either his cell or room phone. I had wanted to go to Ocean City the next day, but Dale's car was not fixed so I cancelled since she usually watched Fluffy at my house. *I know that I wasn't supposed to go; therefore, the Universe blocked my going.*

The next day, Thursday, I went to see Jesse and he couldn't speak very well. He mumbled and when I asked him to repeat what he said, he would get mad. He could get a cigarette in his mouth but could not get it lit. He just sat in the smoke room and when I went to get him the cigarette would be in his mouth backwards and not lit. All of his pants had cigarette burns on them from Jesse nodding off while he was smoking.

He had received a bad report on Tuesday about his blood so he couldn't take any chemotherapy. It would be another two weeks before they would check his blood again.

Jesse's lunch tray came in while I was there and he was given the funeral arrangements that he had taken care of on Tuesday.

Jesse took the arrangements out of the big envelope with his son's name on it and took a piece of bread off his lunch tray and was pressing it on the other envelope the arrangements were in. He was looking around and I asked him, "What are you looking for and what are you trying to do?"

He said he wanted it attached to the envelope.

"I'm going to be put on death row, aren't I?" Jesse asked as he awoke from his nap. His question took me back to the question my dad asked me a day-and-a-half before he died.

"Mary, I'll live if I eat these mashed potatoes? Won't I?"

I replied, "Yes." I wished that I could have told Dad that it was okay to die, but I couldn't say it. Instead I left the room crying.

Now back to Jesse's question as he woke up from his nap. With a knot in my stomach, I responded, "Yes. Wendy says that they would have already put you there, but they don't have any beds available."

After my response, Jesse went back to sleep. The private rooms are what the veterans consider death row, since only patients near death are put in them.

That is when I called his brother and told him I thought he might want to see his brother. He arrived that night and called his sister and told her she might want to come the following night. His brother took him out where there is a fish pond and tables for the veterans and guest. His brother also lit Jesse's cigarette for him.

Jesse was having a hard time zipping up his jacket to go to the smoke room. He would get mad when I would zip it up for him. When he went to the smoke room, he did not smoke. The other men would look at Jesse and knew he wouldn't be around soon. I could see it on their faces. They were looking at the physical decline of his body.

Over the next few days, I would follow Jesse with a wheelchair because he insisted on walking until he could not. He would get mad when he saw me with the wheelchair until he needed it. On Friday, I was pushing Jesse in the wheelchair around the outside of the building, but the cracks in the sidewalk made his kidneys hurt.

Jesse took a shower, which took him over an hour. I kept checking on him and he would get mad when he saw me. He never took his slippers off and complained there were no chairs to sit on in the shower. It was very sad to see him trying to do for himself. He kept trying to get his belt into another hole but it didn't have any more so I brought him a pair of suspenders to keep his pants up.

At dinnertime on Saturday, Jesse slammed down on the tray and said, "You f---ing women."

I didn't care that Jesse was dying and replied, "Not all women are f---ing women." I said this very loudly, even though Jesse's roommate was a wonderful Christian man whom Dale said had so much light coming from him that you could see it spilling from the room into the hallway.

Jesse also couldn't get the straw in the drink to his mouth and would get mad at me when I helped him. I knew he really was mad that he couldn't do it for himself. He would only drink half his drink and only half of the Jell-O or pudding. But after he got angry, he ate almost a third of a large meal.

Jesse had in essence raised his vibration from depression up to anger, which gave him energy to eat. This was what I was reading in *Ask and It Is Given*, by Esther and Jerry Hicks. It was amazing to be given an example of someone raising his vibration right after I read about it.

On Sunday, Jesse continued to look at me with disdain and when his children came to see him, he told me not to go to the smoke room with them. I was delighted not to and left to go to April's for dinner.

While I was at April's, I let out all my frustrations about Jesse and how he was treating me. On the way back to the hospital, I decided I was being abused because I allowed it. When I returned to the V.A. Center, I continued to read, *Ask and It Is Given*. It suggested a process to move your vibration up. So I started to look at things that gave me joy and that I appreciated.

When I glanced at Jesse, I noticed my vibration going down so I immediately looked at the expansive mandala I had created on the first two days I had come to be with Jesse. I then looked at the other mandalas I had drawn and colored. Then I looked at the vase of fresh daffodils I had brought into the room to cheer it up. I kept looking at things that I loved and appreciated.

Since I was hungry, I went down to the lunchroom to get a candy bar. On the way I saw a plant that had beautiful purple tones running through it. When I reached the canteen, there was a man laughing. I received two candy bars instead of one when I put the money in and got 15 cents in change instead of a nickel. In *Ask and It Is Given*, it says you attract that which matches your vibration. *Hmmm that seems to be true.*

The highest vibration of feelings is of joy, love, appreciation, empowerment and knowledge. The lowest vibration of feelings is of grief, depression, despair, fear and powerlessness. There are others in between. I was impressed that it worked and I saw examples right away. *Wow!*

On Monday, Jesse was putting his jacket on with my help. I questioned him. "Jesse, if you were me …"

"Yes."

"And I was you," I continued. "Would you do this for me?"

He responded, "Absolutely."

Jesse never sent me negative energy after that and even thanked me later in the day. *Yea!*

I had made the decision the day before that if Jesse continued to send me negative energy I was not going to come any more even if he was dying. We are only treated the way we allow someone to treat us.

Jesse's health continued to decline and on Tuesday when I was wheeling him back to his room, he doubled over in pain. The staff rushed to him and gave him more pain pills. I called his brother again and he came with a cheeseburger for Jesse. When he got there, Jesse went to the bathroom and we heard him slide down the door to the floor. The nurses all tried to push the door open and move Jesse so they could get him out of the bathroom.

He was put in a diaper. Jesse had to go to the bathroom again and his brother tried to help him (even though he had had heart surgery). And while it was heartwarming to see Jesse's brother trying to help him go to the bathroom, he had to stop because he couldn't do it.

He said to his brother, "I'm sorry Jesse I can't do it." And he helped him back to his bed.

His brother also called his sister and told her that she should come that night because he didn't know if Jesse would be alive the next day. When Jesse's sister and daughter arrived, she walked right past me and went to Jesse. I extended my hand and introduced myself.

She did not extend her hand and said, "I took care of him for 20 years."

Her daughter was very nice. Jesse had introduced me to her when we stopped at their house to pick up his brother-in-law for his hearing.

I received a phone call from her one time because I had tried to do something for Jesse. One of my lessons through Jesse was not to be the third wheel between two people; instead let the two people solve their own situation. Sometimes I forget and get the lesson again. This happened with my daughter; she called and left a message to mind my own business. She was right even though my intentions were to help her.

Wednesday morning I arrived to see Jesse in a lounge chair on wheels positioned in the hallway in front of the nurses' station. I felt so hurt that he was propped up where everyone was walking by. I'd seen other patients sitting in the hall. His roommate told me that Jesse tried to leave by the hallway door and set off the alarm so the nurses stopped him and put him in the chair.

I pushed Jesse back to the hallway near his room and waited for hours for a private room to be prepared for him. On the bare walls, I hung the mandalas and the picture of Jesse and me that Robert Kane Chan had taken when we first met.

At this time Jesse could not talk or barely move. He began thrashing in the bed and I knew he was having morphine withdrawal or maybe he was in pain. It took me back to an earlier day when after he had pain medicine he walked down the hall snickering about the fact that he had convinced the nurses that he was in more pain than he really was so he could get more drugs.

"I fooled them and they gave me more drugs."

I judged Jesse then and was mad, but did not say anything. Now I was in control. Jesse could not speak or walk: he was helpless. I could have chosen to let him thrash around until the nurse came with the scheduled pain medicine. My decision was to go get the nurse, but after the nurse gave him his medication, I knew my personal vibration was lowered with my thoughts, so I opened my heart and only let the love of God enter my heart. I also sent Jesse pink light for love and the golden light to raise his vibration, which also raised mine. *Without the wall of judgment, I could be present for Jesse's passing.*

It was very important that I had my vibration as high as I could because I knew from the experiment with the Leadership class that my thoughts affected Jesse. I was also told that one of the reasons that Jesse and I met was for me to help Jesse go to the Light (God) when he passed over.

When visitors would come, I would get very teary eyed and cry. Even though I knew that Jesse would be going to a better place, I still had feelings of sadness. After they left, I would again look at things and appreciate them in order to raise my vibration.

Often I would put pieces of crushed ice in Jesse's mouth to keep it moist as Dale had told me that it would make his passing easier. The nurses kept wondering why they would have to change him a couple of times a day, which was very painful for Jesse.

On Friday, I was not able to visit Jesse since I was taking my daughter to get an operation and her husband was not in town. Dale sat with him for an hour or two. The next day his lips were stuck to his teeth. I played classical music on his portable DVD player to help his transition.

The nurse came in on Saturday and told me her husband had died of a similar condition and that he would be dead by tomorrow, but Jesse passed that evening. It was a very spiritual and sacred moment. He took one more breath and passed. There was a moment in which time seemed to stand still. I feel it is the moment his soul left the body.

I got the nurse and the doctor came in later and pronounced him dead. In the meantime, I decided to raise my vibration again and I was shocked to see a vision of a large bunch of red roses coming at me. Each rose was approximately five inches across and a hand deep. The bunch must have been almost two feet in diameter. I had never seen roses that big. The vision took my breath away.

I then called Dale to tell her not to bring the DVDs I had asked her to bring.

She said, "Turn around and look through the doorway."

She was already there. She came in and I told her that Jesse had passed. She looked up and said Jesse was almost at the light and was turning back to tell me, "Thank you for helping and staying with me." Then he turned and went to the light with a large angel escorting him.

Dale gasped and fell back into a chair. I later asked her why she gasped and she said the skirt of the angel was so big that it would have filled the room. She was surprised he went to the light since she thought he would linger on the earth plane. Jesse had discussed with me that when he passed he would go to the light.

I had been praying that an angel would help Jesse and on the Saturday before he passed, I looked over at him and was surprised to see about a two-foot golden circle around his right arm. I knew then that my prayers were being answered and that an angel was already helping him.

Red Roses,
Photo by Julie Strong

Jesse's Message to Me, Eulogy and Viewing

Saturday night I called Joy Melchezidek and left a message. She called me back a little after midnight and I informed her that Jesse had passed.

She gave me her condolences and said, "Jesse is here and he wants to talk to you. Do you want to hear?"

I said yes, and Jesse spoke to me through Joy.

"I went to the light. I am still over viewing my life. Your light shining helped me to remember who I am. Tell my children that I love them very much. I didn't say it enough and show it to them. I am going away to study now. I am coming to the memorial services. I will be there. Of course, I will."

He then sent me a bouquet of red roses.

"I see things wiser now," he continued, "sorry I had to go. Sorry for the mean stuff."

He then sent me a bouquet of red roses for the passion in our relationship. He also sent a bouquet of pink roses for the love in our relationship. A single yellow rose for the friendship love and he laid a single white rose with pink edges at my feet for the pure intent of my soul.

Jesse also said, "I did love you. I found comfort in your light. You brought me grace. Your work is not done. You will meet someone new in a little while. You learned the lesson – love without attachment. You will be committed to your purpose and not be swayed in the relationship."

Joy then said that she saw Jesse with a funny hat on and a bottle of beer in one hand with green clovers floating around him. She said that he looked like a leprechaun and was skipping back to the light.

Awesome, the vision I had of the bouquet of red roses coming at me after Jesse passed came from him. The viewing for Jesse was planned for a couple weeks later in West Virginia and the day after he was buried at Quantico National Cemetery in Virginia.

Since there was no service planned, I asked Father Soto to do a service for Jesse. Father Soto showed much love and compassion for Jesse while he was dying in the nursing home at the V. A. Center. When I talked with him, I asked him if Jesse interrogated him the first time he met him.

Father Soto said, "Yes, Jesse did interrogate me."

It had upset him, but he could hardly wait for the next time he would see Jesse so they could continue their discussion.

There were about 20 people at the service. Some were veterans from the post-traumatic stress class, other veterans, employees, my sister and a friend. His close veteran friends Pat, Rich and Trisha came.

I had prepared a eulogy but I wasn't sure if I would perform it until I noticed that the energy of those present had dropped considerably after the priest was done. The eulogy included Jesse's life, except the parts about the war, which all the veterans shook their heads in agreement about omitting. The eulogy expressed my feelings that one of the reasons we met was to give me an understanding of what a soldier went through in Vietnam so I would know how to design an uplifting Pathway of Peace for the Center of Gratitude.

In the eulogy I shared our relationship, the meeting, the breakup, giving up control, the wall, and true love. When I mentioned that I loved Jesse, I began to cry and his close friend, Rich, stood up and put his arms around me to comfort me. Jesse and Rich had had a falling out before Jesse found out he had cancer. I was so glad that Rich came, because Jesse had often called out his name during the days he was passing over.

I spoke about *Ask and It Is Given*, and how I worked on raising my vibration. In the book, it stresses the Law of Attraction, which states that what you think and talk about you get. Whether your thoughts are negative or positive, you will attract what you are thinking about. You will also attract where your vibration is. I also shared with them the 22 levels of emotions and left them with the thought that they could focus on appreciating what they have and what they want.

Another thing I suggested was to raise the vibration of peace by focusing on seeing happy soldiers returning and to visualize people working together for the good of all. They know what war is like. If they think about the war, they give energy to the war and attract it. Give energy to Peace if they so choose. They can make a difference in the world. They can create the 1,000 years of peace for the future.

The eulogy also included Dale's vision when Jesse passed over, my vision, and Jesse's message to me through Joy. I also read the following poems I found on the social worker Bob Smith's door. There was no author given for either one.

Angels walk these halls
In this VA Nursing Home,
Ministering to Veterans
Making them feel less alone.

They give hope where there is little
And tender loving care,
To old warriors who are fading
And starting up heaven's stair.

They have no wings or halos,
These doctors, nurses and aides,

But the smiles they wear and the words they use
Help us be less afraid.

Day and night will be all right
Behind these nursing home walls,
And tonight I'll dream in a peaceful sleep
'Cause angels walk these halls.

Bereavement
I walked a mile with Pleasure
She chattered all the way,
But left me none the wiser
For all she had to Say.

I walked a mile with Sorrow,
And ne'er a word said she,
But, oh, the things I learned from her
When Sorrow walked with me.

The eulogy ended with the message: "Raise your vibration. Create a brilliant light. Love and accept your fellow man. Feel appreciation to God for all you have. And may you skip off to the light of God when you are ready to go." To my surprise many of the mourners stood up and clapped, which meant that their vibration was higher.

At the viewing that night, his sister came up to me and told me that they each were going to say something about Jesse at the burial the next day. All of Jesse's brothers but one came, as well as his step-siblings and his mother.

His brother-in-law came up to me near the end and asked me to tell him what I thought of Jesse. I gave him my feelings and he said that I was the only one there that agreed with him. The others just said he was mean. Perhaps that is why Jesse only wanted me to meet his brother-in-law and his brother who could communicate by mental telepathy with him.

When I mentioned to his brother-in-law about Jesse skipping off to the light looking like a leprechaun, he said he had many stories about

Jesse he would tell. One of the stories would be about the Saint Patrick's Day that Jesse, his sister, and friends went out to celebrate. When they came back, Jesse was wearing a top hat that he wore all evening.

When I spoke with his daughter, she told me that a few months earlier she had found out that their name had an "O" before it and that the "O" was dropped when their descendants came to America. So that explained why Jesse was skipping off to the light dressed as a leprechaun with clovers floating around him! I chose not to attend the burial.

Jesse said he had experienced a lot in his lifetime. He also accomplished his goals after he met me. One was to reunite with his children. The second was to get total disability, which he got after the cancer was found.

Do you have any goals in your life? What do you want to do before you die?

Fluffy,
Photo by Mary B. Reed

The Rest of 2007

The search for land continues; attended an A.R.E. retreat; had some near death experiences; attended a free class; took an energy class, and watched Dale experience her dream.

In April, I looked at land in the area where my grandparents had lived. I loved it and I found it interesting that a year ago when I had told my Aunt Esther that I looked at land in that area, she told me that that was where her mother lived and had died in a car accident. I had a thought that, wouldn't it be something if the church Granddaddy had preached at would be for sale? Well, the land I looked at is a rectangle with a portion indented, which happens to be the cemetery of the church that my grandfather preached at.

I had been looking in that area for a house to live in and there was one that I was interested in because when I got out of my car, I felt like skipping into the house. *How I am feeling when I look at land or houses has become very important to me.*

In June I attended an A. R. E. retreat, which someone else paid for. The Past-Life Regression course and hearing Charles Cayce speaking had also been complimentary, so I knew I was supposed to go. God was supplying the resources to do so. P. M. H. Atwater spoke at the retreat at Shepherd University.

Atwater was fantastic. She had experienced three near deaths and has interviewed close to 4,000 people who also had near death experiences. Atwater stressed how important prayer is and that the last thing a person responds to is your voice. During her third near death, her son found her on the floor, and instead of calling 911 right away, his intuition told him to start talking. Talking brought her back because she was just about to go into the light.

Just before going to the retreat, I met my real estate agent and she said she would treat me to a reading by Donna Sims who had had a near death experience. When I went to see Donna, I had Atwater's book, *You Live Forever*. I asked Donna about her near death experience and she said she normally did not talk about it, but knew that I understood. She had been about eight years old and her family was preparing for her death. When she went to the other side, her grandfather met her and a very beautiful woman whom she did not know. Donna heard her mother praying and told the woman, "I have to go back to my Mommy." The beautiful lady said, "Okay." Then Donna came back.

The Knight's father also had a near death experience after he had surgery for a brain tumor. He said that he could see his wife and both sons whom he was looking down on while the doctors worked on him. He said a voice asked him, "Are you ready?" He said he would never forget that voice and answered, "No." He then returned to his body.

A dear friend of mine told me of the time she was in the back of a truck and it stopped suddenly. She fell out and hit her head. She saw this beautiful white light and all she felt was love and would have stayed, but she glanced back and saw her children and came back. *Do we choose when we are going to die?*

In June, I took a Level IV Medical Intuitive class. I was energetically repairing a vertebra of a fellow student and could actually see in my mind the chip that had been broken off. I also saw a knob like protrusion on it that I energetically sanded down and vacuumed out. I shared with the class that with Jesse the only thing I did during his passing over was to be present for him without the wall or control.

The Peace Gathering in August was facilitated by Lee who performed a Native American opening and vocal blessing, Joyce Gedeon channeled the Fairy God Bunny, Joyce M. led a drumming meditation, Brenda played a flute for all veterans, and Robin led BIJA chants. I said a prayer for Universal Peace. The facilitators came from their hearts and with sincere gratitude to God (Spirit, Source).

I did repairs to my home throughout the year and put in new windows, a new sink, a new countertop, replaced part of a wall and painted the ceilings. A contractor took out the moisture barrier from under the crawl space, put in a new one along with a sump pump and dehumidifier to keep it dry. This was the first time I had climbed into the crawl space and wished I had done it earlier. It wasn't that bad and I could have had things corrected sooner.

One of my clients who used to sell real estate said that homeowners should fix their houses as if they are going to sell them. I have come to the same conclusion after enhancing my house. It is certainly a good Feng Shui practice. The energy in your house will feel better. Just think, every time you look at something that needs to be repaired you are putting negative energy out. It's better to repair and have positive energy. Clutter affects us the same way. I love my house even more now; it lifts my spirit.

I also taught several Reiki Classes and Feng Shui throughout the year and had Free Energy Circles on the first Friday of each month for those wanting to boost their energy levels for healing themselves.

On a Thursday in September, a friend and I went to a free energy class at the Shenandoah Valley School of Therapeutic Massage in Edinburg, Virginia. My friend had made an appointment to have Fernand Poulin (www.whitewinds.com) work on her autistic son since his cranial sacral therapist had recommended him.

I'd told her about the free class to introduce what the Energy Medicine Workshop was about. Going to the free class would give her a chance to see who was going to work on her son. I had forgotten about the free class until she called me the day before and asked if I would pick her up. I knew I was supposed to go.

At the free class, Fernand worked on two different men who both had had heart by-pass operations. One of them was a former classmate and near the end of the class, he stood up and said he had just asked the lady beside him if he had surgery and pulled open his shirt for her to see. He said he didn't feel like he had had surgery after Fernand worked on him, although his chest had been tight and hurting up to the moment before.

It was at this free class that Fernand told me that my maternal Grandmother Rachel was standing behind me and it was through her bloodline that I was given my gift.

I was so impressed that I signed up for the three-day class. There are energy fields around your body and you notice this more when someone comes up from behind you. You will know that they are there because they came into your field. When these fields are not clear, they can cause problems on the physical level. The spiritual field starts approximately six feet from you, and then you have the mental field, next is the emotional field, and last the etheric field that is closest to the physical body.

During November and December I watched my friend, Dale Scully do stand-up comedy three different times. She had wanted to do it all her life and by New Year's Eve she did great. *We could all try to do what we dream of doing, and it was wonderful to see someone actually doing it.*

Mary at stream behind the El Santurio de Chimayo, New Mexico, Photo by Jeanelle

2008

I saw another birth; my daughter was in an accident; I started writing this book; did some vision-boards work; had a magical trip; Suzen helped me; a client shared her abuse story; met a princess; had a bird surprise; received the KOA reward, and my son-in-law was in pain.

I was honored that my friend asked me to be present during the homebirth of her daughter. The father called at around 1:00 a.m. and said that his wife was in labor. I was the first to arrive, which took some of the stress off of him.

He asked me, "Why does birthing have to be so painful?"

"A woman goes through a lot of physical changes before birthing." I answered.

Her labor was short and she gave birth around 4:30 a.m. Her daughter's color changed as she was coming out of the birth canal and I had the opportunity to transfer her from the mid-wife to the mother. It is very overwhelming to see a baby coming into the world. *Welcome to our world, or as Esther Hicks channels from energies called Abraham, "Welcome to planet earth."*

Jeanelle had a car accident in February and called me while she was waiting in the emergency room. A drunk driver hit another car first then sideswiped her on the driver's side of her brand new car. It was fortunate for her that because of the first accident, other drivers were being careful and despite the fact that she was in the middle lane of a three-lane highway, no one else hit her.

She went to the hospital because she was experiencing nausea and pain in her neck, hip, and head.

Just a word of advice; after an accident you are usually in shock and will not feel the pain until the shock wears off. If insured, it is best to go to the hospital in an ambulance because you won't have to wait in the emergency room.

My daughter had to hang up the phone because she was going to be examined. I immediately started doing long-distance Reiki on her after a prayer. Her energy was very irregular at her head and her abdomen. It took me an hour to get her energy calm. She called me back and said when they strapped her on the board that she became very relaxed and knew that I was working on her.

I did a chakra balancing on her also, in which I felt her third eye open wide. The next morning I also did Reiki and worked on clearing her energy fields, which I had learned from Dr. Fernand Poulin, DC. I cleared these fields knowing that the impact from the accident had probably disturbed them.

I also balanced her endocrine system, which I learned from the Medical Intuitive class. My daughter's abdomen energy was almost as bad as her head. The reason for this is your adrenals kick in during stress and can take over the hypothalamus's job (master gland). You feel emotion in the solar plexus. After bringing the endocrine back to balance on my daughter, I worked on my grandson, who said he had a little pain when he got out of the car after the accident. His energy was also irregular.

The family was on their way to one of his baseball games. My daughter called me while the baseball game was being played and thanked me.

She said, "I feel great. They told me I would be in pain, but I am not." She went to her chiropractor, which I had suggested because my sister had found out years after an accident that she had injured her neck and it was too late to claim it on the insurance.

I also suggested she go to a cranial sacral therapist since she had a head injury. It was after a couple of sessions that my daughter came to the decision to go ahead and go to massage school.

Another client I worked on doing long-distance Reiki was suffering with great pain in her feet. She stayed on the phone and asked me what I was doing because her feet were feeling better.

I said, "I haven't gotten to your feet. I am still on your abdomen." When I made contact with the teddy bear I use to represent the client, I felt a large pipe running down the length of her abdomen. I was trying to get it to dissolve since I had never sensed it on anyone before. Several weeks later she went to the hospital and they performed surgery to unblock her main artery. *How marvelous it is that I could feel that!*

Most people can do energy work. It is best to create a sacred space. Pray for protection for you and your client. Let the love and light of your creator (God) come through you to the client. Avoid using your energy, instead see it coming from God (source) and flooding and flowing through you.

If you are angry or mad, it would not be in the client's best interest to do energy healing at that time. Always come from a space of love, not control or ego. A client may not feel anything. You can also do this on yourself. Try it when you have a headache. If you tune in to your intuition, you will be guided as to where you need to work. There is no need to actually touch the person. Always wash your hands in cold water afterwards to disconnect from the person. Remember, you are calming yourself or the other person, so that you or they can heal.

Near the end of February I made the decision that I would write this book. I had started it many different times over the years, along with many of my journals. The day I made the decision that I would write it – no matter what – I met an editor and writer who helped me through part of the process. *It is miraculous how the universe works.*

I decided to get out my vision boards that I had done at the Centre for Positive Living. They were done on an intuitive basis; the leader had us go through magazine, papers, and catalogues and cut out pictures or words that felt like they were right. Afterwards, we took what pictures and words still felt right and designed a vision board.

When I walk in my house, I use my vision boards to visualize what I want to create. After three weeks, Jeanelle called me from Colorado and asked me if I wanted to come out for a week. I said sure. She also wanted to take me to New Mexico to see Sky City and go to the El Santuario de Chimayo. Both of these places were on my vision boards and I had wanted to go there for years. *Remarkable!*

I started to look for a very nice hotel to stay at, but decided to let Jeanelle pick one out. I did not tell her I had looked on-line for a place to stay.

She called and asked me, "Would you like to stay at this retreat in Santa Fe? It is the off-season so we can get a room for $120 a night. It has organic food at the Blue Heron."

Outstanding! You can create your reality. Let go and let God.

God also supplied the money to have fun. The week before I went to Colorado, I had an unusually large amount of clients visit me because I was leaving. This gave me plenty of money to spend and enjoy myself.

My flight was on Easter Day. In the airport, my adventure began. I met a gentleman who was back from Iraq and his arm was in a sling. When I went to sit down, I saw him out of the corner of my eye from a distance and he waved and so did I. He came over and we talked then I offered to do Reiki on him. He is very psychic and shared that his guardian angels helped him to get rid of dark entities from other dimensions. He also told me he could see the energy pouring from me while I did the Reiki and some quantum blasts. He hugged me good-bye when it was time for me to board the airplane.

Before I left on my trip to Colorado, I was experiencing pain in my tendon in my left arm. This was caused by not paying attention to my stiffness in my chord hand while learning to play the organ. I continued keeping it stiff until I had severe pain. The pain would wake me up in the middle of the night. I was doing Reiki, the EFT, quantum charts, ice, and heat. But I was still experiencing pain so the day after arriving in Colorado I got my first acupuncture treatment.

As soon as he put the needles in I could feel energy going to the thumb. When the chiropractor did it again at the end of my stay, I could again feel the energy shooting through my whole arm. While the needles were in my arm a man came and sat beside me.

He said, "I'll be joining you."

He had been in an accident and was getting massages and adjustments to help his head and neck. I offered to do some energy work on him. Afterwards, the chiropractor came out and told the man that he now had blood flow in his head because his face had a pinkish color to it.

The man replied, "My head is buzzing."

The third day Jeanelle and I went to Santa Fe, New Mexico and stayed at the Sunrise Springs Resort Spa. I took a stone from one of my peace gardens and left one for the owner to put in her gardens there. We loved the lake, the atmosphere, and especially the hot tub, which we used both evenings. We saw a turtle and two coyotes the first day.

We went to Sky City (Acoma Pueblo) the next morning. Fred, the tour guide, was very informative. He explained that they bury the dead four levels down in the graveyard and the youngest daughter inherits the property. There is no water, except what is collected on top, and there is one tree where the water is collected. There is also no electricity up there. The houses' walls are one-and-a-half to two-feet thick, which keeps them cool in summer and warm in the winter. You have to pay to take pictures up there, but you cannot take pictures of the missionary. John Wayne made several movies up there, which is why there is a paved road going up to the plateau.

That night we went into Santa Fe and looked around and ate a fabulous meal at the Atomic Grill restaurant. The next morning we had breakfast at the Blue Heron and had a very flavorful organic omelet. A woman named Alicia, who worked there (but not that day), came to our table and suggested the way to go to El Santuario de Chimayo.

She had been there before and agreed that it was a very high spiritual church. Jeanelle did not want to go to Taos because she knew it is at a very high altitude and she has a fear of heights. She did not do the EFT process for heights, but she did do it for getting into the car to drive, since it was a rental and only she would be driving. The lady assured Jeanelle that if we went the route she had suggested to Taos, there were no steep drop offs as it followed the river. So we went to Taos too, but there was a stretch of road where Jeanelle was saying, "La, la, la, la, la."

But before Taos, we went to Chimayo, New Mexico and looked for El Santuario de Chimayo, which is a church I had read about in a newspaper. There is a small pit inside of the church that people come and take some of the soil to take home for healing. People have left their crutches after visiting this Santuario. There are many mementos left here, which are cleared out as they accumulate. The receptionist at my daughter's chiropractor told us she lost her son when he was two years old and when she visited the Santuario, a very old priest took her hand and she saw a vision of her son as if he were nineteen years old. It was very comforting to her.

In Chimayo we went to a church that was opened by a very good-looking priest. We went inside and I had this very depressing feeling, almost like the life was being squeezed out of me. My daughter said she felt nothing. I hurried and looked around for the pit, which I knew was off from the left side of the altar. It wasn't there. It was not the right church. I got out fast.

Had I been in this church in one of my lifetimes? When I got home to West Virginia, I had a dream that seemed very real and it woke me up. I dreamt I was about to have shackles and chains put on my ankles, but woke up.

The church we were looking for was within walking distance of the one that gave me the creeps. When we walked into the El Santuario de Chimayo, I felt like I was expanding out and up. The energy was so high in this church that my neck jerked about five or six times. My neck jerks when I am giving quantum blasts that take, or when I am in a very high energy place or group. I have no control of the jerking of my neck. My daughter loved the energy here also. I took a quart of dirt and gave a semi-precious stone from my peace garden for a gift, as I had been directed to do by a friend. She had told me to always leave a gift of some kind.

We went to the backyard of the church where a small river flowed. This is where my daughter took a picture of me and has put it on her vision board. We then proceeded to Taos, where we stopped in the visitor's center and the Taos Gems and Minerals store that has a humongous supply of semi-precious stones. *Thank you, God.*

On the way home we saw the Eagle's Nest Lake that was still frozen, except around the edges, and there was snow still on the ground. From Taos to Eagle's Nest is part of the Enchanted Circle in New Mexico. It was fabulous.

My grandson had a baseball game on Saturday in Littleton, Colorado. In between games I walked around the park and found the Columbine Memorial. Jeanelle said she didn't think she would get emotional, but she did. I felt that the memorial was extremely well done, and reflected a range of emotions and spiritual essence of the families, faculty, students, and President Clinton.

Jeanelle standing overlooking Columbine Memorial

The Memorial for the 12 students and one teacher was on slanted slab-like tables in a circle. On each was written what the family had to say or some had quotes of the student. The most profound for me was on Rachel Joy Scott's. Part of which is:

"Her middle name described her; she was a joy! Her beauty reflected her kindness and compassion. A month before her death she wrote: "I have this theory that if one person can go out of their way to show compassion, then it will start a chain reaction of the same. People will never know how far a little kindness can go."

Rachel had a sense of destiny and purpose. She also had a premonition her life would be short.

She wrote: "Just passing by, just coming through, not staying long. I always knew this home I have will never last." The day she died she told a teacher: "I'm going to have an impact on the world."

Her final words were testimony to her life. When asked if she believed in God she replied, "You know I do!"

Jeanelle and I agreed that our favorite quote on the retaining wall written by a student was, "People talk about defining moments in their lives, but I didn't let this define me."

I highly recommend that if you are in the area to stop and see this memorial. What a bonus to my trip.

My sister, Ruth, and her husband picked me up at Dulles Airport and took me out to dinner. When I arrived home my friend, Anna Marie, had left me homemade lasagna, which is my favorite dish. What a way to top off a magical trip.

The next day I called my friend, Suzen, who has been working through issues with her cancer. I then called one of my Medical Intuitive instructors and asked what I could do. She suggested that Suzen could make a list of the people she is angry with and why, and that she needed to honor her anger and then write a forgiveness letter to each of them. The letters did not need to be mailed. The most important part was for her to figure out her part in the situation.

My instructor also suggested I do quantum charts on the victim vibration of her family lineage and one on repressed anger. Later I could do one on her worthlessness and on her cancer.

After hearing what to do on Suzen, I decided that since I had done an 88 page summary of my life, that it would be good for me to do the same. My list was almost three full pages. I wanted to clear my energy.

I had also recently written a letter to someone who had verbally and energetically abused me. I thanked the person for giving me the opportunity to make the decision that I would not accept the abuse. But the lady's face haunted me because I saw all this repressed anger on her face. Her face continued to haunt me until I realized the repressed anger on her face had mirrored my repressed anger, and that it was not all about me. After typing all my anger into the computer, I began to laugh uncontrollably for 20 to 30 minutes straight. Laughter is one of the ways that I release built-up emotions. After my laughter stopped, I typed, in big and bold letters, **"I release these to the Universe to transform into positive energy."** *Wow what a relief.*

While I was writing about my mom and composing the letter to the abusive lady, a client of mine came. At the end of the session her head felt like an ice cube, so I did a lot of energy work on it. When she paid me she revealed that her first husband had been very abusive. He drank and came home late at night. One time her daughter pleaded with her to stay and go Christmas caroling with the church members. The daughter then called her father and he agreed. My client then talked to her husband and he told her it was fine to go Christmas caroling. When she arrived home, she went into the dark bedroom and bent down and asked him softly if he was awake. She woke up lying on the floor. Her husband had knocked her out cold. To this day she says she gets nervous and uptight if she is out past dark. She also said she would never talk back or shove her husband, the way my mom did.

Her second husband was better, but he embarrassed her once when she signed up for a health club that was only $25. He went down with her and said he wanted the money back. He then went to a lawyer about the $25.

She said that after watching Dr. Phil on television, when a verbal incident came up with her present husband, she sat him down and repeated the incident to him and told him that she had had a lot of abuse in her life, and she would not accept any abuse – verbal or physical. He apologized and said he would try not to do it again. *It is fascinating how I attracted people to help and support me in my understanding.*

In May, after lunch with my editor friend, I went to the grocery store and a young girl of about four or five years old came up to me and said, "Hello Princess, I am Princess Anna."

I was very astonished and stunned. I responded, "I am Princess Mary and I am glad to meet you, Princess Anna."

Her mother came up to me and said, "My daughter insisted on coming over to meet the Princess."

Did she recognize me from a previous lifetime when I was a princess? She certainly made my day. I felt like skipping.

On a Tuesday in May, I was bent over in my driveway pulling some weeds when a bird flew under my arm. I was astounded and shocked. At SES at least twice, two birds had flown out from under the steps as I was walking down them. When I asked the rest of the women in the office if they ever experienced that, they all said, "No." One time when Jesse was alive, I stood by the red bee bomb in the lantern garden and a hummingbird flew close enough to the top of my head that I felt my hair move. A friend standing near me thought it was going to fly into me.

A friend told me they represent angels being present. *Angels are always with us.* They must have wanted my attention.

In June, I went to the Harpers Ferry KOA to do seated massages during a fund-raiser for the preservation of the waterways in West Virginia. The lady in charge climbed out of the golf cart and came to me. Her driver also came to me and asked if I was the Mary Reed who was the swim coach at Jefferson Park and I said, "Yes." He then told me that he was Mitchell Grove, which I thought was funny because I had been thinking about his grandmother, Terry. She had driven me to the bowling alley almost every Tuesday night when I lived in Ranson, and even when I moved to near Martinsburg. I knew she had been placed in a nursing home a few years ago, and I had not been there to see her. I also met her daughter and husband and she told me that her mother had a couple of strokes and couldn't remember things.

I figured it was time to visit Terry and when I went to see her, she repeated the same questions.

"Who are you? Where did you say you lived?"

I just answered her questions over and over. She would say that she was waiting for her husband who had died years ago. My intuition was not to tell her that her husband was dead.

If you get nothing else from this book please get this. Every time you tell someone who has lost their memory that someone is dead, the person goes through the grieving process for that person.

I gave her my business card and left. When I came back a week or two later, she told me the business card was up on her bulletin board. I brought her a picture of the two of us on a boat in Reno, Nevada.

She said, "I look happy in this picture."

I also brought a newspaper article of when she bowled a perfect 300 game and read it to her. After that I did energy work and noticed that her face had color in it when I left. You only need to be present when you visit someone in a nursing home. Be where they are. It is such a beautiful thing and they love the company.

In July, Jeanelle called and said her husband was having chest pains, nausea, sweating, and pain in his arm. She asked me to do long-distance Reiki on him because she was on the way to pick him up at work because he did not want to go to the hospital in an ambulance. She told me as she was driving to him, "He's got to at least live until our 20th anniversary."

It was not his heart but his gallbladder.

Jeanelle called me a couple of weeks after the hospital trip and told me about a dream she had. In the dream she saw her husband and maybe her son leaving. Then an angel came and took her arm and was pulling sorrow and pain out of her arm. When she told me the dream, I felt that her husband was leaving because of the statement she made on the day he was sick, but I didn't tell her that.

I purchased an anniversary card, which I don't think I had ever done before, and every time I looked at the card I remembered what Jeanelle had said about her husband living at least until their 20th anniversary and about the dream with the angel. I called her a couple of weeks before their anniversary and told her what she had said when she was going to get her husband and about her dream. I suggested that she make a new wish.

She said quickly, "I wish Casey will live a long and happy life." She then said, "I don't remember saying that about Casey and I don't remember the dream."

But Jeanelle had another dream the night before I called. She said that in her dream she and I went on a trip in an airplane and then all of a sudden we were touring. I was asking her in the dream, "Don't you remember the plane landing? Don't you remember seeing this and that?" and she said that in the dream she told me, "No, I don't remember any of that."

Isn't it interesting that Jeanelle couldn't remember in her dream and in reality the very next day? Jeanelle has prophetic dreams. And I am happy to say her husband is still alive and they celebrated their anniversary in August.

Closing

Some of the revelations that came from writing this book were awesome for me. One was when my sister told me that she considered me the weak one. I was a little surprised until I thought back to my childhood. I was weak, especially in my arms, which is surprising since a massage client the other day told me that I have fingers of steel. Both gardening and bowling have made me very strong in my arms along with swimming, yoga, and other exercises I did when my children were young.

I was not only weak in my arms as a child, I was also sick with toothaches, earaches, and eczema on my fingers which would crack, bleed, and itch. The eczema got me out of scrubbing, but I still had to dust every weekend and dry dishes every other week. My sister also considered me weak because I would not defend my frustrated mom when she and Dad were fighting; instead I would run and hide. After telling my sister that I could see that Mom was asking for it, she said that maybe I was the smart one.

Another was the painful experience of reading the letter I had written to the Knight but never gave to him. In it I wrote about the verbal abuse he gave me and I realized that by going further with the relationship, I had set up my personal vibration to that of verbal abuse, and therefore attracted it to me at my job at SES.

Also, while revising this closing another revelation came to me. I realized that my point of view that my parents suffered from low self-esteem was a match for me. Low self-esteem is something I have myself and have raised over the years. Slowly but surely I have come to love myself more. It started with Miss Lloyd teaching me to be able to look at myself in a mirror, but Louise Hay's suggestion in her book, *You Can Heal Your Life*, was more powerful. She suggested that you look at yourself in a mirror and say the words, "I love you." Then notice how you feel.

I keep saying it. It is good for the soul and it raises my energy (vibration).

I've already shared the revelation about acknowledging my anger, forgiving the person/persons, seeing my part in it, and releasing it. Still another revelation while writing this book was the reason why my sister and I were the ones who had to go to the Legion to get Dad. We would have to stand outside and wait for someone to come in or out; then we would ask if our dad was in there. Sometimes Dad came in or out, but I hated the wait and didn't know why we were there, except to get Dad. Mom told me this year that she sent us after him so he wouldn't spend all his money gambling. Because if he did, we would not have any money for food. A friend of mine, whose family was large, went for three days without food because her dad gambled and drank his paycheck away.

Besides these revelations, what did I get from my grandparents and parents? I learned to get the work done and put my feelings last at SES. From the Burkhart's side of the family I learned work ethic (and from the Frazier's side too.) I allowed abuse against me, which I learned from my mom. And I thank God that I chose her for a mother, because after leaving SES, my goal has been to love what I do and work with the people who feel the same way.

From Grandma Burkhart I evidently got her voice. When my oldest sister (whom I had not talked to in years) called, she said, "My God, you sound just like Grandma Burkhart."

I apparently look like both sides of the family: My ex-husband told me that as long as I was alive, my mother would be alive and my cousin Mary Lou, whom I met in college, said, "You look just like my Aunt Carrie," referring to my dad's sister.

I got a strong sense of right and wrong from my mom, which she got from both of her parents. Honesty was handed down (mostly) from Granddaddy Frazier. Mom taught it, but she didn't always practice it, especially when it came to how much money she had.

My father taught me to stand up for what you believe in, and do it your way. He also taught me to enjoy life, but to be able to look yourself in the mirror. He thoroughly enjoyed his life, but he would hide behind sunglasses and arrive late at family functions because he was ashamed. I also learned what alcohol and drugs do to you by observing my dad.

How to be a martyr was learned from Mom, but it was my decision to change the pattern. Taking responsibility and raising my children I learned by Mom's presence and by Dad's absence. *Very often what we lacked in our childhood is what we try to give our children.* One of the things my sister, Virginia, said to me was that the important things she wanted to give her children were love, food, and an education. She remembers when the only thing in the house was catsup and mustard. And I can remember having only onions, butter, and bread many times and sometimes no bread.

Love was the most important thing I wanted to give to my children. I also didn't want to take my unhappiness with my marriage and transfer it to them the way my mom had done to us. In addition, it was also important to give my children social skills and a belief in God.

My children taught me that you can't fulfill your children. They always want more. A parent cannot fulfill their child without giving up their entire life for them. I went to my children's functions to support them in a way that I was not supported. Ironically, one of my daughters only remembers the one event that I did not attend. A parent can teach children to respect and honor themselves, and give them love at the same time, but they will make their own mistakes. Hopefully learn from them--- or repeat them like I have done.

I got spiritualism from Granddaddy Frazier and love of God from both grandparents and Mom. My inventiveness is from Grandma Burkhart. Being wise with money would be from the Fraziers.

Being bossy was handed down from my grandmother to my mom to me. Before a Peace Gathering that my girls attended, I was barking out orders to them. Even though my back was turned, I could feel their shoulders bristling and negative energy coming from them. I immediately changed my orders to, "Would you please do this for me?" Instantly I felt their energy shifted and they helped me. I am still working on asking since the bossy tone comes up once in awhile, especially when I am rushing to get something done.

Why did I choose my parents? I chose them because they were the perfect parents to give me the opportunity to learn the many lessons I have learned.

Did I create my reality? I began this book with the president of SES telling me to cut down on my talking. While I solved the problem with the president by disclosing and revealing the moment of conflict, I didn't deal with the too much talking part.

Too much talking at work was twofold. Out of frustration I would talk, but on a deeper level it had to do with being right. War is about both sides thinking that they are right. On the way home from work, I would be upset with myself for always having to put in my two cents when the secretary voiced her opinion on an issue. When I learned to stop reacting to her comments and keep my point of view to myself, she left.

The Knight and I mirrored the secretary and myself playing the game of being nice to control or change someone. I learned from my mom that hollering and shoving did not change Dad, so I used the strategy of being nice. It took me years to stop playing the game with the Knight. And when I stopped, he drifted further away, perhaps because he liked the game a lot.

Did I create the relationship with my husband? I certainly did. As early as eighth grade I wondered who would take care of me; therefore, I created the situation for my husband to come into my life. Since I did not enjoy my sexual relationship with him, I wanted someone who was good in bed, and the Knight showed up. Except that the Knight used the sex to control me. However, that control was not his fault because it was control I gave to him. I could have dropped the relationship, but instead I held on to something that did not feel good. I kept hoping it would work out. I got what I wanted, but not exactly everything. I had asked for very little in the relationship and got what I asked for.

I wanted to do a Pathway of Peace in the Center of Gratitude, and the Universe supplied Jesse to give me knowledge of what veterans lived through. With this knowledge I was able to design the Pathway of Peace. Almost every girlfriend or wife of a veteran that I have met has told me the veteran would never talk about the war to them. Mainly because the discussion would scare the listener or the listener didn't want to hear it. Also it brought back memories of the war to the veteran. Just before death some veterans do open up, but there are those who never do.

When I first went to Donna Sims for a psychic reading, she asked me to make two silent wishes. Then she told me that the first one was really good and the second was good but further into the future. She also told me after the wishes that I would be getting a marriage proposal soon. I told her that I didn't have a boyfriend, but she said it didn't matter.

The second time I went to Donna I again made two wishes. This time she said they were both good. However, they were a little bit into the future. The third time I went to Donna, I again made two wishes. Then she told me they both were good but further into the future.

At the end of the session, I said, "What is up with you?" I mentioned that the first wish was always about my mate and her response kept putting it further into the future. She did not respond.

While I was writing this book, it dawned on me why the reading about my mate kept changing. I called her to apologize, but before I could do so she asked if I wanted to schedule an appointment since she would be in town that weekend. When I went to see her a couple of months ago, I made two wishes. Donna said they were both good and she didn't see any blockages to them. She then said that my mate was in a relationship with a blonde-haired woman and that the relationship was about to end. She said that she didn't think it was a marriage.

At the end of the reading, I said I wanted to apologize to her. At my first visit to her I had worn earrings that I wanted to wear when I got married. (I wore them and walked in heels for 15 minutes every day while I looked at my vision boards.) The second and third time I went to see her my mind was completely focused on working in my gardens and preparing them. And just two weeks prior to the most recent reading I had worn the earrings and walked in the heels for 15 minutes while I looked at my vision boards, so therefore she saw my mate in my field again.

P.M.H. Atwater said that when she had her three near death experiences, she kept seeing these gray blobs around her. When she asked what they were, she was told they were her thoughts that had not manifested. Because I was working and giving energy on my visions,

Donna could see my mate in my field. *Fascinating, isn't it? I actually see how this works on small things every day. It is fun.*

When Jeanelle replaced her living room floor three times while she lived in Texas, she realized that each time they put the floor down there was something that she didn't like about the end result. The first replacement was because they wanted a wood floor instead of carpet, the second time the commode overflowed while they were gone, and the third time a relatively new hot water heater broke during the night. After Jeanelle realized that she was creating it (the Virgo in her), despite the fact that the floor wasn't perfect the third time, she kept saying, "I love this floor."

The year before I left SES I decided to stop saying, "I don't have enough time to do everything." I then started saying, "I have enough time to do that which I need to do." I was delighted when I had time to go through old files and shred papers that were not necessary for the files. I cleaned up most of the files and boxed what was no longer needed in my office. I also got to read financial magazines that had piled up on a shelf waiting to be read. It was remarkable to see the time I created for myself. I got things done that had been hanging around for over five years.

I wondered last year why I wasn't getting that many clients when it dawned on me that I had been saying I didn't want to pay taxes. Well, if you don't make money you don't have to pay taxes! I started saying that I was happy to pay my share of taxes and this year my revenue from massage has increased over last year. *It pays to be aware of what you think and say because you are creating your reality.*

Be aware of negative thoughts, because the energy you are giving them will bring negativity to you. Your thoughts and words have energy. A positive thought is more powerful than a negative thought. Therefore, when you notice you have thought or said something negative, just change it to something positive---something that you want.

Point of warning – do not try to change anybody or control them. You are only responsible for you. Let other people take care of themselves.

The book, *The Four Agreements*, by Don Miguel Ruiz is well worth reading. My sister, Ruth, says she reads the short version in the cover each day. The four agreements are: do your best (Cub Scout motto), be impeccable with your word (honesty), don't take anything personally, and don't make assumptions. The small book explains each in detail. The agreement of "don't take anything personally" is a lesson I learned while living with the Knight, which served me well with Jesse and everybody I meet. It is very freeing and I feel better when I practice not taking things personally. Also, "don't make assumptions" is a very empowering agreement to practice and one which I am still working on.

Massage, EFT, Reiki, foot reflexology, Medical Intuitive, Shiatsu, yoga, and meditation are different modalities I use to clear my body of toxins and stored up anger. There are also semi-precious stones you can buy as stones or in jewelry that have helped me in my healing process.

Jeanelle had problems with her abdomen and the doctor could not find out what was wrong. She dreamed one night that she had stones in her mouth. The stone was a very poisonous stone, and if you made an elixir out of it you would not put it in your mouth. So she used the indirect method she found on the Internet and drank a safe elixir and got rid of her stomach problems. Most stones only have to be held or worn. I've listed a couple of books in the reading list that give the characteristics of the stones and their healing properties. Most books suggest you seek out a professional if you want to take elixirs since they can be dangerous.

I will leave you with the telephone call my mother made just before the Leadership class presentation.

"Mary, this is important so listen. My father said, 'honesty is the best policy', but never mind that. What my mother said is more important. She said, 'Leave this world a better place than when you came into the world.'"

You can do it by simply healing yourself, loving yourself, working on yourself and not being concerned with changing someone else. By raising your vibration to love, acceptance, and appreciation for all you have, you leave the world a better place. It is your choice. May you let the love of God (source) shine through you.

Love and Light,

Mary

-END-

Appendix

Partial List of Books I have read.

Center of Gratitude

Pathway of Peace

Peace Gardens–to see colored photos go to:
www.healingpointofview.com

Partial List of Books I Have Read

You will be drawn to a book you need. Just say a prayer and ask to be shown which one is for you at this time. Following is a partial list of books I have read. At the bottom is a list of readers that have given me readings.

Ask and It Is Given, Learning to Manifest Your Desires Hicks, Esther and Jerry Hicks, CA, Hay House Inc., 2007.

A Toltec The Mastery of Love Wisdom Book by Don Miguel Ruiz, Amber-Allen Publishing, San Rafael, CA

Meditations from Conversations with God an uncommon dialogue book 1, by Neale Donald Walsch, Berkley Books, New York 1997

The Astonishing Power of Emotions, Let Your Feelings Be Your Guide. Esther and Jerry Hicks by Hay House Inc., CA 2007

The Complete System of Self-Healing Internal Exercises by Dr. Stephen T. Chang, Tao Publishing, San Francisco, CA 1986

The Four Agreements by Don Miguel Ruiz, Amber-Allen Publishing, San Rafael, CA

The Green Pharmacy by James A. Duke, Ph.D., Rodale Press, Emmaus, PA 1997

The Holy Bible Authorized King James Version. Cleveland and New York, The World Publishing Company.

The Law of Attraction, The Basics of the Teachings of Abraham by Esther and Jerry Hicks by Hay House Inc., CA 2007

The Peace Book 108 simple ways to create a more peaceful world by Louise Diamond, Conari Press, Berkeley, CA 2001 ($3 a book) phone (802) 453-7191

The Power of Positive Thinking by Norman Vincent Peale published by Fawcett Crest, New York, NY tenth 1989

The Richest Man in Babylon by George S. Clason, Hawthorn/Dutton, E.P. Dutton a division of NAL Penguin Inc., New York, NY 1955

The Secret Language of Destiny, A Personology Guide to Finding Your Life Purpose. Gary Goldschneider and Joost Elffers. New York, Penguin Group, 1999.

The Secret of Shambhala-In Search of the Eleventh Insight by James Redfield, Warner Books, New York, NY1999

The Tenth Insight Holding the Vision by James Redfield, read by Chris Sarandon, Time Warner Audio Books

You Can Heal Your Life by Louise L Hay, Hay House Inc., CA 1988

You Live Forever: The Real Truth About Death by P. M. H. Atwater, ARE Press, Virginia Beach, VA 2004

Feng Shui
Clear Your Clutter with Feng Shui by Karen Kingston, published by Broadway Books, New York, NY 1999 Originally published in 1998 in Great Britian by Judy Piatkus (Publisher) Limited.

Feng Shui: Harmony by Design by Nancy SantoPietro with a Foreward by Professor Lin Yun, A Perigee Book published by The Berkley Publishing Group, New York, NY, 1996

Interior Design With Feng Shui by Sarah Rossbach, Foreword by Professor Lin Yun, published by Arkana, Penguin Group, Penguin Books USA Inc., New York, NY, 1991

Numerology

Linda Goodman's Star Signs by Linda Goodman, published by St. Martin's Press, New York, 1988

Numerology, The Complete Guide Volume 1, The Personal Reading by Matthew Oliver Goodwin, published by Newcastle Publishing Company, Inc., North Hollywood, CA 1981

Numerology, The Complete Guide Volume Two, The Advanced Personality Analysis and Reading the Past, Present and Future by Matthew Oliver Goodwin, published by Newcastle Publishing Company, Inc., North Hollywood, CA 1981

Crystals

Love is in the Earth, A Kaleidoscope of Crystals Updated by Melody, Earth-LovePublishing House, Wheat Ridge, CO 7th 1998

The Crystal Bible, A Definitive Guide to Crystals by Judy Hall, Walking Stick Press, Cincinnati, OH

Color Therapy

Healing for the Age of Enlightenment –Balanced nutrition Vita Flex Color Therapy by Stanley Burroughs, Burroughs Books, Reno, NV 1993

Readers

Joyce Gedeon (540) 456-6123 email joy_zhel@yahoo.com website www.joycegedeon.com

Joy Melchezidik (717) 944-2188 email joyofunion@hotmail.com

Dale Scully email healthdcs@hotmail.com

Cyndi Wallace website www.cyndiwallace.com and email goldicyn@aol.com

Center of Gratitude

Our Mission is unifying mankind by offering a variety of modalities by which the individual may choose to become self-empowered with an open heart full of gratitude.

See Bahlahnsay in color and map at www.healingpointofview.com.

The Center of Gratitude is the combination of visions of a group of empowered persons and its design has been done using the form school of Feng Shui, the study of energy. An overview of the layout, starting at the center, would begin at placement of the **Gratitude Garden** in the Career section followed by the **Pathway of Peace** and finally at the very center is **Bahlahnsay**, the first building to be built. A connection road encircles these and connects all other buildings. Detail on each section will follow the description of the layout.

The **Information and Counseling Services** building is located in the Travel and Helpful People section. Next is a playground that leads to the **Go-eco Home Store** and **Next Generation Day Care**. In the Marriage and Love section is the **Chapel of Union**. Continuing around the road in the Fame and Reputation area is the **White Buffalo Healing Center**. In the Wealth and Prosperity section are the **Bee Co-op** and the **One World Health Food Store** followed by the **Groovy Garden Restaurant** in the Health and Family area. Finally, in the Knowledge and Spirituality section is the **White Eagle Feather** gift and book store. Framing all of the buildings will be a delivery and access road that connects the final areas and completes the Center of Gratitude.

Caressing the Center of Gratitude at the far end in the Fame and Reputation area is the terraced **Rainbow Garden** where all humanity is invited to bring a flower, rock, crystal or other gift to represent the individual's desire for PEACE. The garden is accessible by a stone bride leading from the **Chapel of Union** and a wooden bridge coming from the **Bee Co-op** or one can park directly behind the garden.

The proposed first building is Bahlahnsay (Bah-lah'-say) its spelling is an English derivative taken from a Spanish pronunciation of the word balance. The design is to bring about balance to each individual who enters. To accomplish this color, sacred geometry, Feng Shui ruler (positive measurements used where possible), and the form school of Feng Shui has been applied.

Bahlahnsay will feature a stage, dance floor, rest rooms, office, gift shop, mechanics room, several storage rooms, kitchen, juice bar, coat room, health store, multi-purpose room, and stage dressing rooms. There is a large entrance way for a water fountain, ticket booths, and information.

This six-sided building with natural light coming from the glass enclosure on the second floor and two groupings of triple windows has a sound system and dance floor for dances, entertainment, speakers, and large conventions.

If you are interested in the Center, you may send comments or inquiries to:

Peace Master, P.O. Box 278, Kearneysville, West Virginia 25430.

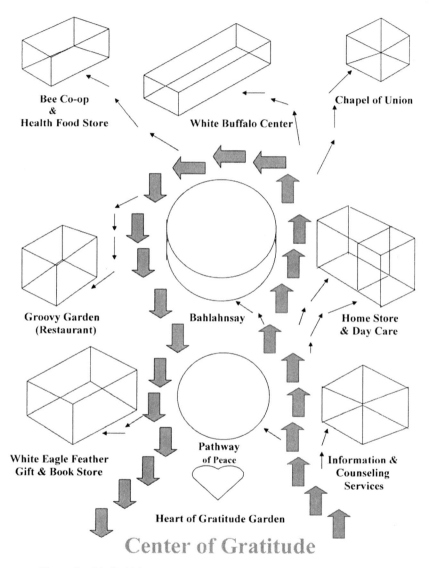

Bee Co-op
&
Health Food Store

White Buffalo Center

Chapel of Union

Groovy Garden
(Restaurant)

Bahlahnsay

Home Store
& Day Care

White Eagle Feather
Gift & Book Store

Pathway
of Peace

Information &
Counseling
Services

Heart of Gratitude Garden

Center of Gratitude

Photos of model of Bahlahnsay on other side were taken by John Baker of JRB Associates.

Map of Center of Gratitude

Pathway of Peace

The purpose of the Pathway of Peace is to aid in the healing and empowering of those who walk the pathway. It honors warriors who died giving service to their country and it also honors, uplifts, and supports healing for warriors who gave of themselves serving their country. In addition, its purpose is to give the energy of Peace to those who travel it.

The Pathway will be on an acre or two of land and will be in the shape of a man walking. The concrete pathway will have bricks with names of men and women who gave their life in the fight for Peace. This pathway will be surrounded by a square walkway with brick with the names of warriors who fought, but did not die, in a war. This will be encompassed by a circle walkway that will have bricks with the names of people who support Peace.

There will be gardens intertwined between these pathways and there will also be words to inspire uplifting of the people who walk these paths, such as:

You are forgiven.

When the power of Love is stronger than the love of the power, we will have Peace.

Peace is where it is at.

You are wonderful.

We are one.

You are blessed.

You make a difference.

Love conquers all.

Hope.

Faith.

Be a light in the world.

There will also be benches, a sweat lodge, a water fountain and an octagon building with stained-glass windows where healings, meetings, and gatherings can take place. If you are interested in the Pathway of Peace, you may send comments or inquiries to:

Peace Master, P.O. Box 278, Kearneysville, West Virginia 25430.

Pathway of Peace

Pathway that will have bricks with the names of People who support Peace.

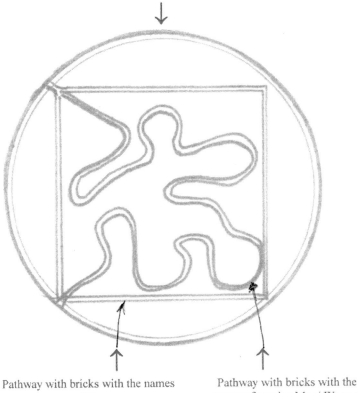

Pathway with bricks with the names of Veterans

Pathway with bricks with the names of service Men/ Women who died while serving their country

Map of Pathway to Peace

Peace Gardens

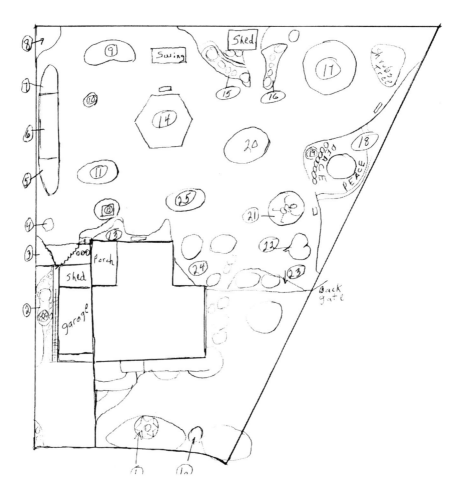

Peace Gardens
To see colored photos go to:
www.healingpointofview.com

About the Author

Mary Burkhart Reed is Nationally Certified in Therapeutic Massage and Bodywork, a Reiki Master, and a Peace Facilitator. She also holds a Bachelor of Science Degree in Business Administration. Mary is a Certified Public Accountant (CPA) who was a controller for over fourteen years.

She is a happy and successful survivor from a violent and abusive childhood. She shared her childhood with four sisters in a small railroad town in Brunswick, Maryland. At the tender age of 15, she escaped into a loveless marriage when only in the tenth grade. As a loving and devoted housewife and mother of four children, she kept the family unit together for almost 27 years.

Mary is also a passionate gardener who has designed over 27 serene gardens in West Virginia, which are dedicated to Peace every year. Her life is now dedicated to helping others overcome and heal their past in order to empower themselves so they can live and enjoy life to the fullest.

Workshops are given that may just give you the courage and determination to do what inner work is necessary to go forward in your life. You may contact Mary by mail at: Peace Master, P.O. Box 278, Kearneysville, WV 25430.

For colored pictures of gardens go to www.Healingpointofview.com.

LaVergne, TN USA
12 May 2010
182498LV00003B/9/P

9 781449 022136